G K Chesterton was born in London in 1874 and was educated at St Paul's School. He became a journalist and began writing for *The Speaker* with his friend Hilaire Belloc. His first novel, *The Napoleon of Notting Hill,* was published in 1904. In this book Chesterton developed his political attitudes in which he attacked socialism, big business and technology and showed how they become the enemies of freedom and justice. These were themes which were to run through his other works.

Chesterton converted to Catholicism in 1922. He explored his belief in his many religious essays and books. The best known is *Orthodoxy,* his personal spiritual odyssey.

His output was prolific. He wrote a great variety of books from biographies on Shaw and Dickens to literary criticism. He also produced poetry and many volumes of political, social and religious essays. His style is marked by vigour, puns, paradoxes and a great intelligence and personal modesty.

Chesterton is perhaps best known for his Father Brown stories. Father Brown is a modest Catholic priest who uses careful psychology to put himself in the place of the criminal in order to solve the crime.

Chesterton died in 1936.

G K CHESTERTON

Autobiography

HOUSE OF
STRATUS

This edition published in 2001 by House of Stratus, an imprint of House of Stratus Ltd, Thirsk Industrial Park, York Road, Thirsk, North Yorkshire, YO7 3BX, UK.

www.houseofstratus.com

Typeset by House of Stratus, printed and bound by Short Run Press Limited.

A catalogue record for this book is available from the British Library and the Library of Congress.

ISBN 1-84232-983-9

Contents

I

HEARSAY EVIDENCE

Bowing down in blind credulity, as is my custom, before mere authority and the tradition of the elders, superstitiously swallowing a story I could not test at the time by experiment of private judgment, I am firmly of opinion that I was born on the 29th of May, 1874, on Campden Hill, Kensington; and baptised according to the formularies of the Church of England in the little church of St George opposite the large Waterworks Tower that dominated that ridge. I do not allege any significance in the relation of the two buildings; and I indignantly deny that the church was chosen because it needed the whole water-power of West London to turn me into a Christian.

Nevertheless, the great Waterworks Tower was destined to play its part in my life, as I shall narrate on a subsequent page; but that story is connected with my own experiences, whereas my birth (as I have said) is an incident which I accept, like some poor ignorant peasant, only because it has been handed down to me by oral tradition. And before we come to any of my own experiences it will be well to devote this brief chapter to a few of the other facts of my family and environment which I hold equally precariously on mere hearsay evidence. Of course what many call hearsay evidence, or what I call human evidence, might be questioned in theory, as in the Baconian controversy or a good deal of the Higher Criticism. The story of my birth might be untrue. I might be the long-lost heir of the Holy Roman Empire, or an infant left by ruffians from Limehouse on a doorstep in Kensington, to develop in later life a hideous criminal heredity. Some of the sceptical methods applied to the world's origin might be applied to my origin, and a grave and earnest enquirer come to the conclusion that I was never born at all. But I prefer to believe that common sense is something that my readers and I have in common and that they will have patience with a dull summary of the facts.

I was born of respectable but honest parents, that is, in a world where the word "respectability" was not yet exclusively a term of abuse, but retained some dim philological connection with the idea of being respected. It is true that even in my own youth the sense of the word was changing, as I remember in a conversation between my parents, in which it was used with both implications. My father, who was serene, humorous and full of hobbies, remarked casually that he had been asked to go on what was then called The Vestry. At this my mother, who was more swift, restless and generally Radical in her instincts, uttered something like a cry of pain; she said, "Oh, Edward, don't! You will be so respectable! We never have been respectable yet; don't let's begin now." And I remember my father mildly replying, "My dear, you present a rather alarming picture of our lives, if you say that we have never for one single instant been respectable." Readers of *Pride and Prejudice* will perceive that there was something of Mr Bennet about my father; though there was certainly nothing of Mrs Bennet about my mother.

Anyhow, what I mean here is that my people belonged to that rather old-fashioned English middle-class; in which a businessman was still permitted to mind his own business. They had been granted no glimpse of our later and loftier vision, of that more advanced and adventurous conception of commerce, in which a businessman is supposed to rival, ruin, destroy, absorb and swallow up everybody else's business. My father was a Liberal of the school that existed before the rise of Socialism; he took it for granted that all sane people believed in private property; but he did not trouble to translate it into private enterprise. His people were of the sort that were always sufficiently successful, but hardly, in the modern sense, enterprising. My father was the head of a hereditary business of house-agents and surveyors, which had already been established for some three generations in Kensington; and I remember that there was a sort of local patriotism about it and a little reluctance in the elder members, when the younger first proposed that it should have branches outside Kensington. This particular sort of unobtrusive pride was very characteristic of this sort of older businessmen. I remember that it once created a comedy of cross-purposes, which could hardly have occurred unless there had been some such secret self-congratulation upon any accretion of local status. The incident is in more ways than one a glimpse of the tone and talk of those distant days.

My grandfather, my father's father, was a fine-looking old man with white hair and beard and manners that had something of that rounded solemnity that went with the old-fashioned customs of proposing toasts and sentiments. He kept up the ancient Christian custom of singing at the dinner-table, and it did not seem incongruous when he sang "The Fine Old English

Gentleman" as well as more pompous songs of the period of Waterloo and Trafalgar. And I may remark in passing that, having lived to see Mafeking Night and the later Jingo lyrics, I have retained a considerable respect for those old and pompous patriotic songs. I rather fancy it was better for the tradition of the English tongue to hear such rhetorical lines as these, about Wellington at the death-bed of William the Fourth,

> For he came on the Angel of Victory's wing
> But the Angel of Death was awaiting the King,

than to be entirely satisfied with howling the following lines, heard in all music-halls some twenty years afterwards

> And when we say we've always won
> And when they ask us how it's done
> We proudly point to every one
> Of England's soldiers of the Queen.

I cannot help having a dim suspicion that dignity has something to do with style; but anyhow the gestures, like the songs, of my grandfather's time and type had a good deal to do with dignity. But, used as he was to ceremonial manners, he must have been a good deal mystified by a strange gentleman who entered the office and, having conferred with my father briefly on business, asked in a hushed voice if he might have the high privilege of being presented to the more ancient or ancestral head of the firm. He then approached my grandfather as if the old gentleman had been a sort of shrine, with profound bows and reverential apostrophes.

"You are a Monument," said the strange gentleman, "Sir, you are a Landmark."

My grandfather, slightly flattered, murmured politely that they had certainly been in Kensington for some little time.

"You are an Historical Character," said the admiring stranger. "You have changed the whole destiny of Church and State."

My grandfather still assumed airily that this might be a poetical manner of describing a successful house-agency. But a light began to break on my father, who had thought his way through all the High Church and Broad Church movements and was well-read in such things. He suddenly remembered the case of "Westerton versus Liddell," in which a Protestant churchwarden prose-cuted a parson for one of the darker crimes of Popery, possibly wearing a surplice.

"And I only hope," went on the stranger firmly, still addressing the Protestant Champion, "that the services at the Parish Church are now conducted in a manner of which you approve."

My grandfather observed in a genial manner that he didn't care how they were conducted. These remarkable words of the Protestant Champion caused his worshipper to gaze upon him with a new dawn of wonder, when my father intervened and explained the error, pointing out the fine shade that divides Westerton and Chesterton. I may add that my grandfather, when the story was told, always used to insist that he had added to the phrase, "I don't care how they're conducted," the qualifying words (repeated with a grave motion of the hand) "provided it is with reverence and sincerity." But I grieve to say that sceptics in the younger generation believed this to have been an afterthought.

The point is, however, that my grandfather was pleased, and not really very much amazed, to be called a monument and a landmark. And that was typical of many middle-class men, even in small businesses, in that remote world. For the particular sort of British *bourgeoisie* of which I am speaking has been so much altered or diminished, that it cannot exactly be said to exist today. Nothing quite like it at least can be found in England; nothing in the least like it, I fancy, was ever found in America. One peculiarity of this middle-class was that it really was a class and it really was in the middle. Both for good and evil, and certainly often to excess, it was separated both from the class above it and the class below. It knew far too little of the working-classes, to the grave peril of a later generation. It knew far too little even of its own servants. My own people were always very kind to servants; but in the class as a whole there was neither the coarse familiarity in work, which belongs to democracies and can be seen in the clamouring and cursing housewives of the Continent, nor the remains of a feudal friendliness such as lingers in the real aristocracy. There was a sort of silence and embarrassment. It was illustrated in another hearsay anecdote, which I may here add to the anecdote of the Protestant Champion. A lady of my family went to live in a friend's house in the friend's absence; to be waited on by a sort of superior servant. The lady had got it fixed in her head that the servant cooked her own meals separately, whereas the servant was equally fixed on the policy of eating what was left over from the lady's meals. The servant sent up for breakfast, say, five rashers of bacon; which was more than the lady wanted. But the lady had another fixed freak of conscience common in the ladies of the period. She thought nothing should be wasted; and could not see that even a thing consumed is wasted if it is not wanted. She ate the five rashers and the servant consequently sent up seven rashers. The lady paled a little, but followed the path of duty and ate them all. The servant, beginning to feel that she too would like a little breakfast, sent up nine or ten rashers. The lady, rallying all her powers, charged at them with her head down, and swept them from the field. And so, I suppose, it went on; owing to the polite silence between the two social classes. I dare not think how it ended. The logical conclusion would seem to be that the servant starved and the lady burst. But I suppose that, before they reached that point, some communications had been opened between two people living on two floors of the same house. But that was certainly the weak side of that world; that it did not extend its domestic confidence to domestic servants. It smiled and felt superior when reading of the old-world vassals who dined below the salt, and continued to feel equally superior to its own vassals, who dined below the floor.

But however we may criticise the old middle-class, and however heartily we may join in these immortal words of the Song of the Future, which are said to run;

> Class-conscious we are, class-conscious we'll be;
> Till our foot's on the necks of the *bourgeoisie,*

it has a right to historical justice; and there are other points to remember. One point is that it was partly the real "culture conquests" of this stratum of the middle-class, and the fact that it really was an educated class, that made it unduly suspicious of the influence of servants. It attached rather too much importance to spelling correctly; it attached enormous importance to speaking correctly. And it did spell and speak correctly. There was a whole world in which nobody was any more likely to drop an *h* than to pick up a title. I early discovered, with the malice of infancy, that what my seniors were really afraid of was any imitation of the intonation and diction of the servants. I am told (to quote another hearsay anecdote) that about the age of three or four, I screamed for a hat hanging on a peg, and at last in convulsions of fury uttered the awful words, "If you don't give it me, I'll say 'at." I felt sure that would lay all my relations prostrate for miles around.

And this care about education and diction, though I can see much to criticise in it now, did really have its good side. It meant that my father knew all his English literature backwards, and that I knew a great deal of it by heart, long before I could really get it into my head. I knew pages of Shakespeare's blank verse without a notion of the meaning of most of it; which is perhaps the right way to begin to appreciate verse. And it is also recorded of me that, at the age of six or seven, I tumbled down in the street in the act of excitedly reciting the words,

> Good Hamlet, cast thy nightly colour off,
> And let thine eye look like a friend on Denmark,
> Do not for ever with thy vailed lids
> Seek for thy noble father in the dust,

at which appropriate moment I pitched forward on my nose.

What is perhaps even less appreciated is that the particular class I mean was not only cut off from what are called the lower classes, but also quite as sharply from what are called the upper classes. Since then we may say, with all graceful apologies, that this class has split up into the two great sections of the Snobs and the Prigs. The first are those who want to get into Society; the second are those who want to get out of Society, and into Societies. I mean Vegetarian Societies and Socialist Colonies and things of that sort. But the people I mean were not cranks, and, what is more, they were not snobs. There were plenty of people in their time, of course, who were snobbish; but those I mean were really a class apart. They never dreamed of knowing the aristocracy except in business. They had, what has since become almost incredible in England, a pride of their own.

For instance, almost all that district of Kensington was and is laid out like a chart or plan to illustrate Macaulay's Essays. Of course we read Macaulay's Essays; and in our simple isolation, often even believed them. We knew all the great names of the Whig aristocrats who had made the Revolution (and incidentally their own fortunes) and those names were written conspicuously all over the Kensington estates. Every day we passed Holland House, that opened its hospitality to Macaulay, and the statue of Lord Holland inscribed with the boast that he was the nephew of Fox and the friend of Grey. The street opposite where we came to live bore the name of Addison; the street of our later sojourn the name of Warwick the stepson of Addison. Beyond was a road named after the house of Russell, to the south another with the name of Cromwell. Near us, on our original perch in Campden Hill, was the great name of Argyll. Now all these names thrilled me like trumpet, as they would any boy reading Macaulay. But it never so much as crossed my mind that we should ever know any people who bore them, or even especially want to. I remember making my father laugh very much by telling him of the old Scots ballad with the line,

There fell about a great dispute between Argyle and Airlie.

For he knew, as a house-agent, that Lord Airlie's house was actually quite close to Argyll Lodge; and that nothing was more likely than that there might fall about a great dispute, directly affecting his own line of business. He knew the old Duke of Argyll in purely business relations, and showed me a letter from him as a curiosity; but to me it was like a delightful curiosity in a museum. I no more thought of expecting McCallum More to come in any way into my own social existence, than I expected Graham of Claverhouse to ride up on his great black horse to the front-door, or Charles the Second to drop in to tea. I regarded the Duke living at Argyll Lodge as an historical character. My people were interested in an aristocracy because it was still an historical thing. The point is worth mentioning, because it is exactly this difference, whether for good or evil, that justifies a fight or feud of which I shall have to write on a later page. Long afterwards, I had the luck to figure in a political row about the Sale of Peerages; and many said that we were wasting our energies in denouncing it. But we were not. The treatment of a title did make a difference; and I am just old enough to be able to measure the difference it has really made. If, regarding Lord Lorne with historical respect, I had been introduced to an unknown Lord Leatherhead, I should have respected him also as something historical. If I were to meet him now, I should know he might be any pawnbroker from any gutter in Europe. Honours have not been sold; they have been destroyed.

One considerable family connected with the family business, merely in the way of business, may be worth mentioning for quite other reasons. The firm was, and indeed still is, agent for the large Phillimore Estate then owned by two brothers who both played considerable public parts; Admiral Phillimore who died long ago and Lord Justice Phillimore, one of the most famous of the modern English judges, who died more recently. We had nothing to do with such people, nor tried to, though I remember more than one quite independent testimony to the magnanimity of the old Admiral. But I mention this vague background of the great Kensington Estate for another reason. For the name of Phillimore was destined in a strange and double and rather ironic fashion, to be entwined with my subsequent adventures in life. The Admiral I never saw; but his son, who must have been a child of about my own age, I was long afterwards to know and love and lose, as a friend and an ally in a cause which would then have seemed fantastically far away from our boyhoods. And the Judge I was destined to see sitting on the seat of judgment, and to give evidence before him on behalf of my brother, who stood in the dock at the Old Bailey and was found guilty of patriotism and public spirit.

My mother's family had a French surname; though the family, as I knew it by experience as well as tradition, was entirely English in speech and social habit. There was a sort of family legend that they were descended from a French private soldier of the Revolutionary Wars, who had been a prisoner in England and remained there; as some certainly did. But on the other side my mother came of Scottish people, who were Keiths from Aberdeen; and for several reasons, partly because my maternal grandmother long survived her husband and was a very attractive personality, and partly because of a certain vividness in any infusion of Scots blood or patriotism, this northern affiliation appealed strongly to my affections; and made a sort of Scottish romance in my childhood. But her husband, my maternal grandfather whom I never saw, must have been an interesting person too; and something of an historical type, if not an historical character. He had been one of the old Wesleyan lay-preachers and was thus involved in public controversy, a characteristic which has descended to his grandchild. He was also one of the leaders of the early Teetotal movement; a characteristic which has not. But I am quite sure there was a great deal in him, beyond anything that is implied in mere public speaking or teetotalism. I am quite sure of it, because of two casual remarks he made; which are indeed the only two remarks I ever heard of him making. Once, when his sons were declaiming against mode and convention in the manner of all liberal youth, he said abruptly: "Ah, they talk a lot about fashion; but fashion is civilisation." And in the other case, the same rising generation were lightly tossing about that pessimism which is only possible in the happy time of youth. They were criticising the General Thanksgiving in the Prayer-Book, and remarking that a good many people have very little reason to be thankful for their creation. And the old man, who was then so old that he hardly ever spoke at all, said suddenly out of his silence, "I should thank God for my creation if I knew I was a lost soul."

Of the other side of my family I may say more when I come to my own memories; but I put this side of the matter first because there is so much more of it that I have received only at second-hand. And this is the part of the book which is forced to be biography and cannot be autobiography. It deals with the things that were just behind me and merely threw their shadows on my earliest path; the things I saw in reflection rather than reality. Of these there were more on my mother's side; especially that historical interest in the house of Keith which was mixed up with my general historical interest in things like the house of Argyll. But on my father's side also there were legends; the nearest and most eminent figure being that Captain Chesterton, who was famous in his day as a reformer of prisons. He was a friend of Dickens, and, I suspect, himself something of a Dickens character. But indeed these first memories and rumours suggest that there were a good many Dickens characters in the days of Dickens. I am far from denying the inference; that a good many Dickens characters are humbugs. It would not be fair to say all I have said in praise of the old Victorian middle-class, without admitting that it did sometimes produce pretty hollow and pompous imposture. A solemn friend of my grandfather used to go for walks on Sunday carrying a prayer-book, without the least intention of going to church. And he calmly defended it by saying, with uplifted hand: "I do it, Chessie, as an example to others." The man who did that was obviously a Dickens character. And I am disposed to think that, in being a Dickens character, he was in many ways rather preferable to many modern characters. Few modern men, however false, would dare to be so brazen. And I am not sure he was not really a more genuine fellow than the modern man who says vaguely that he has doubts or hates sermons, when he only wants to go and play golf. Hypocrisy itself was more sincere. Anyhow, it was more courageous.

What I can but call a Great Gusto breathed out of that epoch; something now only remembered in the rich and rollicking quotations of Swiveller and Micawber. But the point is that the savour of it could then be found in scores of quite worthy and obscure people; certainly much more worthy than the blatantly Pecksniffian person with the prayer-book; and much more obscure than the eccentric, but efficient, and even eminent, prison governor and reformer. To use a trade term of the period, this indescribable sort of relish was by no means only a gentlemen's relish. It was the effect, I think, of that popular humour, which is still perhaps our only really popular institution, working upon the remains of the rhetoric of the eighteenth-century orators, and the almost equally rhetorical rhetoric of the nineteenth-century poets, like Byron and Moore. Anyhow, it was evidently common to countless common or average people, and rather specially to commercial clerks. The clerk came afterwards to figure rather as a mere cheap Cockney with clipped speech; a sort of broken English that seems broken by accident; chipped rather than clipped. But there was a race that really dealt in periods as rounded as Christmas platters and punchbowls. My father told me of a fellow-clerk of his youth, or boyhood, who took leave of the tavern or chop-house with a stately message of thanks, which he delivered in a big booming voice, before stalking into the street: "Tell Mrs Bayfield that the steak was excellent; the potatoes done to a turn; in short a dinner fit for an Emperor." Is not that exactly like "F B" in the moments when Thackeray was most Dickensian? From the same remote source, I recall another quite Dickensian scene; a bland, round-faced little man in spectacles, the sort that is always chaffed anywhere; and a fellow-clerk named Cart, of more mysterious humours; both ghosts from my father's time of apprenticeship. At intervals the more sombre clerk would call out across the office: "Mr Hannay!" The round face, bright with its smile and spectacles, would bob up with never-failing freshness and expectation: "Yes, Mr Carr." Then Mr Carr would fix him with a sphinx-like visage and say in hollow, but resounding tones: "Boundless Space!" And then Mr Carr would turn more briskly to the other clerks, shaking his head, and repeating in a hopeless tone: "He can't grasp it!" I do not know what either of them would have thought of the idea of Professor Einstein entering the office and avenging Mr Hannay on Mr Carr, by suggesting that space is not boundless at all. The point is that there is this element of pomp and ritual about jokes; even about practical jokes; indeed even about practical deceptions. It was known in humbler walks, among mountebanks and even monstrosities, as well Dickens knew; and there was something as stately about the cheap-jacks demanding money as the orators demanding fame. One of my own earliest memories is of looking from a balcony above one of the big residential roads of a watering-place, and seeing a venerable party with white hair solemnly taking off a white hat as he walked down the centre of the street, and saying to nobody in particular in the loud voice of a lecturer: "When I first came into Cannon Street – I beg your pardon, Cannon Place…" a performance which he repeated every day, always falling into the same error to be followed by the same apology. This gave me, I know not why, enormous pleasure; partly, I think, from the feeling that a gigantic clockwork doll had been added to what Mr Maurice Baring calls the puppet-show of memory. But his importance here is that the rest of his speech seemed all the more polished and faultless for that one strangely recurrent fault; and it always ended with a beautiful peroration, about recalling in the distant future, and in the hour of death, "the kindness I have met with in Cannon Place." Later, I remember the same seaside paths paraded by a yet more loquacious public character wearing cap and gown, I fear with but little academic authority; but I think he marked a much later stage, because he was acrid and antagonistic, and appealed to his audience by calling them hypocrites and whited sepulchres; which had the curious effect upon that very English crowd of causing them to throw pennies into his mortar-board. But in the earlier stage which concerns me here, a glow of convivial courtesy covered everything; and the wing of friendship could never moult a feather. The amazing patience of our populace then went with a certain pomp, but it was a pompous geniality; and even their jeers were still jovial. Their mockery and their heroism still remain, heaven knows; but they no longer thus combine in the mock heroic. But anybody who heard, or heard of, the men I mention, will be certain to his dying day that Dick Swiveller did say: "When he who adores thee has left but the name – in case of letters or parcels," or that the poor usher at the party did whisper to each lady in turn: "Had I a heart for falsehood framed I ne'er could injure you." There was a glow in it; not to be copied by sparks, even when they really sparkle. The world is less gay for losing that solemnity.

Another real Victorian virtue, not to be discredited by many imaginary Victorian virtues, belongs not so much to my generation as to my father's and grandfather's; or at least, if I was specially lucky, to my father and grandfather. It should, therefore, be mentioned in this place, as it is illustrated by incidents within my own memory. My own people in any case had a strict standard of commercial probity; but I fancy the standard was stricter in all that more stolid commercial class than in a later time, when the notion of success was mixed up not only with cynicism, but with a queer sort of piratical romance. The change may be felt, as in the word "respectable," in the very atmosphere of certain words. The favourite modern ideal in morals and even in religion, especially the religion popularised in the papers for millions of modern business men, is the word "adventure." The most menacing monster in morals, for the business men of my old middle-class, was branded with the title of "adventurer." In later times, I fancy, the world has defended some pretty indefensible adventurers by implying the glamour of adventure.

Anyhow, this is not merely my own belated opinion in an age of reaction. It was the opinion of the best even of the old optimists and orthodox economists, who lived when the change was beginning, and believed they were living in an age of reform. My own father and uncles were entirely of the period that believed in progress, and generally in new things, all the more because they were finding it increasingly difficult to believe in old things; and in some cases in anything at all. But though as Liberals they believed in progress, as honest men they often testified to deterioration.

I remember my father telling me how much he had begun to be pestered by great swarms of people wanting private commissions upon transactions, in which they were supposed to represent another interest. He mentioned it not only with the deepest disgust, but more or less as if it were a novelty as well as a nuisance. He was himself in the habit of meeting these unpleasant people with a humorously simulated burst of heartiness and even hilarity; but it was the only sort of occasion on which his humour might be called grim and even ferocious. When the agent, bargaining for some third party, hinted that an acceptable trifle would smooth the negotiations, he would say with formidable geniality: "Oh, certainly! certainly! So long as we are all friends and everything is open and above-board! I am sure your principals and employers will be delighted to hear from me that I'm paying for a small – " He would then be interrupted with a sort of shriek of fear and the kind diplomatic gentleman would cover his tracks as best he could in terror. "And doesn't that prove to you," said my father with innocent rationalism, "the immorality of such a proposal ?"

My Uncle Sidney, who was his partner in the business, was a more unanswerable witness, because a more unwilling witness. My father was very universal in his interests and very moderate in his opinions; he was one of the few men I ever knew who really listened to argument; moreover, he was more traditional than many in the liberal age; he loved many old things, and had especially a passion for the French cathedrals and all the Gothic architecture opened up by Ruskin in that time. It was not quite so inconceivable that he might admit another side to modern progress. But my uncle was the very reverse of a *laudator temporis acti*. He was one of those sensitive and conscientious men, very typical of the modern world, who had the same scrupulous sense of the duty of accepting new things, and sympathising with the young, that older moralists may have had about preserving old things and obeying the elders. I remember him assuring me quite eagerly of the hopeful thoughts aroused in him by the optimistic official prophecies of the book called, *Looking Backwards*; a rather ironical title, seeing that the one thing forbidden to such futurists was Looking Backwards. And the whole philosophy, afterwards sublimated by the genius of Mr Wells, was the duty of Looking Forwards. My uncle, much more than my father, was this

11

scrupulously sanguine sort of man; and the last man in the world to hold any brief for the good old times. But he was also a quite transparently truthful man; and I remember him telling me, with that wrinkle of worry in his brow, which confessed his subconscious and sensitive anxiety: "I'm bound to confess that commercial morality has got steadily worse through my lifetime."

Of course I admit, or rather I boast, that in anything like sympathy with any such Utopia, such individuals were in advance of the times. But I boast much more that, in the great modern growth of high finance, they were behind the times. The class as a whole was, indeed, dangerously deaf and blind upon the former question of economic exploitation; but it was relatively more vigilant and sensitive upon the latter question of financial decency. It never occurred to these people that anybody could possibly admire a man for being what we call "daring" in speculation, any more than a woman for being what we call "daring" in dress. There was something of the same atmospheric change in both cases. The absence of social ambition had a great deal to do with it. When the restrictions really were stuffy and stupid, they were largely those of ignorance; but this was nothing like so evil and ruinous as the ignorance of the real wrongs and rights of the working-classes. Heaven knows, it is even possible that in some cases the reader knows, that I am no admirer of the complacent commercial prosperity of England in the nineteenth century. At the best it was an individualism that ended by destroying individuality; an industrialism which has done nothing except poison the very meaning of the word industry. At the worst it turned at last into a vulgar victory of sweating and swindling. I am only pointing out a particular point about a particular group or class, now extinct; that if they were ignorant of, or often indifferent to the sweating, they were really indignant at the swindling. In the same way, few will accuse me of Puritanism; but I think it due to the Puritan tradition to say that certain notions of social sobriety did have something to do with delaying the full triumph of flashy finance and the mere antics of avarice. Anyhow, there has been a change from a middle-class that trusted a businessman to look after money because he was dull and careful, to one that trusts a businessman to get more money because he is dashing and worldly. It has not always asked itself for whom he would get more money, or whose money he would get.

I know well I was very fortunate in my own family. But even those less fortunate were not subject to the special evils now commonly labelled Victorian. Indeed, in the modern sense, Victorianism was not at all Victorian. It was a period of increasing strain. It was the very reverse of solid respectability; because its ethics and theology were wearing thin throughout. It may have been orderly compared with what came after; but not compared with the centuries that came before. It sometimes boasted of being domestic; but the Englishman's home was not half so domestic as that of the horrid foreigner, the profligate Frenchman. It was the age when the Englishman sent all his sons to boarding-school and sent all his servants to coventry. I cannot imagine why anybody ever said that the Englishman's house was his castle, since he was one of the few Europeans who did not even own his house; and his house was avowedly a dull box of brick, of all the houses the least like a castle. Above all, so far from being stiff with orthodox religion, it was almost the first irreligious home in all human history. Theirs was the first generation that ever asked its children to worship the hearth without the altar. This was equally true, whether they went to church at eleven o'clock, with more decent thoroughness than the gay deceiver with the prayer-book, or were reverently agnostic or latitudinarian, as was much of my own circle. For the most part, it was family life stripped of its festivals and shrines and private cults, which had been its poetry in the past. It was a joke to talk of the heavy father's heavy furniture, and call the chairs and tables his household gods. It was the fact that he was the first man, for whom there were no household gods but only furniture.

That was the duller side; but there has been even more exaggeration about the darker side. I mean that modern novelists and others have started a trick of writing as if the old middle-class home was almost always a private lunatic asylum, with the lunatic in charge; as in the case of the exceedingly Mad Hatter who inhabited Hatter's Castle. This is a grotesque exaggeration; there were parents with this savage degree of selfishness; I recall not many more than three of them in the whole of our old social circle; but the wrong associations are attached even to them. A few of them may have been religious fanatics. I remember one, who locked up his daughters like prisoners; one of whom said to me: "You see he thinks nobody else can think at all, except himself and Herbert Spencer." I remember another who was an extreme Radical, a champion of liberty everywhere except at home. The point is of some historic importance. Tyrants, religious or irreligious, turn up anywhere. But this type of tyrant was the product of the precise moment when a middle-class man still had children and servants to control; but no longer had creeds or guilds or kings or priests or anything to control him. He was already an anarchist to those above him; but still an authoritarian to those below. But he was an abnormal fellow anyhow; and none of my people bore the least resemblance to him.

What Puritanic element there was in this forgotten society must certainly be allowed for as a part of the picture. It was mostly, among my people, a rather illogical disapproval of certain forms of luxury and expenditure. Their tables would groan under far grander dinners than many aristocrats eat today. But they had, for instance, a fixed feeling that there was something rather raffish about taking a cab. It was probably connected with their sensitive pride about not aping the aristocracy. I can remember my grandfather, when he was nearly eighty and able to afford any number of cabs, standing in the pouring rain while seven or eight crowded omnibuses went by; and afterwards whispering to my father (in a hushed voice lest the blasphemy be heard by the young): "If three more omnibuses had gone by, upon my soul I think I should have taken a cab." In the matter of driving about in cabs, I cannot claim to have kept the family escutcheon unspotted, or to have lived up to the high standard of my sires. But in the matter of their motive for not doing so, I am disposed to defend them, or at least to say that they are much misunderstood. They were the last descendants of Mrs Gilpin, who told the chaise to stop a few doors from her house, lest the neighbours should think her proud. I am not sure that she was not a healthier person than the smart lady who will be seen in anybody's Rolls Royce, lest the neighbours should think her humble.

Such, so far as I know it, was the social landscape in which I first found myself; and such were the people among whom I was born. I am sorry if the landscape or the people appear disappointingly respectable and even reasonable, and deficient in all those unpleasant qualities that make a biography really popular. I regret that I have no gloomy and savage father to offer to the public gaze as the true cause of all my tragic heritage; no pale-faced and partially poisoned mother whose suicidal instincts have cursed me with the temptations of the artistic temperament. I regret that there was nothing in the range of our family much more racy than a remote and mildly impecunious uncle; and that I cannot do my duty as a true modern, by cursing everybody who made me whatever I am. I am not clear about what that is; but I am pretty sure that most of it is my own fault. And I am compelled to confess that I look back to that landscape of my first days with a pleasure that should doubtless be reserved for the Utopias of the Futurist. Yet the landscape, as I see it now, was not altogether without a visionary and symbolic character. And among all the objects in that landscape, I find myself returning at the last to those which I mentioned first. In one way and another, those things have come to stand for so many other things, in the acted allegory of a human existence; the little church of my baptism and the waterworks, the bare, blind, dizzy tower of brick that seemed, to my first upward starings, to take hold upon the stats. Perhaps there was something in the confused and chaotic notion of a tower of water; as if the sea itself could stand on one end like a water-spout. Certainly later, though I hardly know how late, there came into my mind some fancy of a colossal water-snake that might be the Great Sea Serpent, and had something of the nightmare nearness of a dragon in a dream. And, over against it, the small church rose in a spire like a spear; and I have always been pleased to remember that it was dedicated to St George.

II

THE MAN WITH THE GOLDEN KEY

The very first thing I can ever remember seeing with my own eyes was a young man walking across a bridge. He had a curly moustache and an attitude of confidence verging on swagger. He carried in his hand a disproportionately large key of a shining yellow metal and wore a large golden or gilded crown. The bridge he was crossing sprang on the one side from the edge of a highly perilous mountain chasm, the peaks of the range rising fantastically in the distance; and at the other end it joined the upper part of the tower of an almost excessively castellated castle. In the castle tower there was one window, out of which a young lady was looking. I cannot remember in the least what she looked like; but I will do battle with anyone who denies her superlative good looks.

To those who may object that such a scene is rate in the home life of house-agents living immediately to the north of Kensington High Street, in the later seventies of the last century, I shall be compelled to admit, not that the scene was unreal, but that I saw it through a window more wonderful than the window in the tower; through the proscenium of a toy theatre constructed by my father; and that (if I am really to be pestered about such irrelevant details) the young man in the crown was about six inches high and proved on investigation to be made of cardboard. But it is strictly true to say that I saw him before I can remember seeing anybody else; and that, so far as my memory is concerned, this was the sight on which my eyes first opened in this world. And the scene has to me a sort of aboriginal authenticity impossible to describe; something at the back of all my thoughts; like the very back-scene of the theatre of things. I have no shadow of recollection of what the young man was doing on the bridge, or of what he proposed to do with the key; though a later and wearier knowledge of literature and legend hints to me that he was not improbably going to release the lady from captivity. It is a not unamusing detail of psychology that, though I can remember no other characters in the story, I do remember noting that the crowned gentleman had a moustache and no beard, with a vague inference that there was another crowned gentleman who had a beard as well. We may safely guess, I imagine, that the bearded one was by way of being a wicked king; and we should not need much more converging evidence to convict him of having locked up the lady in the tower. All the rest is gone; scenes, subject, story, characters; but that one scene glows in my memory like a glimpse of some incredible paradise; and, for all I know, I shall still remember it when all other memory is gone out of my mind.

Apart from the fact of it being my first memory, I have several reasons for putting it first. I am no psychologist, thank God; but if psychologists are still saying what ordinary sane people have always said: that early impressions count considerably in life, I recognise a sort of symbol of all that I happen to like in imagery and ideas. All my life I have loved edges; and the boundary-line that brings one thing sharply against another. All my life I have loved frames and limits; and I will maintain that the largest wilderness looks larger seen through a window. To the grief of all grave dramatic critics, I will still assert that the perfect drama must strive to rise to the higher ecstasy of the peep-show. I have also a pretty taste in abysses and bottomless chasms and everything else that emphasises a fine shade of distinction between one thing and another; and the warm affection I have always felt for bridges is connected with the fact that the dark and dizzy arch accentuates the chasm even more than the chasm itself. I can no longer behold the beauty of the princess; but I can see it in the bridge that the prince crossed to reach her. And I believe that in feeling these things from the first, I was feeling the fragmentary suggestions of a philosophy I have since found to be the truth. For it is upon that point of truth that there might perhaps be a quarrel between the more material psychologists and myself. If any man tells me that I only take pleasure in the mysteries of the window and the bridge because I saw these models of them when I was a baby, I shall take the liberty of telling him that he has not thought the thing out. To begin with, I must have seen thousands of other things before as well as after; and there must have been an element of selection and some reason for selection. And, what is still more obvious, to date the occasion does not even begin to deal with the fact. If some laborious reader of little books on child psychology cries out to me in glee and cunning: "You only like romantic things like toy theatres because your father showed you a toy theatre in your childhood," I shall reply with gentle and Christian patience: "Yes, fool, yes. Undoubtedly your explanation is, in that sense, the true one. But what you are saying, in your witty way, is simply that I associate these things with happiness because I was so happy. It does not even begin to consider the question of why I was so happy. Why should looking through a square hole, at yellow pasteboard, lift anybody into the seventh heaven of happiness at any time of life? Why should it specially do so at that time of life? That is the psychological fact that you have to explain; and I have never seen any sort of rational explanation."

I apologise for this parenthesis; and for mentioning child psychology or anything else that can bring a blush to the cheek. But it happens to be a point on which I think some of our psychoanalysts display rather unblushing cheek. I do not wish my remarks confused with the horrible and degrading heresy that our minds are merely manufactured by accidental conditions, and therefore have no ultimate relation to truth at all. With all possible apologies to the freethinkers, I still propose to hold myself free to think. And anybody who will think for two minutes will see that this thought is the end of all thinking. It is useless to argue at all, if all our conclusions are warped by our conditions. Nobody can correct anybody's bias, if all mind is all bias.

The interlude is now over, thank you; and I will proceed to the more practical relations between my memory and my story. And it will first be necessary to say something about memory itself; and the reliability of such stories. I have begun with this fragment of a fairy play in a toy theatre, because it also sums up most clearly the strongest influences upon my childhood. I have said that the toy theatre was made by my father; and anybody who has ever tried to make such a theatre or mount such a play, will know that this alone stands for a remarkable round of crafts and accomplishments. It involves being in much more than the common sense the stage carpenter, being the architect and the builder and the draughtsman and the landscape-painter and the story-teller all in one. And, looking back on my life, and the relatively unreal and indirect art that I have attempted to practise, I feel that I have really lived a much narrower life than my father's.

His mere name, of course, is enough to recall wider memories. One of my first memories is playing in the garden under the care of a girl with ropes of golden hair; to whom my mother afterwards called out from the house: "You are an angel;" which I was disposed to accept without metaphor. She is now living in Vancouver as Mrs Kidd; and she and her sister had more to do with enlivening my early years than most. Since then, I have met what used to be called the wits of the age; but I have never known wittier conversation. Among my first memories also are those seascapes that were blue flashes to boys of my generation; North Berwick with the cone of green hill that seemed like the hill absolute; and a French seaside associated with little girls, the daughters of my father's old friend Mawer Cowtan, whom I shall not forget. But indeed I had a whole background of cousins; Tom Gilbert (my godfather, who gave me his last and my first name) had a large family of daughters, and my uncle Sidney a large family of sons; and they all still move in my memory almost like

17

a male and female chorus in a great Greek play. The eldest of the boys, the one whom I once knew best, was killed with my brother in the Great War; but many of the others, I am glad to say, are still friends as well as relations. All these are memorable memories; but they do not resolve that first individual speculation about memory itself. The girl with the yellow hair is an early memory, in the sense in which some of the others have inevitably become later memories, at once expanded and effaced.

Really, the things we remember are the things we forget. I mean that when a memory comes back sharply and suddenly, piercing the protection of oblivion, it appears for an instant exactly as it really was. If we think of it often, while its essentials doubtless remain true, it becomes more and more our own memory of the thing rather than the thing remembered. I had a little sister who died when I was a child. I have little to go on; for she was the only subject about which my father did not talk. It was the one dreadful sorrow of his abnormally happy and even merry existence; and it is strange to think that I never spoke to him about it to the day of his death. I do not remember her dying; but I remember her falling off a rocking-horse. I know, from experience of bereavements only a little later, that children feel with exactitude, without a word of explanation, the emotional tone or tint of a house of mourning. But in this case, the greater catastrophe must somehow have become confused and identified with the smaller one. I always felt it as a tragic memory, as if she had been thrown by a real horse and killed. Something must have painted and repainted the picture in my mind; until I suddenly became conscious about the age of eighteen that it had become the picture of Amy Robsart lying at the foot of the stairs, flung down by Varney and another villain. This is the real difficulty about remembering anything; that we have remembered too much – for we have remembered too often.

I will take another example of this psychological trick, though it involves the anticipation of much later events in my life. One of these glimpses of my own prehistoric history is a memory of a long upper room filled with light (the light that never was on sea or land) and of somebody carving or painting with white paint the deal head of a hobby-horse; the head almost archaic in its simplification. Ever since that day my depths have been stirred by even a wooden post painted white; and more so by any white horse in the street; and it was like meeting a friend in a fairy-tale to find myself under the sign of the White Horse at Ipswich on the first day of my honeymoon. But for that very reason, this image has remained and memory has constantly returned to it; and I have even done my best to deface and spoil the purity of the White Horse by writing an interminable ballad about it. A man does not generally manage to forget his wedding-day; especially such a highly comic wedding-day as mine. For the family remembers against me a number of now familiar legends, about the missing of trains, the losing of luggage, and other things counted yet more eccentric. It is alleged against me, and with perfect truth, that I stopped on the way to drink a glass of milk in one shop and to buy a revolver with cartridges in another. Some have seen these as singular wedding-presents for a bridegroom to give to himself; and if the bride had known less of him, I suppose she might have fancied that he was a suicide or a murderer or, worst of all, a teetotaller. They seemed to me the most natural things in the world. I did not buy the pistol to murder myself or my wife; I never was really modern. I bought it because it was the great adventure of my youth, with a general notion of protecting her from the pirates doubtless infesting the Norfolk Broads, to which we were bound; where, after all, there are still a suspiciously large number of families with Danish names. I shall not be annoyed if it is called childish; but obviously it was rather a reminiscence of boyhood, and not of childhood. But the ritual consumption of the glass of milk really was a reminiscence of childhood. I stopped at that particular dairy because I had always drunk a glass of milk there when walking with my mother in my infancy. And it seemed to me a fitting ceremonial to unite the two great relations of a man's life. Outside the shop there was the figure of a White Cow as a sort of pendant to the figure of the White Horse; the one standing at the beginning of my new journey and the other at the end. But the point is here that the very fact of these allegories having been acted over again, at the stage of marriage and maturity, does in a sense transform them, and does in some sense veil even while it invokes the original visions of the child. The sign of the White Horse has been repainted, and only in that sense painted out. I do not so much remember it as remember remembering it.

But if I really want to be realistic about those remote days, I must scratch around till I find something not too much blunted to scratch me; something sufficiently forgotten to be remembered. I make the experiment at this moment as I write. Searching for those lost surroundings, I recall for the first time, at this moment, that there was another shop, next to the milk-shop, which had some mysterious charm for my childhood; and then I recall that it was an oil and colour shop, and they sold gold paint smeared inside shells; and there was a sort of pale pointed chalks I have been less familiar with of late. I do not think here of the strong colours of the common paint-box, like crimson-lake and Prussian-blue, much as I exulted and still exult in them. For another boy called Robert Louis Stevenson has messed about with my colours upon that sort of palette; and I have grown up to enjoy them in print as well as in paint. But when I remember that these forgotten crayons contained a stick of "light-red," seemingly a more commonplace colour, the point of that dull red pencil pricks me as if it could draw red blood.

From this general memory about memory I draw a certain inference. What was wonderful about childhood is that anything in it was a wonder. It was not merely a world full of miracles; it was a miraculous world. What gives me this shock is almost anything I really recall; not the things I should think most worth recalling. This is where it differs from the other great thrill of the past, all that is connected with first love and the romantic passion; for that, though equally poignant, comes always to a point; and is narrow like a rapier piercing the heart, whereas the other was more like a hundred windows opened on all sides of the head.

I have made here a sort of psychological experiment in memory. I have tried to think of the things I forget adjoining the things I remember; and in the childish case, though they are without form, I am sure they are of the same tint. I have long remembered the milk shop; I have only just remembered the oil-shop; I have no notion at all about the next shop to the oil shop. I am sure it was a shop shining with the same lost light of morning; because it was in the same street under the same sky. I have no notion on what street the row of windows in the long uplifted room looked out, when the white horse head was carved. But I feel in a flash that it was a happy street; or, if we must be pedantic, a street in which I should have been happy. Now it is not like that with even the happiest hours of the later things called love-affairs. I have already mentioned how my honeymoon began before the White Cow of my childhood; but of course I had in my time been myself a calf, not to say a moon-calf, in the sort of calf-love that dances in the moonshine long before the honeymoon. Those day-dreams also are wrecks of something divine; but they have the colour of sunset rather than the broad daylight. I have walked across wide fields at evening and seen, as a mere distant dot in a row of houses, one particular window and just distinguishable head; and been uplifted as with roaring trumpets as if by the salute of Beatrice. But it did not, and does not, make me think the other windows and houses were all almost equally interesting; and that is just what the glimpse of the babies' wonderland does. We have read countless pages about love brightening the sun and making the flowers more flamboyant; and it is true in a sense; but not in the sense I mean. It changes the world; but the baby lived in a changeless world; or rather the man feels that it is he who has changed. He has changed long before he comes neat to the great and glorious trouble of the love of woman; and that has in it something new and concentrated and crucial; crucial in the true sense of being as near as Cana to Calvary. In the later case, what is loved becomes *instantly* what may be lost.

My point here is that we can test the childish mood by thinking, not only of what was there, but of what must have been there. I think of the backs of houses of which I saw only the fronts; the streets that stretched away behind the streets I knew; the things that remained round the corner; and they still give me a thrill. One of the sports of the imagination, a game I have played all my life, was to take a certain book with pictures of old Dutch houses, and think not of what was in the pictures, but of all that was out of the pictures, the unknown corners and side-streets of the same quaint town. The book was one my father had written and illustrated himself, merely for home consumption. It was typical of him that, in the Pugin period he had worked at Gothic illumination; but when he tried again, it was in another style of the dark Dutch Renaissance, the grotesque scroll-work that suggests wood-carving more than stone-cutting. He was the sort of man who likes to try everything once. This was the only book he ever wrote; and he never bothered to publish it.

My father might have reminded people of Mr Pickwick, except that he was always bearded and never bald; he wore spectacles and had all the Pickwickian evenness of temper and pleasure in the humours of travel. He was rather quiet than otherwise, but his quietude covered a great fertility of notions; and he certainly liked taking a rise out of people. I remember, to give one example of a hundred such inventions, how he gravely instructed some grave ladies in the names of flowers; dwelling especially on the rustic names given in certain localities. "The country people call them Sailors' Pen-knives," he would say in an off-hand manner, after affecting to provide them with the full scientific name, or, "They call them Bakers' Bootlaces down in Lincolnshire, I believe"; and it is a fine example of human simplicity to note how far he found he could safely go in such instructive discourse. They followed him without revulsion when he said lightly: "Merely a sprig of wild bigamy." It was only when he added that there was a local variety known as Bishop's Bigamy, that the full depravity of his character began to dawn on their minds. It was possibly this aspect of his unavailing amiability that is responsible for an entry I find in an ancient minute-book, of mock trials conducted by himself and his brothers; that Edward Chesterton was tried for the crime of Aggravation. But the same sort of invention created for children the permanent anticipation of what is profoundly called a Surprise. And it is this side of the business that is relevant here.

His versatility both as an experimentalist and a handy man, in all such matters, was amazing. His den or study was piled high with the stratified layers of about ten or twelve creative amusements; water-colour painting and modelling and photography and stained glass and fretwork and magic lanterns and medieval illumination. I have inherited, or I hope imitated, his habit of drawing; but in every other way I am emphatically an unhandy man. There had been some talk of his studying art professionally in his youth; but the family business was obviously safer; and his life followed the lines of a certain contented and ungrasping prudence, which was extraordinarily typical of him and all his blood and generation. He never dreamed of turning any of these plastic talents to any mercenary account, or of using them for anything but his own private pleasure and ours. To us he appeared to be indeed the Man with the Golden Key, a magician opening the gates of goblin castles or the sepulchres of dead heroes; and there was no incongruity in calling his lantern a magic lantern. But all this time he was known to the world, and even the next-door neighbours, as a very reliable and capable though rather unambitious businessman. It was a very good first lesson in what is also the last lesson of life; that in everything that matters, the inside is much larger than the outside. On the whole I am glad that he was never an artist. It might have stood in his way in becoming an amateur. It might have spoilt his career; his private career. He could never have made a vulgar success of all the thousand things he did so successfully.

If I made a generalisation about the Chestertons, my paternal kinsfolk (which may be dangerous, for there are a lot of them still alive), I should say that they were and are extraordinarily English. They have a perceptible and prevailing colour of good nature, of good sense not untinged with dreaminess, and a certain tranquil loyalty in their personal relations which was very notable even in one, like my brother Cecil, who in his public relations was supremely pugnacious and provocative. I think this sort of sleepy sanity rather an English thing; and in comparison it may not be entirely fanciful to suppose there was something French, after all, in the make-up of my mother's family; for, allowing for the usual admixture, they ran smaller in stature, often darker in colouring, tough, extraordinarily tenacious, prejudiced in a humorous fashion and full of the fighting spirit. But whatever we may guess in such matters (and nobody has yet done anything but guess about heredity), it was for another purpose that I mentioned the savour of something racial about such a stock. English in so many things, the Chestertons were supremely English in their natural turn for hobbies. It is an element in this sort of old English businessman which divides him most sharply from the American businessman; and to some extent from the new English businessman, who is copying the American. When the American begins to suggest that, "salesmanship can be an art," he means that an artist ought to put all his art into his salesmanship. The old-fashioned Englishman, like my father, sold houses for his living, but filled his own house with his life.

A hobby is not a holiday. It is not *merely* a momentary relaxation necessary to the renewal of work; and in this respect it must be sharply distinguished from much that is called sport. A good game is a good thing, but it is not the same thing as a hobby; and many go golfing or shooting grouse because this is a concentrated form of recreation; just as what our contemporaries find in whisky is a concentrated form of what our fathers found diffused in beer. If half a day is to take a man out of himself, or make a new man of him, it is better done by some sharp competitive excitement like sport. But a hobby is not half a day, but half a lifetime. It would be truer to accuse the hobbyist of living a double life. And hobbies, especially such hobbies as the toy theatre, have a character that runs parallel to practical professional effort, and is not merely a reaction from it. It is not merely taking exercise; it is doing work. It is not merely exercising the body instead of the mind, an excellent, but now largely a recognised thing. It is exercising the rest of the mind; now an almost neglected thing. When Browning, that typical Victorian, says that he likes to know a butcher paints and a baker writes poetry, he would not be satisfied with the statement that a butcher plays tennis or a baker golf. And my father and uncles, also typical Victorians of the sort that followed Browning, were all marked in varying degrees by this taste for having their own tastes. One of them gave all his spare time to gardening and has somewhere in the horticultural records a chrysanthemum named after him, dating from the first days when chrysanthemums came to us from the islands of the Rising Sun. Another travelled in an ordinary commercial fashion, but made a most amazing collection of cranks and quacks, fitted to fill a far better memoir than this, whom he had met in his wanderings, and with whom he had argued and sympathised and quoted Browning and George Macdonald, and done I fancy not a little good, for he was himself a most interesting man; above all, interesting because he was interested. But in my own household, as I have said, it was not a question of one hobby, but a hundred hobbies, piled on top of each other; and it is a personal accident, or perhaps a personal taste, that the one which has clung to my memory through life is the hobby of the toy theatre. In any case, watching such work has made one great difference to my life and views to this day.

I cannot do much, by the standard of my nursery days. But I have learned to love seeing things done; not the handle that ultimately causes them to be done, but the hand that does them. If my father had been some common millionaire owning a thousand mills that made cotton, or a million machines that made cocoa, how much smaller he would have seemed. And this experience has made me profoundly sceptical of all the modern talk about the necessary dullness of domesticity; and the degrading drudgery that only has to make puddings and pies. Only to make things! There is no greater thing to be said of God Himself than that He makes things. The manufacturer cannot even manufacture things; he can only pay to have them manufactured. And (in the same way) I am now incurably afflicted with a faint smile, when I hear a crowd of frivolous people, who could not make anything to save their lives, talking about the inevitable narrowness and stuffiness of the Victorian home. We managed to make a good many things in our Victorian home which people now buy at insane prices from Art and Craft Shops; the sort of shops that have quite as much craft as art. All the things that happened in the house, or were in any sense done on the premises, linger in my imagination like a legend; and as much as any, those connected with the kitchen or the pantry. Toffee still tastes nicer to me than the most expensive chocolates which Quaker millionaires sell by the million; and mostly because we made toffee for ourselves.

No. 999 in the vast library-catalogue of the books I have never written (all of them so much more brilliant and convincing than the books that I have written) is the story of a successful city man who seemed to have a dark secret in his life; and who was eventually discovered by the detectives still playing with dolls or tin soldiers or some undignified antic of infancy. I may say with all modesty that I am that man, in everything except his solidity of repute and his successful commercial career. It was perhaps even more true, in that sense, of my father before me; but I for one have never left off playing, and I wish there were more time to play. I wish we did not have to fritter away on frivolous things, like lectures and literature, the time we might have given to serious, solid and constructive work like cutting out cardboard figures and pasting coloured tinsel upon them. When I say this, I come to the third reason for taking the toy theatre as a text; and it is one about which there will be much misunderstanding, because of the repetitions and the stale sentiment that have somehow come to cling to it. It is one of those things that are always misunderstood, because they have been too often explained.

I am inclined to contradict much of the modern Cult of the Child at Play. Through various influences of a recent and rather romantic culture, the Child has become rather the Spoilt Child. The true beauty has been spoilt by the rather unscrupulous emotion of mature persons, who have themselves lost much of their sense of reality. The worst heresy of this school is that a child is concerned only with make-believe. For this is interpreted in the sense, at once sentimental and sceptical, that there is not much difference between make-belief and belief. But the real child does not confuse fact and fiction. He simply likes fiction. He acts it, because he cannot as yet write it or even read it; but he never allows his moral sanity to be clouded by it. To him no two things could possibly be more totally contrary than playing at robbers and stealing sweets. No possible amount of playing at robbers would ever bring him an inch nearer to thinking it is really right to rob. I saw the distinction perfectly clearly when I was a child; I wish I saw it half as clearly now. I played at being a robber for hours together at the end of the garden; but it never had anything to do with the temptation I had to sneak a new paint-box out of my father's room. I was not *being* anything false; I was simply writing before I could write. Fortunately, perhaps, for the condition of the back-garden, I early transferred my dreams to some rude resemblance to writing; chiefly in the form of drawing straggling and sprawling maps of fabulous countries, inhabited by men of incredible shapes and colours and bearing still more incredible names. But though I might fill the world with dragons, I never had the slightest real doubt that heroes ought to fight with dragons.

I must stop to challenge many child-lovers for cruelty to children. It is quite false to say that the child dislikes a fable that has a moral. Very often he likes the moral more than the fable. Adults are reading their own more weary mockery into a mind still vigorous enough to be entirely serious. Adults liked the comic Sandford and Merton. Children liked the real Sandford and Merton. At least I know I liked it very much, and felt the heartiest faith in the Honest Farmer and the Noble Negro. I venture to dwell on the point if only in parenthesis: for on this also there is a current misunderstanding. Indeed there is what may be called a current cant; and none the less so because it is a cant against cant. It is now so common as to be conventional to express impatience with priggish and moralising stories for children; stories of the old-fashioned sort that concern things like the sinfulness of theft; and as I am recalling an old-fashioned atmosphere, I cannot refrain from testifying on the psychology of the business.

Now I must heartily confess that I often adored priggish and moralising stories. I do not suppose I should gain a subtle literary pleasure from them now; but that is not the point in question. The men who denounce such moralisings are men; they are not children. But I believe multitudes would admit their early affection for the moral tale, if they still had the moral courage. And the reason is perfectly simple. Adults have reacted against such morality, because they know that it often stands for immorality. They know that such platitudes have been used by hypocrites and pharisees, by cunning or perversion. But the child knows nothing about cunning or perversion. He sees nothing but the moral ideals themselves, and he simply sees that they are true. Because they are.

There is another blunder made by the modern cynic about the moralising story-teller. The former always imagines that there is an element of corruption, in his own cynical manner, about the idea of reward, about the position of the child who can say, as in Stevenson's verses: "Every day when I've been good, I get an orange after food." To the man made ignorant by experience this always appears as a vulgar *bribe* to the child. The modern philosopher knows that it would require a very large bribe indeed to induce *him* to be good. It therefore seems to the modern philosopher what it would seem to the modern politician to say: "I will give you fifty thousand pounds when you have, on some one definite and demonstrated occasion, kept your word." The solid price seems something quite distinct from the tare and reluctant labour. But it does not seem like that to the child. It would not seem like that to the child, if the Fairy Queen said to the Prince: "You will receive the golden apple from the magic tree when you have fought the dragon." For the child is not a Manichee. He does not think that good things are in their nature separate from being good. In other words, he does not, like the reluctant realist, regard goodness as a bad thing. To him the goodness and the gift and the golden apple, that is called an orange, are all parts of one substantial paradise and naturally go together. In other words, he regards himself as normally on amiable terms with the natural authorities; not normally as quarrelling or bargaining with them. He has the ordinary selfish obstacles and misunderstandings; but he does not, in his heart, regard it as odd that his parents should be good to him, to the extent of an orange, or that he should be good to them, to the extent of some elementary experiments in good behaviour. He has no sense of being corrupted. It is only we, who have eaten the forbidden apple (or orange) who think of pleasure as a bribe.

My main purpose here, however, is to say this. To me my whole childhood has a certain quality, which may be indescribable but is not in the least vague. It is rather more definite than the difference between pitch dark and daylight, or between having a toothache and not having a toothache. For the sequel of the story, it is necessary to attempt this first and hardest chapter of the story: and I must try to state somehow what I mean by saying that my own childhood was of quite a different kind, or quality, from the rest of my very undeservedly pleasant and cheerful existence.

Of this positive quality, the most general attribute was clearness. Here it is that I differ, for instance, from Stevenson, whom I so warmly admire; and who speaks of the child as moving with his head in a cloud. He talks of the child as normally in a dazed day-dream, in which he cannot distinguish fancy from fact. Now children and adults are both fanciful at times; but that is not what, in my mind and memory, distinguishes adults from children. Mine is a memory of a sort of white light on everything, cutting things out very clearly, and rather emphasising their solidity. The point is that the white light had a sort of wonder in it, as if the world were as new as myself; but not that the world was anything but a real world. I am much more disposed *now* to fancy that an apple-tree in the moonlight is some sort of ghost or grey nymph; or to see the furniture fantastically changing and crawling at twilight, as in some story of Poe or Hawthorne. But when I was a child I had a sort of confident astonishment in contemplating the apple-tree as an apple-tree. I was quite sure of it, and also sure of the surprise of it; as sure, to quote the perfect popular proverb, as sure as God made little apples. The apples might be little as I was: but they were solid and so was I. There was something of an eternal morning about the mood; and I liked to see a fire lit more than to imagine faces in the firelight. Brother Fire, whom St Francis loved, did seem more like a brother than those dream-faces which come to men who have known other emotions than brotherhood. I do not know whether I ever, as the phrase goes, cried for the moon; but I am sure that I should have expected it to be solid like some colossal snowball; and should always have had more appetite for moons than for mere moonshine. Only figures of speech can faintly express the fact; but it was a fact and not a figure of speech. What I said first about the toy theatre may be urged in contradiction, and as an example of delight in a mere illusion.

In that case, what I said first about the toy theatre will be entirely misunderstood. In fact, there was in that business nothing of illusion or of disillusion. If this were a ruthless realistic modern story, I should of course give a most heartrending account of how my spirit was broken with disappointment, on discovering that the prince was only a painted figure. But this is not a ruthless realistic modern story. On the contrary, it is a true story. And the truth is that I do not remember that I was in any way deceived or in any way undeceived. The whole point is that I did like the toy theatre even when I knew it was a toy theatre. I did like the cardboard figures, even when I found they were of cardboard. The white light of wonder that shone on the whole business was not any sort of trick; indeed the things that now shine most in my memory were many of them mere technical accessories; such as the parallel sticks of white wood that held the scenery in place; a white wood that is still strangely mixed in my imaginative instincts with all the holy trade of the Carpenter. It was the same with any number of other games or pretences in which I took delight; as in the puppet-show of Punch and Judy. I not only knew that the figures were made of wood, but I wanted them to be made of wood. I could not imagine such a resounding thwack being given except by a wooden stick on a wooden head. But I took the sort of pleasure that a primitive man might have taken in a primitive craft, in seeing that they were carved and painted into a startling and grimacing caricature of humanity. I was pleased that the piece of wood was a face; but I was also pleased that the face was a piece of wood. That did not mean that the drama of wood, like the other drama of cardboard, did not reveal to me real ideas and imaginations, and give me glorious glimpses into the possibilities of existence. Of course, the child did not analyse himself then; and the man cannot analyse him now. But I am certain he was not merely tricked or trapped. He enjoyed the suggestive function of art exactly as an art critic enjoys it; only he enjoyed it a jolly sight more. For the same reason I do not think that I myself was ever very much worried about Santa Claus, or that alleged whisper of the little boy that Father Christmas "is only your father." Perhaps the word "only" would strike all children as the *mot juste*.

My fixed idolatry of Punch and Judy illustrated the same fact and the same fallacy. I was not only grateful for the fun, but I came to feel grateful for the very fittings and apparatus of the fun; the four-cornered tower of canvas with the one square window at the top, and everything down to the minimum of conventional and obviously painted scenery. Yet these were the very things I ought to have torn and rent in rage, as the trappings of imposture, if I had really regarded the explanation as spoiling the experience. I was pleased, and not displeased, when I discovered that the magic figures could be moved by three human fingers. And I was right; for those three human fingers are more magical than any magic fingers; the three fingers which hold the pen and the sword and the bow of the violin; the very three fingers that the priest lifts in benediction as the emblem of the Blessed Trinity. There was no conflict between the two magics in my mind.

I will here sum up in four statements, which will look very like puzzles upon this page. I can assure the reader that they have a relevance to the ultimate upshot of this book. Having littered the world with millions of essays for a living, I am doubtless prone to let this story stray into a sort of essay; but I repeat that it is not an essay but a story. So much so, that I am here employing a sort of device from a detective story. In the first few pages of a police novel, there are often three or four hints rather to rouse curiosity than allay it; so that the curate's start of recognition, the cockatoo's scream in the night, the burnt blotting-paper or the hasty avoidance of the subject of onions, is exhibited in the beginning though not explained until the end. So it is with the dull and difficult interlude of this chapter; a mere introspection about infancy which is not introspective. The patient reader may yet discover that these dark hints have something to do with the ensuing mystery of my misguided existence, and even with the crime that comes before the end. Anyhow, I will set them down here, without discussion of anything which they foreshadow.

First; my life unfolded itself in the epoch of evolution, which really only means unfolding. But many of the evolutionists of that epoch really seemed to mean by evolution the unfolding of what is not there. I have since, in a special sense, come to believe in development; which means the unfolding of what is there. Now it may seem both a daring and a doubtful boast, if I claim that in my childhood I was all there. At least, many of those who knew me best were quite doubtful about it. But I mean that the distinctions I make here were all there; I was not conscious of them but I contained them. In short, they existed in infancy in the condition called implicit; though they certainly did not then express themselves in what is commonly called implicit obedience.

Second; I knew, for instance, that pretending is not deceiving. I could not have defined the distinction if it had been questioned; but that was because it had never occurred to me that it could be questioned. It was merely because a child understands the nature of art, long before he understands the nature of argument. Now it is still not uncommon to say that images are idols and that idols are dolls. I am content to say here that even dolls are not idols, but in the true sense images. The very word images means things necessary to imagination. But not things contrary to reason; no, not even in a child. For imagination is almost the opposite of illusion.

Third; I have noted that I enjoyed Punch and Judy as a drama and not a dream; and indeed the whole extraordinary state of mind I strive to recapture was really the very reverse of a dream. It was rather as if I was more wide-awake then than I am now, and moving in broader daylight, which was to our broad daylight what daylight is to dusk. Only, of course, to those seeing the last gleam of it through the dusk, the light looks more uncanny than any darkness. Anyhow, it looks quite different; of that I am absolutely and solidly certain; though in such a subjective matter of sensation there can be no demonstration. What was the real meaning of that difference? I have some sort of a notion now; but I will not mention it at this stage of the story.

Fourth: it will be quite natural, it will also be quite wrong, to infer from all this that I passed a quite exceptionally comfortable childhood in complete contentment; or else that my memory is merely a sundial that has only marked the sunny hours. But that is not in the least what I mean; that is quite a different question. I was often unhappy in childhood like other children; but happiness and unhappiness seemed of a different texture or held on a different tenure. I was very often naughty in childhood like other children; and I never doubted for a moment the moral of all the moral tales; that, as a general principle, people ought to be unhappy when they have been naughty. That is, I held the whole idea of repentance and absolution implicit but not unfolded in my mind. To add to all this, I was by no means unacquainted with pain, which is a pretty unanswerable thing; I had a fair amount of toothache and especially earache; and few can bemuse themselves into regarding earache as a form of epicurean hedonism. But here again there is a difference. For some unaccountable reason, and in some indescribable way, the pain did not leave on my memory the sort of stain of the intolerable or mysterious that it leaves on the mature mind. To all these four facts I can testify; exactly as if they were facts like my loving a toy gun or climbing a tree. Their meaning, in the murder or other mystery, will appear later.

For I fear I have prolonged preposterously this note on the nursery; as if I had been an unconscionable time, not dying but being born, or at least being brought up. Well, I believe in prolonging childhood; and I am not sorry that I was a backward child. But I can only say that this nursery note is necessary if all the rest is to be anything but nonsense; and not even nursery nonsense. In the chapters that follow, I shall pass to what are called real happenings, though they are far less real. Without giving myself any airs of the adventurer or the globetrotter, I may say I have seen something of the world; I have travelled in interesting places and talked to interesting men; I have been in political quarrels often turning into faction fights; I have talked to statesmen in the hour of the destiny of States; I have met most of the great poets and prose writers of my time; I have travelled in the track of some of the whirlwinds and earthquakes in the ends of the earth; I have lived in houses burned down in the tragic wars of Ireland; I have walked through the ruins of Polish palaces left behind by the Red Armies; I have heard talk of the secret signals of the Ku Klux Klan upon the borders of Texas; I have seen the fanatical Arabs come up from the desert to attack the Jews in Jerusalem. There are many journalists who have seen more of such things than I; but I have been a journalist and I have seen such things; there will be no difficulty in filling other chapters with such things; but they will be unmeaning, if nobody understands that they still mean less to me than Punch and Judy on Campden Hill.

In a word; I have never lost the sense that this was my real life; the real beginning of what should have been a more real life; a lost experience in the land of the living. It seems to me that when I came out of the house and stood on that hill of houses, where the roads sank steeply towards Holland Park, and terraces of new red houses could look out across a vast hollow and see far away the sparkle of the Crystal Palace (and seeing it was a juvenile sport in those parts), I was subconsciously certain then, as I am consciously certain now, that there was the white and solid road and the worthy beginning of the life of man; and that it is man who afterwards darkens it with dreams or goes astray from it in self-deception. It is only the grown man who lives a life of make-believe and pretending; and it is he who has his head in a cloud.

At this time, of course, I did not even know that this morning light could be lost; still less about any controversies as to whether it could be recovered. So far the disputes of that period passed over my head like storms high up in air; and as I did not foresee the problem I naturally did not foresee any of my searches for a solution. I simply looked at the procession in the street as I looked at the processions in the toy theatre; and now and then I happened to see curious things, twopence coloured rather than a penny plain, which were worthy of the wildest pageants of the toy theatre. I remember once walking with my father along Kensington High Street, and seeing a crowd of people gathered by a rather dark and narrow entry on the southern side of that thoroughfare. I had seen crowds before; and was quite prepared for their shouting or shoving. But I was not prepared for what happened next. In a flash a sort of ripple ran along the line and all these eccentrics went down on their knees on the public pavement. I had never seen people play any such antics except in church; and I stopped and stared. Then I realised that a sort of little dark cab or carriage had drawn up opposite the entry; and out of it came a ghost clad in flames. Nothing in the shilling paint box had ever spread such a conflagration of scarlet, such lakes of lake; or seemed so splendidly likely to incarnadine the multitudinous sea. He came on with all his glowing draperies like a great crimson cloud of sunset, lifting long frail fingers over the crowd in blessing. And then I looked at his face and was startled with a contrast; for his face was dead pale like ivory and very wrinkled and old, fitted together out of naked nerve and bone and sinew; with hollow eyes in shadow;

but not ugly; having in every line the ruin of great beauty. The face was so extraordinary that for a moment I even forgot such perfectly scrumptious scarlet clothes.

We passed on; and then my father said, "Do you know who that was? That was Cardinal Manning."

Then one of his artistic hobbies returned to his abstracted and humorous mind; and he said: "He'd have made his fortune as a model."

III

HOW TO BE A DUNCE

The change from childhood to boyhood, and the mysterious transformation that produces that monster the schoolboy, might be very well summed up in one small fact. To me the ancient capital letters of the Greek alphabet, the great Theta, a sphere barred across the midst like Saturn, or the great Upsilon; standing up like a tall curved chalice, have still a quite unaccountable charm and mystery, as if they were the characters traced in wide welcome over Eden of the dawn. The ordinary small Greek letters, though I am now much more familiar with them, seem to me quite nasty little things like a swarm of gnats. As for Greek accents, I triumphantly succeeded, through a long series of school terms, in avoiding learning them at all; and I never had a higher moment of gratification than when I afterwards discovered that the Greeks never learnt them either. I felt, with a radiant pride, that I was as ignorant as Plato and Thucydides. At least they were unknown to the Greeks who wrote the prose and poetry that was thought worth studying; and were invented by grammarians, I believe, at the time of the Renaissance. But it is a simple psychological fact, that the sight of a Greek capital still fills me with happiness, the sight of a small letter with indifference tinged with dislike, and the accents with righteous indignation reaching the point of profanity. And I believe that the explanation is that I learnt the large Greek letters, as I learnt the large English letters, at home. I was told about them merely for fun while I was still a child; while the others I learnt during the period of what is commonly called education; that is, the period during which I was being instructed by somebody I did not know, about something I did not want to know.

But I say this merely to show that I was a much wiser and wider-minded person at the age of six than at the age of sixteen. I do not base any educational theories upon it, heaven forbid. This work cannot, on some points, avoid being theoretical; but it need not add insult to injury by being educational. I certainly shall not, in the graceful modern manner, turn round and abuse my schoolmasters because I did not choose to learn what they were quite ready to teach. It may be that in the improved schools of today, the child is so taught that he crows aloud with delight at the sight of a Greek accent. But I fear it is much more probable that the new schools have got rid of the Greek accent by getting rid of the Greek. And upon that point, as it happens, I am largely on the side of my schoolmasters against myself. I am very glad that my persistent efforts not to learn Latin were to a certain extent frustrated; and that I was not entirely successful even in escaping the contamination of the language of Aristotle and Demosthenes. At least I know enough Greek to be able to see the joke, when somebody says (as somebody did the other day) that the study of that language is not suited to an age of democracy. I do not know what language he thought democracy came from; and it must be admitted that the word seems now to be a part of the language called journalese. But my only point for the moment is personal or psychological; my own private testimony to the curious fact that, for some reason or other, a boy often does pass, from an early stage when he wants to know nearly everything, to a later stage when he wants to know next to nothing. A very practical and experienced traveller, with nothing of the mystic about him, once remarked to me suddenly: "There must be something rottenly wrong with education itself. So many people have wonderful children and all the grown-up people are such duds." And I know what he meant; though I am in doubt whether my present duddishness is due to education, or to some deeper and mote mysterious cause.

Boyhood is a most complex and incomprehensible thing. Even when one has been through it, one does not understand what it was. A man can never quite understand a boy, even when he has been the boy. There grows all over what was once the child a sort of prickly protection like hair; a callousness, a carelessness, a curious combination of random and quite objectless energy with a readiness to accept conventions. I have blindly begun a lark which involved carrying on literally like a lunatic; and known all the time that I did not know why I was doing it. When I first met my best friend in the playground, I fought with him wildly for three-quarters of an hour; not scientifically and certainly not vindictively (I had never seen him before and I have been very fond of him ever since) but by a sort of inexhaustible and insatiable impulse, rushing hither and thither about the field and rolling over and over in the mud. And all the time I believe that both our minds were entirely mild and reasonable; and when we desisted from sheer exhaustion, and he happened to quote Dickens or the Bab Ballads, or something I had read, we plunged into a friendly discussion on literature which has gone on, intermittently, from that day to this. There is no explaining these things; if those who have done them cannot explain them. But since then I have seen boys in many countries and even of many colours; Egyptian boys in the bazaars of Cairo or mulatto boys in the slums of New York. And I have found that by some primordial law they all tend to three things; to going about in threes; to having no apparent object in going about at all; and, almost invariably speaking, to attacking each other suddenly and equally suddenly desisting from the attack.

Some may still question my calling this conduct conventional; from a general impression that two bankers or business partners do not commonly roll each other head-over-heels for fun, or in a spirit of pure friendship. It might be retorted, that two business partners are not always by any means such pure friends. But in any case, it is true to call the thing a convention in more than the verbal sense of a collision. And it is exactly this convention that really separates the schoolboy from the child. When I went to St Paul's School, in Hammersmith, there really was a sort of convention of independence; which was in a certain degree a false independence; because it was a false maturity. Here we must remember once more the fallacy about "pretending" in childhood. The child does not really pretend to be a Red Indian; any more than Shelley pretended to be a cloud or Tennyson to be a brook. The point can be tested by offering a political pamphlet to the cloud, a peerage to the brook, or a penny for sweets to the Red Bull of the Prairies. But the boy really is pretending to be a man; or even a man of the world; which would seem a far more horrific metamorphosis. Schoolboys in my time could be blasted with the horrible revelation of having a sister, or even a Christian name. And the deadly nature of this blow really consisted in the fact that it cracked the whole convention of our lives; the convention that each of us was on his own; an independent gentleman living on private means. The secret that each of us did in fact possess a family, and parents who paid for our support, was conventionally ignored and only revealed in moments of maddened revenge. But the point is that there was already a faint touch of corruption in this convention; precisely because it was more serious and less frank than the tarradiddles of infancy. We had begun to be what no children are; snobs. Children disinfect all their dramatic impersonations by saying "Let us pretend." We schoolboys never said "Let us pretend;" we only pretended.

Boys, I have said, wander in threes. Three is certainly the symbolic number for comradeship, even if it is not always exactly the same as friendship. I have had the good luck to enjoy both, as did the Three Musketeers or the Three Soldiers of Mr Kipling. The first of my friends, with whom I fought in the field, has since written the best detective story of modern times and still conceals a very powerful sense of humour under the almost impenetrable disguise of a writer on the *Daily Telegraph*. He was, and indeed still is, remarkable for the combination of an extraordinary gravity of visage with extreme agility and quickness of movement. I used to say that he had the head of a professor on the body of a harlequin. It was a poetic pleasure to see him walk, a little pompously, down the street and suddenly scale a lamp-post like a monkey, with the alleged intention of lighting a cigarette, and then drop down and resume his walk with an unchanged expression of earnestness and serenity. He had extraordinarily well-balanced brains and could do almost anything with them; even writing an ordinary leading article for a London daily. But he could write clear and unadulterated nonsense with the same serious simplicity. It was he who invented that severe and stately form of Free Verse which has since been known by his own second name as "the Clerihew" (his name is Edmund Clerihew Bentley) or "Biography for Beginners"; which dates from our days at school, when he sat listening to a chemical exposition, with his rather bored air and a blank sheet of blotting paper before him. On this he wrote, inspired by the limpid spirit of song, the unadorned lines:

> Sir Humphrey Davy
> Abominated gravy
> He lived in the odium
> Of having discovered sodium.

Even in those days I used to draw pictures, or what were called pictures, to illustrate these biographical rhymes; though of course it was not till decades afterwards that we either of us had the notion of publishing a book, or of publishing anything. Long after we had both become incurable scribblers, we remained inconspicuous schoolboys; we never thought we could be anything else; I do not think we very clearly realised that we ever should be anything else; or that our schoolboy days would ever end. In that sense we were as unambitious as children whispering a secret language. Our jokes were all domestic or developed out of the daily affairs of the school; but they covered enough waste paper to stock a library. I remember an interminable romance, for which I was always drawing pictures, and which I still think had a touch of wild fancy. It arose merely from our walking behind three of the masters; two of them, who were young and tall, had between them a third, who was old and very small; so that there seemed a vague suggestion that they were supporting him. On this was based the great constructive theory that the elder master (who was one of the most important persons in the school) was in fact only a clockwork figure, which they carried about with them and wound up to go through his daily round. The dummy and the two conspirators were dragged through an endless reel of long-drawn (and badly drawn) adventures, some scraps of which must still be kicking about the world somewhere. But needless to say, we never thought of doing anything with them, except enjoying them. It has sometimes struck me as not being a bad thing to do with things.

My friend Bentley, indeed, had and has a natural talent for these elaborate strategic maps of nonsense, or the suggestion of such preposterous plots. It is something like the industry which accompanies the fantasy of Father Ronald Knox, when he makes a detailed map of the Barsetshire of Trollope or works out an incredible cryptogram to show that Queen Victoria wrote "In Memoriam." I remember one day when the whole school assembled for a presentation to a master who was leaving us to take up a fellowship at Peterhouse. The congratulatory speech was made by one of the upper masters who happened to be a learned but heavy and very solemn old gentleman, whose manner and diction were alike ponderous and prosaic. My friend and I were sitting side by side, hopeless of any enlivenment except from the speaker's solemnity; when the whole assembly was startled as by a thunder-clap. The old gentleman had made a joke. What was even more shocking, it was quite a good joke. He remarked that, in sending our friend from this school to that college, we were robbing Paul to pay Peter. We looked at each other with a wild surmise. We shook our heads gravely. It could not be explained. But Bentley afterwards produced a most convincing and exhaustive explanation. He insisted that the elder schoolmaster had devoted his whole life to planning and preparations for that one joke. He had used his interest with the High Master to obtain for the junior master a place on the staff. He had intrigued with the University authorities to get him a Fellowship at that college. He had lived for that hour. He had now made his first and last joke; and probably would soon pass away in peace.

It was the third member of our original trio who brought into our secrets the breath of ambition and the air out of the great world. He was a dark and very thin youth, named Lucian Oldershaw, who looked and in some ways was very sensitive; but about those larger matters he was much less shy than we were. He was the son of an actor and had travelled about the country more than the rest of us; he had been to other schools and he knew much more of the variety of life. Above all, there possessed him, almost feverishly, a vast, amazing and devastating idea, the idea of *doing* something; of doing something in the manner of grown-up people, who were the only people who could be conceived as doing things. I well remember how my hair stood on end, when he first spoke casually about the official School Magazine; which was to me something like the School Prayers or the School Foundation. None of us had ever dreamed of contributing to it, any more than to the Encyclopaedia Britannica. And my new friend, who was somewhat younger than I, spoke lightly about an old idea he had had of establishing some co-operation between all the great school magazines, those of Eton, Harrow,

Winchester and the rest. If he had proposed that we should conquer and rule the British Empire, I could not have been more staggered; but he dismissed it as casually as he had called it up, and then proposed in cold blood that we should publish a magazine of our own; and have it printed at a real printer's. He must have possessed considerable persuasive powers; because we actually did. We also founded a small society of boys of our own age, and called it the Junior Debating Club; though nobody, so far as I know, has ever heard of the Senior Debating Club. There was the Union, to which you belonged when you were in the top form, as you did other awful and appalling things, such as dining with the High Master. But we no more anticipated that, at our age, than we anticipated death.

Our debates are still recorded in stray volumes of our strange little paper; the persons of the play being mysteriously represented by their initials, as if they were members of a secret society in a sensational novel; as "Mr B emphatically disputed the last speaker's statement," or "These remarks provoked an indignant protest from Mr C." This and other deadly fascinations render these old volumes the favourite reading of my friend, Mr Edward Fordham, who was himself a member of the club and delighted in decorating its chronicle with the most magnificent and florid journalese, and in making game in it of himself and others. He is still, I believe, especially attached to a passage in the reports which states, of one of the little boys who formed this society, "Mr L-D briefly described the Governments of France, America, Germany, Austria, Italy and Spain." Sometimes, however, Fordham's own burlesque rhetoric recoiled on his own head. He described one of the innumerable riots of our tea-table by writing, "A penny bun of the sticky order caressingly stung the chairman's honoured cheek, sped on its errand of mercy by the unerring hand of Mr F." I may remark that I was the chairman; and I was generally honoured in that way. But the printer avenged me; for he rendered the missile as "A peony but of the stick order;" a most suggestive botanical formula. It was the beginning of a long career of martyrdom from misprints; which reached its crown when I wrote of a Nonconformist minister, "a distinguished correspondent," and it came out as, "a distinguished co-respondent."

Our debating club was actually founded and did actually debate, if it can be called debating. This part of the matter did not alarm me much; for I had debated off and on ever since I was born; certainly with my brother, probably with my nurse. But, what was infinitely more blood-curdling, our paper did actually appear in print; and I contributed to its turgid poems, in which bad imitations of Swinburne were so exactly balanced with worse imitations of the Lays of Ancient Rome, that many of my simpler friends fell under the illusion that I had a style of my own. I have never read those verses since; there are limits to the degradation and despair which even autobiography demands.

But I must admit that, for whatever reason, they attracted a certain amount of attention; and our experiment began to float to the surface of the school life and come within the range of official attention, which was the last thing I had ever desired. It is only right to say that the magazine contained probably better, and certainly better educated, poetry than mine. Among the small group of twelve that formed our society was Robert Vernède, who also imitated Swinburne, but who was capable of appreciating how well Swinburne imitated the Greek poets. It is melancholy and amusing to reflect that of all those eager Swinburnian echoes, I can only remember an echo of parody; in which the style of Vernède's first choruses, *à la* Atalanta, were rendered by Bentley in the form of a farewell to him when he departed from the tea-table:

> Let the milk that was poured
> Be the draught of the cat,
> For from under the board
> From the seat where he sat
> The feet of his boots are departed; he has widowed the hall of
> his hat.

Vernède and Bentley were very intimate; and had something in common in their union of immobility and activity; but the immobility of Vernède was not dry and earnest like the other; but somnolent and oriental, like that of a Buddha, or (as his early friends were more prone to inform him) of a cat. He had that oval, almost Japanese face that can be seen in some of the Southern French blood of which he came. He lived to be a fine and promising poet and to write, on the outbreak of the fighting, a noble invocation to the English Sea, which multitudes must still remember. But his full promise as a poet he did not keep; because he kept a better one, and is dead on the field of honour.

For the rest, it is very typical of the difference between the two or three types that the work of E C B, my first and in every sense original friend, was the only work in the whole paper which might have been published by the same person fifteen years afterwards. Whatever the other relative merits of our minds, his was by far the most mature; perhaps for the very reason that it largely confined itself to being critical or flippant. Anyhow, the nonsense fables that he wrote for the paper would have made excellent paragraphs in any real paper. There was nothing particularly juvenile about them; and, of all men I have known, he is the man whose mind has least changed, has least lost its balance and, above all, had least of the first youthful blunders in finding its balance. He had also, as I have said, a sort of calm versatility; he could carry out other people's plans and improve them; he could, as the phrase goes, turn his hand to anything. On this absurd little rag of a school paper, the original three wrote letters in rotation, in three imaginary characters; and I think his were the best. Twenty years afterwards, when Belloc and I started a scheme of Ballades for the *Eye Witness*, Bentley was brought in afterwards, in the same fashion; and I think his were the best. But he was at this time, and perhaps for long after, too detached and ironic to become conspicuous in connection with a cause, or any of the things in which youth is generally both communal and combative. When some of us were pretending to be Knights of the Round Table, he was content to be Dagonet the fool, or in other words, the wise man. And it was in the character of a portentously solemn buffoon that he began to draw the attention of the elders. When the old High Master of St Paul's School ran his eye through a version of the Dog in the Manger, which described the cattle as being prevented "from refreshing their inner cows" he went into unearthly convulsions of his own extraordinary laughter which, like the other movements of his extraordinary voice, began like an organ and ended like a penny whistle. "That boy looks at the world standing on his head," said the High Master of St Paul's School; and instantly we were in the full blaze of the spotlight.

It is time that something should be said about the masters, and especially the High Master. Immensely important as we thought ourselves in comparison with those remote but respectable enemies, after all they did have something to do with the school. The most eccentric and entertaining of them Mr Elam has already been sketched in brilliant black and white by the pen of Mr Compton Mackenzie. I have forgotten whether Mr Mackenzie mentioned what always struck me as the most disturbing eccentricity of that eccentric; the open derision with which he spoke of his own profession and position, of those who shared it with him and even of those who were set over him in its exercise. He would explain the difference between satire and the bitterness of the *risus sardonicus* by the helpful parable, "If I were walking along the street and fell down in the mud, I should laugh a sardonic laugh. But if I were to see the High Master of this school fall down in the mud, I should laugh a sarcastic laugh." I chiefly mention his name here for another reason; because he once vented his scorn for what he called "the trade of an usher" in the form of a rhetorical question addressed to a boy: "Why are boys sent to school, Robinson?" Robinson, with downcast eyes and an air of offensive virtue, replied faintly, "To learn, sir." "No, boy, no," said the old gentleman wagging his head, "it was because one day at breakfast Mr Robinson said to Mrs Robinson, 'My dear, we must do something about that boy. He's a nuisance to me and he's a nuisance to you and he's a perfect plague to the servants.'" Then, with an indescribable extreme of grinding and grating contempt: "'So we'll Pay Some Man...'"

I say I introduce this ancient anecdote for another reason; and it is partly because I would suggest another answer. If ever the problem troubled me in

my boyhood, it did not force me in the direction of the lofty morality of
Robinson. The idea that I had come to school to work was too grotesque to
cloud my mind for an instant. It was also in too obvious a contrast with the
facts and the result, I was very fond of my friends; though, as is common at
such an age, I was much too fond of them to be openly emotional about it.
But I do remember coming, almost seriously, to the conclusion that a boy
must go to school to study the characters of his schoolmasters. And I still think
that there was something in it. After all, the schoolmaster is the first educated
grown-up person that the boy comes to see constantly, after having been
introduced at an early age to his father and mother. And the masters at St
Paul's were very interesting; even those of them who were not so obviously
eccentric as the celebrated Mr Elam. To one very distinguished individual, my
own personal debt is infinite; I mean, the historian of the Indian Mutiny and
of the campaigns of Caesar: Mr T Rice Holmes. He managed, heaven knows
how, to penetrate through my deep and desperately consolidated desire to
appear stupid; and discover the horrible secret that I was, after all, endowed
with the gift of reason above the brutes. He would suddenly ask me questions
a thousand miles away from the subject in hand, and surprise me into
admitting that I had heard of the Song of Roland, or even read a play or two
of Shakespeare. Nobody who knows anything of the English schoolboy at that
date will imagine that there was at the moment any pleasure in such
prominence or distinction. We were all hag ridden with a horror of showing
off, which was perhaps the only coherent moral principle we possessed. There
was one boy, I remember, who was so insanely sensitive on this point of
honour, that he could hardly bear to hear one of his friends answer an
ordinary question right. He felt that his comrade really ought to have
invented some mistake, in the general interest of comradeship. When my
information about the French epic was torn from me, in spite of my efforts,
he actually put his head in his desk and dropped the lid on it, groaning in a
generous and impersonal shame and faintly and hoarsely exclaiming, "Oh,
shut it... Oh, shut up!" He was an extreme exponent of the principle; but it
was a principle which I fully shared. I can remember running to school in
sheer excitement repeating militant lines of *Marmion* with passionate
emphasis and exultation; and then going into class and repeating the same
lines in the lifeless manner of a hurdy-gurdy, hoping that there was nothing
whatever in my intonation to indicate that I distinguished between the sense
of one word and another.

Nobody, I think ever got past my guard in this matter except Mr T R
Holmes and Mr R F Cholmeley, who afterwards became the form-master of
my two intimate friends, and who, I am glad to say, has often joined us in later
years in our reunions of remembrance. But, somehow or other, a rumour
must have begun to circulate among the authorities that we were not such

fools as we looked. One day, to my consternation, the High Master stopped me in the street and led me along, roaring in my deafened and bewildered ears that I had a literary faculty which might come to something if somebody could give it solidity. Sometime after that, to my cowering terror, he bellowed aloud to a whole crowd of parents and other preposterous intruders, on the occasion of a prize day, that our little magazine showed signs of considerable talent, though it was an unofficial publication on which he "might have hesitated to set his *Imprimatur.*" Somehow we felt it would have been even more crushing if he had set his *Imprimatur*. It sounded like the thumb of a giant.

Frederick Walker, High Master of Manchester and afterwards High Master of St Paul's School, was, as most people know by this time, a very remarkable man. He was the sort of man who may live in anecdotes, like Dr Johnson; indeed in some respects he was not unlike Dr Johnson. He was like him in the startling volume of his voice, in his heavy face and figure, and in a certain tendency to explode at what did not seem to be exactly the appropriate moment; he would talk with perfect good humour and rationality and rend the roof over what seemed a trifle. In essential matters, however, his hard-hitting was generally quite right; and had even about it a homely and popular character, that somehow smacked of the north country. It is he of whom the famous tale is told that, when a fastidious lady wrote to ask him what was the social standing of the boys at his school, he replied, "Madam, so long as your son behaves himself and the fees are paid, no questions will be asked about his social standing."

One day I was frozen with astonishment to find my name in an announcement on the notice-board, saying that I was to be accorded the privileges of the highest form, though I did not belong to it. It produced in me a desire to be accorded the privileges and protection of the coal-cellar and never to come out again. At the same time I learned that a special branch of the highest form had actually been created for my two principal friends, in order that they might study for History Scholarships at the Universities. All this seemed like the very universe breaking up and turning topsy-turvy; and indeed all sorts of things happened about this time that seemed to be quite outside the laws of nature. I got a prize, for instance; what was called the Milton Prize for what was called a prize poem; I imagine it was about as bad as all other prize poems, but I am happy to say that I cannot recall a single syllable of it. I do, however, recall the subject, not without a faint thrill of irony; for the subject was St Francis Xavier, the great Jesuit who preached to the Chinese. I recall these things, so contrary to the previous course of my school life, because I am not sorry to be an exception to the modern tendency to reproach the old Victorian schoolmaster with stupidity and neglect and to represent the rising generation as a shining band of Shelleys inspired by light and liberty to rise. The truth is that in this case it was I who exhibited the stupidity; though I really think it was largely an affected stupidity. And certainly it was I who rejoiced in the neglect, and who asked for nothing better than to be neglected. It was, if anything, the authorities who dragged me, in my own despite, out of the comfortable and protected atmosphere of obscurity and failure. Personally, I was perfectly happy at the bottom of the class.

For the rest, I think the chief impression I produced, on most of the masters and many of the boys, was a pretty well-founded conviction that I was asleep. Perhaps what nobody knew, not even myself, was that I was asleep and dreaming. The dreams were not much more sensible or valuable than they commonly are in persons in such profound slumber; but they already had this obscure effect on my existence; that my mind was already occupied, though I myself was idle. Before forming the few special friendships of which I speak, I was somewhat solitary; not sharply unpopular or in any sense persecuted, but solitary. But though I was solitary, I was not sorry; and I think I can claim that I was not sulky. One effect of this was that my first acquaintances, as distinct from my ultimate friends, were odd and scrappy sort of people like myself. These individuals were accidents; one or two of them I fear were disasters. I remember one youth who made one appearance in my daily life, that puzzled me like a detective story. I cannot imagine how I came to cultivate his society; still less how he came to cultivate mine. For he was a brilliant mathematician, and must presumably have worked hard at mathematics; whereas I worked less at mathematics, if possible, than at anything else. Moreover, I was very untidy and he was very tidy, with a large clean collar and an Eton jacket, also a large head very neatly brushed but something odd and perhaps too mature about his froglike face. One day he asked me whether I could lend him a Hall & Knight's Algebra. So far as enthusiasm for that study was concerned I could answer, "Thy need is greater than mine," with all the gesture of Sir Philip Sidney; but I had to observe some minimum of attention to the mathematical class; so in lending him the book, I told him I should want it back sometime next week. As the time approached, I was much mystified by the fact that I found it quite difficult to get it back. He gave evasive replies; he interposed postponements and hazy promises; till at last I quarrelled with him, using the words of action which are really commoner among schoolboys as words than as actions; but anyhow indicating that I should make an earnest effort to punch his head. To this threat he ultimately capitulated; and eventually led me to his locker, which he reluctantly opened. And his locker was stuffed from top to bottom with about twenty-five identical copies of Hall & Knight's Algebra, which he had presumably collected by similar arts from similar acquaintances. I believe he left the school later, without any particular scandal; and I hope the poor fellow recovered his mental balance somewhere else. I write in no superior spirit; I was quite capable myself at many earlier stages of going mad in a quiet way; but not by an exaggerated appetite for Hall & Knight's Algebra.

There was another little boy with whom I walked to school in the same fortuitous fellowship; a very prim and proper little boy, as became the son of the venerable and somewhat ponderous clergyman who held one of the highest scholastic posts in the school. He also was very neat, he also was quite an industrious pupil; and he also had a peculiarity. He was the most fertile, fluent and really disinterested liar I have ever had the pleasure of knowing. There was nothing base or materialistic about his mendacity; be was not trying to cheat anybody or to get anything; he simply boasted like Baron Munchausen in quiet and even tones all the way from Holland Park to Hammersmith. He told the most staggering stories about himself, without lifting his voice or showing the faintest embarrassment; and there was nothing else notable about him at all. I have often wondered what became of him; and whether he followed his father into the Church. It may be retorted by the light-minded, that he may have fallen so low as to write stories, even crime stories, like myself; which some regard as almost tantamount to joining the criminal classes. But I do not believe any of his stories would be probable enough for fiction.

Perhaps the same chapter of accidents, that threw me first in the way of these human curiosities, was responsible for another social accident, of which I am very glad; for it led to my seeing both sides of a very difficult social question; about which a great deal of nonsense is talked on both sides; and the worst nonsense of all by those who talk as if there were no question at all. It must be explained that St Paul's School, in schoolboy language, was more than most others a school of "swots." I need hardly clear myself of the charge of swottishness; and, of course, there were many lazy boys, and some almost as lazy as I. But the diligent type was in a larger proportion than is usual; for the school was chiefly celebrated for winning scholarships at the Universities, rather than for athletics or other forms of fame. And there was another reason why this particular type was conspicuous. To put the point in popular language, there were a great many swots partly because there were a great many Jews.

Oddly enough, I lived to have later on the name of an Anti-Semite; whereas from my first days at school I very largely had the name of a Pro-Semite. I made many friends among the Jews, and some of these I have retained as lifelong friends; nor have our relations ever been disturbed by differences upon the political or social problem. I am glad that I began at this end; but I have not really ended any differently from the way in which I began. I held by instinct then, and I hold by knowledge now, that the right way is to be interested in Jews as Jews; and then to bring into greater prominence the very much neglected Jewish virtues, which are the complement and sometimes even the cause of what the world feels to be the Jewish faults. For instance, one of the great Jewish virtues is gratitude. I was criticised in early days for quixotry and priggishness in protecting Jews; and I remember once extricating a strange swarthy little creature with a hooked nose from being bullied, or rather being teased; for the worst torture really consisted of his being lightly tossed from one boy to another amid wild stares of wide-eyed scientific curiosity and questions like, "What is it?" and "Is it alive?" Thirty years afterwards, when that little goblin was a great grown bearded man, utterly remote from me in type and trade and interests and opinions, he had a sort of permanent fountain of thanks for that trifling incident, which was quite embarrassing. In the same way, I noted that strong family bond among the Jews which, as I noted, was not merely disguised but denied among most normal schoolboys. Doubtless, I came to know the Jews because in this sense they were a little abnormal, as I was then becoming a little abnormal myself. Yet there is nothing I have come to count more normal, and nothing I desire more to restore to its normal place, than those two things; the family and the theory of thanks. And then, in the light of these virtues as seen from within, it was often possible to understand the origin and even the justification of much of the Anti-Semitic criticism from without. For it is often the very loyalty of the Jewish family which appears as disloyalty to the Christian state. As the reader will realise before the end, it was partly what I admired in private friends, especially in two brothers named Solomon, which I came ultimately to denounce in political enemies, in two brothers named Isaacs. The first were good by every standard, the second vulnerable even by their own standard: and yet they had the same virtue.

I am not at all ashamed of having asked Aryans to have more patience with Jews or for having asked Anglo-Saxons to have more patience with Jew-baiters. The whole problem of the two entangled cultures and traditions is much too deep and difficult, on both sides, to be decided impatiently. But I have very little patience with those who will not solve the problem, on the ground that there is no problem to solve. I cannot explain the Jews; but I certainly will not explain them away. Nor have the Jews a worse enemy than the sort of Jew sceptic who sometimes tries to explain himself away. I have seen a whole book full of alternative theories of the particular historic cause of such a delusion about a difference; that it came from medieval priests or was burnt into us by the Inquisition; that it was a tribal theory arising out of Teutonism; that it was revolutionary envy of the few Jews who happened to be the big bankers of Capitalism; that it was Capitalist resistance to the few Jews who happened to be the chief founders of Communism. All these separate theories are false in separate ways; as in forgetting that medieval heresy-hunts spared Jews more and not less than Christians; or that Capitalism and Communism are so very nearly the same thing, in ethical essence, that it would not be strange if they did take leaders from the same ethnological elements. But broadly, the evasions are contrary to common sense; as they were contrary even to the common sense of a boy of thirteen. I do not believe that a crowd on a race-course is poisoned by medieval theology; or the navvies in a Mile End pub misled by the ethnology of Gobineau or Max Muller; nor do I believe that a mob of little boys fresh from the cricket-field or the tuckshop were troubled about Marxian economics or international finance. Yet all these people recognise Jews as Jews when they see them; and the schoolboys recognised them, not with any great hostility except in patches, but with the integration of instinct. What they saw was not Semites or Schismatics or capitalists or revolutionists, but foreigners; only foreigners that were not called foreigners. This did not prevent friendship and affection, especially in my own case; but then it never has prevented it in the case of ordinary foreigners. One of these early friends of mine, now Professor of Latin at University College, happened to have all the Jewish virtues, and also all the others there are; he afterwards became a member of the little club already described; and passed through Oxford with distinction; probably greater distinction than my other friends.

Most of the members of our little club, however, thus passed on to the older Universities and were promising figures either on the academic or the social and political side; two of them being Presidents of the Oxford and two of the Cambridge Union. Oldershaw, characteristically enough, was almost instantly found immersed and entangled in the establishment of yet another unofficial paper, called the J C R, in which were not a few memorable curiosities of literature; including the first work of a pen then unknown to me, but recognisable enough now in lines like, "We slumbered on the fire lit ground beside the guns in Burgundy." Bentley, on being requested by a poetical lady to write something suitable to Wordsworth's Seat, did not relax his rigid flippancy and composed the simple lines that end:

> It is annoying to reflect
> That two such men as we
> By such a trifle as the grave
> Should separated be.
> 'Twas ever thus. We might have had
> A pleasant afternoon,
> But man is always born too late
> Or else he dies too soon

while Lawrence Solomon, the learned Jewish friend of whom I have spoken, wrote about the best of the parodies of FitzGerald's *Omar*, then a fashionable theme, warning undergraduates not to expect a Blue or a First; "For they were not for me. How shall they be for you?" As a fact, I think he did get a First; but all of them must have lived to realise the further moral:

> For what remains, however great thy fame?
> For thee, for me, for all the end's the same –
> To climb the dark stairs to my old College rooms,
> Look o'er the door and read another's name.

There seemed a general tendency of these schoolfellows of mine to excel in light verse; Fordham, who went to Cambridge, has written many satiric lyrics which have been published and many satiric dramas which ought to be published. If I wind up here some of the stories of my old friends, it is not because I dismiss them from my memories, but because I must admit a multitude of much less interesting people into my memoirs. One contrast in their subsequent careers has always struck me as a curious case of the incalculable individuality and freewill of man. A friend of Fordham, normal, virile and ambitious, popular rather in the sense of fashionable, always struck me as the sort of man who could wear a uniform in camp or court, serving the obvious virtues. When the Great War came, he became an uncompromising and unconventional Pacifist agitator. Another, a friend of Vernède, one of those rare spiritual types in which a Puritan tradition has really flowered into a full Hellenic culture, is the most unselfish man I ever knew in my life, of the sort that is still unsatisfied even with its own unselfishness. I should say he was something rather like a saint; but I should never have been surprised if he had been a Conscientious Objector. As a fact, he went to the Front in a flash like fire; and had his leg shot off in his first battle,

But all this time very queer things were groping and wrestling inside my own undeveloped mind; and I have said nothing of them in this chapter; for it was the sustained and successful effort of most of my school life to keep them to myself. I said farewell to my friends when they went up to Oxford and Cambridge; while I, who was at that time almost wholly taken up with the idea of drawing pictures, went to an Art School and brought my boyhood to an end.

IV

HOW TO BE A LUNATIC

I deal here with the darkest and most difficult part of my task; the period of youth which is full of doubts and morbidities and temptations; and which, though in my case mainly subjective, has left in my mind for ever a certitude upon the objective solidity of Sin. And before I deal with it in any detail, it is necessary to make a prefatory explanation upon one point. In the matter of religion, I have been much concerned with controversies about rather provocative problems; and have finally adopted a position which to many is itself a provocation. I have grieved my well-wishers, and many of the wise and prudent, by my reckless course in becoming a Christian, an orthodox Christian, and finally a Catholic in the sense of a Roman Catholic. Now in most of the matters of which they chiefly disapprove, I am not in the least ashamed of myself. As an apologist I am the reverse of apologetic. So far as a man may be proud of a religion rooted in humility, I am very proud of my religion; I am especially proud of those parts of it that are most commonly called superstition. I am proud of being fettered by antiquated dogmas and enslaved by dead creeds (as my journalistic friends repeat. with so much pertinacity), for I know very well that it is the heretical creeds that are dead, and that it is only the reasonable dogma that lives long enough to be called antiquated. I am very proud of what people call priestcraft; since even that accidental term of abuse preserves the medieval truth that a priest like every other man, ought to be a craftsman. I am very proud of what people call Mariolatry; because it introduced into religion in the darkest ages that element of chivalry which is now being belatedly and badly understood in the form of feminism. I am very proud of being orthodox about the mysteries of the Trinity or the Mass; I am proud of believing in the Confessional; I am proud of believing in the Papacy.

But I am not proud of believing in the Devil. To put it more correctly, I am not proud of knowing the Devil. I made his acquaintance by my own fault; and followed it up along lines which, had they been followed further, might have led me to devil-worship or the devil knows what. On this doctrine, at least, there is, mingling with my knowledge, no shadow of self-satisfaction any more than of self-deception. On this one matter, a man may well be intellectually right only through being morally wrong. I am not impressed by the ethnical airs and graces of sceptics on most of the other subjects. I am not over-awed by a young gentleman saying that he cannot submit his intellect to dogma; because I doubt whether he has even used his intellect enough to define dogma. I am not impressed very seriously by those who call Confession cowardly; for I gravely doubt whether they themselves would have the courage to go through with it. But when they say, "Evil is only relative. Sin is only negative. There is no positive badness; it is only the absence of positive goodness" – then I know that they are talking shallow balderdash only because they are much better men than I; more innocent and more normal and more near to God.

What I may call my period of madness coincided with a period of drifting and doing nothing; in which I could not settle down to any regular work. I dabbled in a number of things; and some of them may have had something to do with the psychology of the affair. I would not for a moment suggest it as a cause, far less as an excuse, but it is a contributory fact that among these dabblings in this dubious time, I dabbled in Spiritualism without having even the decision to be a Spiritualist. Indeed I was, in a rather unusual manner, not only detached but indifferent. My brother and I used to play with planchette, or what the Americans call the ouija board; but we were among the few, I imagine, who played in a mere spirit of play. Nevertheless I would not altogether rule out the suggestion of some that we were playing with fire; or even with hell-fire. In the words that were written for us there was nothing ostensibly degrading, but any amount that was deceiving. I saw quite enough of the thing to be able to testify, with complete certainty, that something happens which is not in the ordinary sense natural, or produced by the normal and conscious human will. Whether it is produced by some subconscious but still human force, or by some powers, good, bad or indifferent, which are external to humanity, I would not myself attempt to decide. The only thing I will say with complete confidence, about that mystic and invisible power, is that it tells lies. The lies may be larks or they may be lures to the imperilled soul or they may be a thousand other things; but whatever they are, they are not truths about the other world; or for that matter about this world.

I will give one or two examples. We asked planchette, in our usual random fashion, what advice it would give to an acquaintance of ours, a solid and rather dull Member of Parliament who had the misfortune to be an authority on education. Planchette wrote down with brazen promptitude (in these later times it was always very prompt, though not always very clear) the simple words, "Get a divorce." The wife of the politician was so respectable, and I will add so hideous, that the materials of a scandalous romance seemed to be lacking. So we sternly enquired of our familiar spirit what the devil he meant; possibly an appropriate invocation. The result was rather curious. It wrote down very rapidly an immensely and indeed incredibly long word, which was at first quite illegible. It wrote it again; it wrote it four or five times; it was always quite obviously the same word; and towards the end it was apparent that it began with the three letters " O R R" I said, "This is all nonsense; there is no word in the English language beginning O R R, let alone a word as long as that." Finally it tried again and wrote the word out quite clearly; and it ran: "Orrible revelationsinighlife."

If it was our subconsciousness, our subconsciousness at least had a simple sense of humour. But that it was our subconsciousness rather than our consciousness (if it was not something outside both) is proved by the practical fact that we did go on puzzling over the written word, when it was again and again rewritten, and really never had a notion of what it was, until it burst upon us at last. Nobody who knew us, I think, would suppose us capable of playing such a long and solemn and silly deception on each other. We also, like our subconsciousness, had a sense of humour. But cases of this kind fill me with wonder and a faint alarm, when I consider the number of people who seem to be taking spirit communications seriously, and founding religions and moral philosophies upon them. There would indeed have been some Orrible Revelations in Igh Life, and some Orrible Revelations about our own mental state and moral behaviour, if we had trotted off to the M P with our little message from the higher sphere.

Here is another example of the same thing. My father, who was present while my brother and I were playing the fool in this fashion, had a curiosity to see whether the oracle could answer a question about something that he knew and we did not. He therefore asked the maiden name of the wife of an uncle of mine in a distant country; a lady whom we of the younger generation had never known. With the lightning decision of infallibility, the spirit pen said, "Manning." With equal decision my father said, "Nonsense." We then approached our tutelary genius with its lamentable romancing and its still more lamentable rashness. The spirit, never to be beaten, wrote down the defiant explanation, "Married before." And to whom, we asked with some sternness, had our remote but respected aunt been secretly married before? The inspired instrument instantly answered, "Cardinal Manning."

Now I will pause here in passing to ask what exactly would have happened to me and my social circle, what would have ultimately been the state of my mind or my general conception of the world in which I lived, if I had taken these spiritual revelations as some spiritualists seem to take some spiritual revelations; in short, if we had taken them seriously? Whether this sort of thing be the pranks of some Puck or Poltergeist, or the jerks of some subliminal sense, or the mockery of demons or anything else, it obviously is not true in the sense of trustworthy. Anybody who had trusted it as true would have landed very near to a lunatic asylum. And when it comes to selecting a spiritual philosophy, among the sects and schools of the modern world, these facts can hardly be entirely forgotten. Curiously enough, as I have already recorded, Cardinal Manning had crossed my path as a sort of flaming wraith even in my childhood. Cardinal Manning's portrait hangs now at the end of my room, as a symbol of a spiritual state which many would call my second childhood. But anyone would admit that both states are rather saner than my condition would have been, had I begun to dig up The Crime of the Cardinal, by delving in the distant past of a colonial aunt.

Well, even the guidance of higher and wiser intelligences in a better world did not drive me quite so raving mad as that. But I have sometimes fancied since that this practice, of the true psychology of which we really know so little, may possibly have contributed towards the disturbed or even diseased state of brooding and idling through which I passed at that time. I would not dogmatise either way; it is possible that it had nothing to do with it; it is possible that the whole thing was merely mechanical or accidental. I would leave planchette with a playful farewell, giving her the benefit of the doubt; I would allow that she may have been a joke or a fancy or a fairy or anything else; with the proviso that I would not touch her again with a bargepole. There are other aspects, concerning things much more my own fault, in which a barge-pole would have been useful; but I may as well finish here the trail of my merely trivial and accidental relations to psychical research; as there will be no need to return to that aspect of it; and I should never think of judging it seriously by such trifles. This progress of the preternatural has gone on spreading and strengthening through my whole life. Indeed my life happens to cover the precise period of the real change; not realised by those occupied only with later changes or alternative spiritual solutions. When I was quite a boy, practically no normal person of education thought that a ghost could possibly be anything but a turnip-ghost; a thing believed in by nobody but the village idiot. When I was a young man, practically every person with a large circle had one or two friends with a fancy for what would still have been called mediums and moonshine. When I was middle-aged, great men of science of the first rank like Sir William Crookes and Sir Oliver Lodge claimed to have studied spirits as they might have studied spiders, and discovered ectoplasm exactly as they discovered protoplasm. At the time I write, the thing has grown into a considerable religious movement, by the activity of the late Sir Arthur Conan Doyle, much less of a scientist, but much more of a journalist. I hope nobody will think me such a fool as to offer these fragments of random experience as affecting the real controversy. In the controversy, indeed, through most of my life, I have defended Spiritualism against scepticism; though I should now naturally defend Catholicism even against Spiritualism. But in the times of which I am writing, little crossed our path except stray stories; and the phantoms were sometimes rather phantasmal. There was some talk of wraiths or presences precipitated into distant places, which included a story about a man seen going into a public-house, who afterwards testified that he had not been present in the body in any such place or for any such errand. There were plenty of other and more plausible stories, which my brother and I repeated with a sort of vague vicarious excitement, without any definite deduction of doctrine; but my father, whose placid Victorian agnosticism on the point we strove in vain to pierce, would listen to a toll of spiritual revelations and shake his head and say, "Ah, it's all very well to talk about these lights and trumpets and voices; but I pin my faith to the man who said he didn't go into the public-house."

Most of this happened when I was at the art school; but even when I had left it, this very casual connection was continued, in a queer way, by the coincidence that I worked for a short time in the office of a publisher who rather specialised in spiritualistic and theosophical literature, known under the general title of the occult. It was not entirely my fault, if it was not the fault of the real spiritualists or the real spirits, if I blundered into rather queer and uncomfortable corners of Spiritualism. On my first day in the office I had my first insight into the occult; for I was very vague about the business, as about most other businesses. I knew we had just published a big and vigorously boomed book of the Life and Letters of the late Dr Anna Kingsford, of whom I had never heard, though many of our customers seemed to have heard of hardly anybody else. My full enlightenment came when a distraught lady darted into the office and began to describe her most complex spiritual symptoms and to demand the books most suited to her complaint, which I was quite incompetent to select. I timidly offered the monumental Life and Letters; but she shrank away with something like a faint shriek, "No, no," she cried, "I mustn't! Anna Kingsford says I mustn't." Then, with more control, "Anna Kingsford told me this morning that I must not read her Life; it would be very bad for me, she said, to read her Life." I ventured to say, or stammer, with all the crudity of common speech, "But Dr Anna Kingsford is dead." "She told me this morning," repeated the lady, "that I must *not* read the book." "Well," I said, "I hope Dr Kingsford hasn't been giving that advice to many people; it would be rather bad for the business. It seems rather malicious of Dr Kingsford."

I soon found that malicious was a mild word for Dr Anna Kingsford. With all respect to her shade, which is to me the shadow of a shade, I should have said then, and I think I should say now, that the more charitable word was "mad." I mention the matter here because, while it involves no contradiction of the cosmic theory of Spiritualism, it does illustrate the accident by which I bumped into a queer sort of Spiritualist; and it has some relation to a more general view of reason and religion. The lady celebrated in this book was at least queer. Her boast was that she had killed a number of men merely by thinking about them; her excuse was that they were men who defended vivisection. She also had very visionary, but very intimate interviews with various eminent public men, apparently in places of torment; I remember one with Mr Gladstone, in which a discussion about Ireland and the Sudan was interrupted by Mr Gladstone gradually growing red-hot from inside. "Feeling that he would wish to be alone," said Dr Anna Kingsford with delicacy, "I passed out;" and she must now, I fear, pass out of this fragmentary narrative. I hope I do her no injustice; I am fairly sure she was full of many generous enthusiasms; but I pin my faith, as my father would say, to that fine tact and sense of social decorum, which told her that turning completely red-hot is what no gentleman would desire to do in the presence of a lady.

On the whole, the jolliest Spiritualist I ever met, at least until long afterwards, and the psychic enquirer for whom I felt the most immediate sympathy, was a man who firmly believed that he had once got a successful tip for the Derby out of some medium somewhere, and was still pursuing mediums for information of the same kind. I suggested to him that he should purchase *The Pink-'un* and turn it into a paper combining the two interests, and sold at every bookstall under the name of *The Sporting and Spiritual Times*. This, I said, could not fail to lift bookmakers and jockeys into a loftier sphere of spiritual contemplation, not to mention owners, who probably need it quite as much; while it would give to Spiritualism a sound, shrewd and successful business side, vastly increase its popularity, and give to some of its followers an indefinable air of contact with concrete objective matters and what is coarsely called commonsense, which some of them, as I felt at the time, seemed in some fashion to lack. I need not speculate on it here.

For the rest, while I am on the topic, I may assure the reader that I have never experienced anything called psychical, which might be a desperate excuse for my subsequent belief in the things called spiritual. I have hardly happened to strike even the queer psychic coincidences that strike almost anybody; unless we count the story treasured in my household as that of the Wraith of Sarolea. Dr Sarolea, that fiery Flemish Professor of French, is certainly one of the most striking men I have known; but he never struck my path till long afterwards; but it is undoubtedly the fact that we were expecting him to dinner and my wife beheld the unmistakable long figure and pointed beard from a window; after which he vanished utterly from the landscape. What made the story really creepy was that just afterwards a very young Scotsman appeared at the door, asking for Dr Sarolea. The Scotsman remained to dinner; but not the wraith. He was to have come down with the wraith; who (as it turned out afterwards) had awaited him with some irritation at the National Liberal Club. One theory was that his rage had precipitated his astral body down to Beaconsfield, but was spent just before he reached the house. Another obvious theory, which my more materialistic mind naturally preferred, was that he had been murdered by the young man and hidden in the pond in my garden; but subsequent detective search found this to be unsound. I only mention my alternative theory, which I very much prefer, because it is impossible to mention Dr Sarolea, even at this premature stage of the story, without saying something about him. Dr Sarolea is one of the most learned linguists in Europe; he learns a new language every week or so. His library is one of the wonders of the world, not to say the monstrosities of the world. When last I saw him he gave me the impression of buying the neighbouring houses right and left to find room for his library. What, I asked myself, what is more probable than that a man of this sort should find himself in later life in the exact position of Faust? And what is more reasonable, what more probable, than that Mephistopheles should have met him at the corner of the road as he came up from Beaconsfield station; and propounded the old contract, by which, with a single blast of magic, he should be turned into the handsome young man who a moment later was knocking at my door? This psychic theory would be supported by the fact that the young man is now doing well in politics; and quite unshaken, of course, by the fact that Dr Sarolea (I am happy to say) is still alive and active in Edinburgh. The only difficulty about it is one which also affects my triumphant theory that Shakespeare wrote Bacon (controversially far stronger than the converse), which paralysed my father's faith in the story of the public-house; and leads me to suspect that this rather odd incident was one of those fairly ordinary oddities; as when we mistake a stranger for a friend; and then meet the friend afterwards. In short, the only objection to my complete and convincing psychic theory is that I do not believe a word of it.

All this, of course, happened ages afterwards: I only mention it here in order to disclaim any intention of taking my psychic experience seriously. But touching that early period directly described in this chapter, I have the same reason for alluding to the topic. I merely begin with this example of amateur psychical research, because the very fact that I indulged in it without reason and without result, that I did not come to any conclusion, or really even try to come to any conclusion, illustrates the fact that this is a period of life in which the mind is merely dreaming and drifting; and often drifting on to very dangerous rocks.

In this chapter, the period covered is roughly that of my going to an art school and is doubtless also coloured by the conditions of such a place. There is nothing harder to learn than painting and nothing which most people take less trouble about learning. An art school is a place where about three people work with feverish energy and everybody else idles to a degree that I should have conceived unattainable by human nature. Moreover, those who work are, I will not say the least intelligent, but, by the very nature of the case, for the moment the most narrow; those whose keen intelligence is for the time narrowed to a strictly technical problem.

They do not want to be discursive and philosophical; because the trick they are trying to learn is at once incommunicable and practical; like playing the violin. Thus philosophy is generally left to the idle; and it is generally a very idle philosophy. In the time of which I write it was also a very negative and even nihilistic philosophy. And though I never accepted it altogether, it threw a shadow over my mind and made me feel that most profitable and worthy ideas were, as it were on the defensive. I shall have more to say of this aspect of the matter later on; the point is for the moment that an art school can be a very idle place and that I was then a very idle person.

Art may be long, but schools of art are short and very fleeting; and there have been five or six since I attended an art school. Mine was the time of Impressionism; and nobody dared to dream there could be such a thing as Post-Impressionism or Post-Post-Impressionism. The very latest thing was to keep abreast of Whistler, and take him by the white forelock, as if he were Time himself. Since then that conspicuous white forelock has rather faded into a harmony of white and grey, and what was once so young has in its turn grown hoary. But I think there was a spiritual significance in Impressionism, in connection with this age as the age of scepticism. I mean that it illustrated scepticism in the sense of subjectivism. Its principle was that if all that could be seen of a cow was a white line and a purple shadow, we should only render the line and the shadow; in a sense we should only believe in the line and the shadow, rather than in the cow. In one sense the Impressionist sceptic contradicted the poet who said he had never seen a purple cow. He tended rather to say that he had only seen a purple cow; or rather that he had not seen the cow but only the purple. Whatever may be the merits of this as a method of art, there is obviously something highly subjective and sceptical about it as a method of thought. It naturally lends itself to the metaphysical suggestion that things only exist as we perceive them, or that things do not exist at all. The philosophy of Impressionism is necessarily close to the philosophy of Illusion. And this atmosphere also tended to contribute, however indirectly, to a certain mood of unreality and sterile isolation that settled at this time upon me; and I think upon many others.

What surprises me in looking back on youth, and even on boyhood, is the extreme rapidity with which it can think its way back to fundamental things; and even to the denial of fundamental things. At a very early age I had thought my way back to thought itself. It is a very dreadful thing to do; for it may lead to thinking that there is nothing but thought. At this time I did not very clearly distinguish between dreaming and waking; not only as a mood, but as a metaphysical doubt, I felt as if everything might be a dream. It was as if I had myself projected the universe from within, with all its trees and stars; and that is so near to the notion of being God that it is manifestly even nearer to going mad. Yet I was not mad, in any medical or physical sense; I was simply carrying the scepticism of my time as far as it would go. And I soon found it would go a great deal further than most of the sceptics went. While dull atheists came and explained to me that there was nothing but matter, I listened with a sort of calm horror of detachment, suspecting that there was nothing but mind. I have always felt that there was something thin and third-rate about materialists and materialism ever since. The atheist told me so pompously that he did not believe there was any God; and there were moments when I did not even believe there was any atheist.

And as with mental, so with moral extremes. There is something truly menacing in the thought of how quickly I could imagine the maddest, when I had never committed the mildest crime. Something may have been due to the atmosphere of the Decadents, and their perpetual hints of the luxurious horrors of paganism; but I am not disposed to dwell much on that defence; I suspect I manufactured most of my morbidities for myself. But anyhow, it is true that there was a time when I had reached that condition of moral anarchy within, in which a man says, in the words of Wilde, that "Atys with the blood-stained knife were better than the thing I am." I have never indeed felt the faintest temptation to the particular madness of Wilde; but I could at this time imagine the worst and wildest disproportions and distortions of more normal passion; the point is that the whole mood was overpowered and oppressed with a sort of congestion of imagination. As Bunyan, in his morbid period, described himself as prompted to utter blasphemies, I had an overpowering impulse to record or draw horrible ideas and images; plunging deeper and deeper as in a blind spiritual suicide. I had never heard of Confession, in any serious sense, in those days; but that is what is really needed in such cases. I fancy they are not uncommon cases. Anyhow, the point is here that I dug quite low enough to discover the devil; and even in some dim way to recognise the devil. At least I never, even in this first vague and sceptical stage, indulged very much in the current arguments about the relativity of evil or the unreality of sin. Perhaps, when I eventually emerged as a sort of a theorist, and was described as an Optimist, it was because I was one of the few people in that world of diabolism who really believed in devils.

In truth, the story of what was called my Optimism was rather odd. When I had been for some time in these, the darkest depths of the contemporary pessimism, I had a strong inward impulse to revolt; to dislodge this incubus or throw off this nightmare. But as I was still thinking the thing out by myself, with little help from philosophy and no real help from religion, I invented a rudimentary and makeshift mystical theory of my own. It was substantially this: that even mere existence, reduced to its most primary limits, was extraordinary enough to be exciting. Anything was magnificent as compared with nothing. Even if the very daylight were a dream, it was a day-dream; it was not a nightmare. The mere fact that one could wave one's arms and legs about (or those dubious external objects in the landscape which were called one's arms and legs) showed that it had not the mere paralysis of a nightmare. Or if it was a nightmare, it was an enjoyable nightmare. In fact, I had wandered to a position not very far from the phrase of my Puritan grandfather, when he said that he would thank God for his creation if he were a lost soul. I hung on to the remains of religion by one thin thread of thanks. I thanked whatever gods might be, not like Swinburne, because no life lived for ever, but because any life lived at all; not, like Henley, for my unconquerable soul (for I have never been so optimistic about my own soul as all that), but for my own soul and my own body, even if they could be conquered. This way of looking at things, with a sort of mystical minimum of gratitude, was of course, to some extent assisted by those few of the fashionable writers who were not pessimists; especially by Walt Whitman, by Browning and by Stevenson; Browning's, "God must be glad one loves his world so much," or Stevenson's, "belief in the ultimate decency of things." But I do not think it is too much to say that I took it in a way of my own; even if it was a way I could not see clearly or make very clear. What I meant, whether or no I managed to say it, was this; that no man knows how much he is an optimist, even when he calls himself a pessimist, because he has not really measured the depths of his debt to whatever created him and enabled him to call himself anything. At the back of our brains, so to speak, there was a forgotten blaze or burst of astonishment at our own existence. The object of the artistic and spiritual life was to dig for this submerged sunrise of wonder; so that a man sitting in a chair might suddenly understand that he was actually alive, and be happy. There were other aspects of this feeling, and other arguments about it, to which I shall have to return. Here it is only a necessary part of the narrative; as it involves the fact that, when I did begin to write, I was full of a new and fiery resolution to write against the Decadents and the Pessimists who ruled the culture of the age.

Thus, among the juvenile verses I began to write about this time was one called, "The Babe Unborn," which imagined the uncreated creature crying out for existence and promising every virtue if he might only have the experience of life. Another conceived the scoffer as begging God to give him eyes and lips and a tongue that he might mock the giver of them; a more angry version of the same fancy. And I think it was about this time that I thought of the notion afterwards introduced into a tale called, "Manalive;" of a benevolent being who went about with a pistol, which he would suddenly point at a pessimist, when that philosopher said that life was not worth living. This was not printed until long afterwards; but the verses were collected into a little volume; and my father was so imprudent as to help me to get them published under the title of *The Wild Knight*. And this is an important part of the story, in so far as any part of the story is important, because it did involve my introduction to literature and even to literary men.

My little volume of verse was reviewed with warm and almost overwhelming generosity by Mr James Douglas, then almost entirely known as a leading literary critic. Impetuosity as well as generosity was always one of Mr Douglas' most attractive qualities. And he insisted, for some reason, on affirming positively that there was no such person as G K Chesterton; that the name was obviously a *nom de plume*; that the work was obviously not that of a novice, but a successful writer; and finally that it could be none other than Mr John Davidson. This naturally brought an indignant denial from Mr John Davidson. That spirited poet very legitimately thanked the Lord that he had never written such nonsense; and I for one very heartily sympathised with him. Not very long afterwards, when Mr John Lane had accepted the manuscript of *The Napoleon of Notting Hill*, I was lunching with that publisher and fell into a very pleasant conversation with a fair-haired young man on my left, a little older than myself. A more odd-looking man, a little like an elf, bald, black-haired and with a Mephistophelean tuft and monocle, joined in the conversation across the table; and we found that we agreed on a large number of literary subjects and formed, I think I may say, a lasting liking for each other. It was only afterwards that I discovered that the first man was Mr James Douglas and the second man was Mr John Davidson.

I am here advancing my story along the literary line, to a point which I have not yet reached on other lines that were rather political or social; but, for the sake of convenience, I may as well complete this part of my rather erratic development here. Perhaps the next most important accident that favoured me, and brought me into relation with the world of letters, was the fact that I wrote a long review on a book about Stevenson; perhaps the first of the rather stupid books that have been written to belittle Stevenson. I defended Stevenson with so much vehemence, not to say violence, that I had the good fortune to attract the attention of very distinguished writers who, though themselves certainly neither violent nor vehement, were very specially Stevensonian. I received a charming letter, and later a great deal of hospitality and encouragement, from Sir Sidney Colvin; to whose house I often went, where I had the pleasure of meeting the lady who was afterwards Lady Colvin, and where I heard Stephen Phillips read aloud his play of *Ulysses*. Nobody could have been more magnanimous and considerate than Colvin always was to me; but I think we could never have been at one, as he was at one with Stevenson or even Stephen Phillips. For, except on the subject of Stevenson, we differed upon every subject in earth and heaven; he was both an Imperialist in politics and a Rationalist in religion; and with all his frigid refinement, he was whatever he was with an unquenchable pertinacity. He hated Radicals and Christian mystics and romantic sympathisers with small nationalities, and in fact everything that I had any tendency to be. But the same link of the love of Stevenson attached me a little later to another very eminent man of letters; Sir Edmund Gosse. In some way I always felt far more at home with Sir Edmund Gosse; because he despised all opinions, and not merely my opinions. He had an extraordinary depth of geniality in his impartial cynicism. He had the art of snubbing without sneering. We always felt that he had not enjoyed snubbing but the snub itself, as a sort of art for art's sake, a million miles from any personal malice. It was all the more artistic because of the courtly and silken manner that he commonly assumed. I was very fond of him; and it gives me great happiness to think that one of the last things he must have done was to write me a letter thanking me for another and much later vindication of Stevenson, in a book I wrote long afterwards, indeed only a few years ago. In this letter he said of Stevenson, with a very powerful simplicity coming from such a man: "I loved him; I love him still." I have no right to use such strong terms in my case; but I feel something like that about Gosse.

About this time I discovered the secret of amiability in another person with a rather misleading reputation for acidity. Mr Max Beerbohm asked me to lunch; and I have ever since known that he is himself the most subtle of his paradoxes. A man with his reputation might well find offence in the phrase amiability; I can only explain to so scholarly a wit that I put it in Latin or French because I dare not put it in English. Max played in the masquerade of his time, which he has described so brilliantly; and he dressed or overdressed the part. His name was supposed to be a synonym for Impudence; for the undergraduate who exhibited the cheek of a guttersnipe in the garb of a dandy. He was supposed to blow his own trumpet with every flourish of self-praise; countless stories were told about the brazen placidity of his egoism. How, when he had hardly written anything more than a few schoolboy essays, he bound them under the stately title of *The Works of Max Beerbohm*. How he projected a series of biographies called "Brothers of Great Men;" the first volume being *Herbert Beerbohm Tree*. And the first moment I heard his voice, or caught sight of the expression of his eyes, I knew that all this was the flat contrary of the truth. Max was and is a remarkably humble man, for a man of his gifts and his period. I have never known him, by a single phrase or intonation, claim to know more or judge better than he does; or indeed half so much or so well as he does. Most men spread themselves a little in conversation, and have their unreal victories and vanities; but he seems to me more moderate and realistic about himself than about anything else. He is more sceptical about everything than I am, by temper; but certainly he does not indulge in the base idolatry of believing in himself. On this point I wish I were so good a Christian as he. I hope, for the sake of his official or public personality, that he will manage to live down this last affront. But the people who could not see this fact, because an intelligent undergraduate enjoyed an intellectual rag, have something to learn about the possible combination of humility and humour.

Finally, a crown of what I can only call respectability came to me from the firm of Macmillan; in the form of a very flattering invitation to write the study of Browning for the English Men of Letters Series. It had just arrived when I was lunching with Max Beerbohm, and he said to me in a pensive way: "A man ought to write on Browning while he is young." No man knows he is young while he is young. I did not know what Max meant at the time; but I see now that he was right; as he generally is. Anyhow, I need not say that I accepted the invitation to write a book on Browning. I will not say that I wrote a book on Browning; but I wrote a book on love, liberty, poetry, my own views on God and religion (highly undeveloped), and various theories of my own about optimism and pessimism and the hope of the world; a book in which the name of Browning was introduced from time to time, I might almost say with considerable art, or at any rate with some decent appearance of regularity. There were very few biographical facts in the book, and those were nearly all wrong. But there is something buried somewhere in the book; though I think it is rather my boyhood than Browning's biography.

I have pursued this literary part of my own biography in advance of the rest. But long before this it was apparent that the centre of gravity in my existence had shifted from what we will (for the sake of courtesy) call Art to what we will (for the sake of courtesy) call Literature. The agent in this change of intention was, in the first instance, my friend Ernest Hodder Williams, afterwards the head of the well-known publishing firm. He was attending Latin and English lectures at University College while I was attending, or not attending, to the art instructions of the Slade School. I joined him in following the English course; and for this reason I am able to boast myself among the many pupils who are grateful to the extraordinarily lively and stimulating learning of Professor W P Ker. Most of the other students were studying for examinations; but I had not even that object in this objectless period of my life. The result was that I gained an entirely undeserved reputation for disinterested devotion to culture for its own sake; and I once had the honour of constituting the whole of Professor Ker's audience. But he gave as thorough and thoughtful a lecture as I have ever heard given, in a slightly more colloquial style; asked me some questions about my reading; and, on my mentioning something from the poetry of Pope, said with great satisfaction: "Ah, I see you have been well brought up." Pope had much less than justice from that generation of the admirers of Shelley and Swinburne. Hodder Williams and I often talked about literature, following on these literary lectures; and he conceived a fixed notion that I could write; a delusion which he retained to the day of his death. In consequence of this, and in connection with my art studies, he gave me some books on art to review for the *Bookman*, the famous organ of his firm and family. I need not say that, having entirely failed to learn how to draw or paint, I tossed off easily enough some criticisms of the weaker points of Rubens or the misdirected talents of Tintoretto. I had discovered the easiest of all professions; which I have pursued ever since.

When I look back on these things, and indeed on my life generally, the thing that strikes me most is my extraordinary luck. I have already pleaded for the merits of the Moral Tale; but it is against all the proper principles that even any such measure of good fortune should have come to the Idle Apprentice. In the case of my association with Hodder Williams, it was against all reason that so unbusinesslike a person should have so businesslike a friend. In the case of the choice of a trade, it was outrageously unjust that a man should succeed in becoming a journalist merely by failing to become an artist. I say a trade and not a profession; for the only thing I can say for myself, in connection with both trades, is that I was never pompous about them. If I have had a profession, at least I have never been a professor. But in another sense there was about these first stages an element of luck, and even of accident. I mean that my mind remained very much abstracted and almost stunned; and these opportunities were merely things that happened to me, almost like calamities. To say that I was not ambitious makes it sound far too like a virtue, when it really was a not very disgraceful defect; it was that curious blindness of youth which we can observe in others and yet never explain in ourselves. But, above all, I mention it here also because it was connected with the continuity of that unresolved riddle in the mind, which I mentioned at the beginning of this chapter. The essential reason was that my eyes were turned inwards rather than outwards; giving my moral personality, I should imagine, a very unattractive squint. I was still oppressed with the metaphysical nightmare of negations about mind and matter, with the morbid imagery of evil, with the burden of my own mysterious brain and body; but by this time I was in revolt against them; and trying to construct a healthier conception of cosmic life, even if it were one that should err on the side of health. I even called myself an optimist, because I was so horribly near to being a pessimist. It is the only excuse I can offer. All this part of the process was afterwards thrown up in the very formless form of a piece of fiction called *The Man Who Was Thursday*. The title attracted some attention at the time; and there were many journalistic jokes about it. Some, referring to my supposed festive views, affected to mistake it for "The Man Who Was Thirsty." Others naturally supposed that Man Thursday was the black brother of Man Friday. Others again, with more penetration, treated it as a mere title out of topsy-turvydom; as if it had been "The Woman Who Was Half Past Eight," or "The Cow Who Was Tomorrow Evening." But what interests me about it was this; that hardly anybody who looked at the title ever seems to have looked at the subtitle; which was "A Nightmare," and the answer to a good many critical questions.

I pause upon the point here, because it is of some importance to the understanding of that time. I have often been asked what I meant by the monstrous pantomime ogre who was called Sunday in that story; and some have suggested, and in one sense not untruly, that he was meant for a blasphemous version of the Creator. But the point is that the whole story is a nightmare of things, not as they are, but as they seemed to the young half-pessimist of the '90s; and the ogre who appears brutal but is also cryptically benevolent is not so much God, in the sense of religion or irreligion, but rather Nature as it appears to the pantheist, whose pantheism is struggling out of pessimism. So far as the story had any sense in it, it was meant to begin with the picture of the world at its worst and to work towards the suggestion that the picture was not so black as it was already painted. I explained that the whole thing was thrown out in the nihilism of the '90s in the dedicatory lines which I wrote to my friend Bentley, who had been through the same period and problems; asking rhetorically: "Who shall understand but you?" In reply to which a book-reviewer very sensibly remarked that if nobody understood the book except Mr Bentley, it seemed unreasonable to ask other people to read it.

But I speak of it here because, though it came at the beginning of the story, it was destined to take on another meaning before the end of it. Without that distant sequel, the memory may appear as meaningless as the book; but for the moment I can only leave on record here the two facts to which I managed somehow and in some sense to testify. First, I was trying vaguely to found a new optimism, not on the maximum, but the minimum of good. I did not so much mind the pessimist who complained that there was so little good. But I was furious, even to slaying, with the pessimist who asked what was the good of good. And second, even in the earliest days and even for the worst reasons, I already knew too much to pretend to get rid of evil. I introduced at the end one figure who really does, with a full understanding, deny and defy the good. Long afterwards Father Ronald Knox told me, in his whimsical manner, that he was sure that the test of the book would be used to prove that I was a Pantheist and a Pagan, and that the Higher Critics of the future would easily show that the episode of the Accuser was an interpolation by priests.

This was not the case; in fact it was quite the other way. At this time I should have been quite as annoyed as anybody else for miles round, if I had found a priest interfering with my affairs or interpolating things in my manuscript. I put that statement into that story, testifying to the extreme evil (which is merely the unpardonable sin of not wishing to be pardoned), not because I had learned it from any of the million priests whom I had never met, but because I had learned it from myself. I was already quite certain that I could if I chose cut myself off from the whole life of the universe. My wife, when asked who converted her to Catholicism, always answers, "the Devil."

But all that was so long afterwards, that it has no relation to the groping and guesswork philosophy of the story in question. I would much rather quote a tribute from a totally different type of man, who was nevertheless one of the very few men who, for some reason or other, have ever made head or tail of this unfortunate romance of my youth. He was a distinguished psycho-analyst, of the most modern and scientific sort. He was not a priest; far from it; we might say, like the Frenchman asked if he had lunched on the boat, "*au contraire.*" He did not believe in the Devil; God forbid, if there was any God to forbid. But he was a very keen and eager student of his own subject; and he made my hair stand on end by saying that he had found my very juvenile story useful as a corrective among his morbid patients; especially the process by which each of the diabolical anarchs turns out to be a good citizen in disguise. "I know a number of men who nearly went mad," he said quite gravely, "but were saved because they had really understood *The Man Who Was Thursday.*" He must have been rather generously exaggerative; he may have been mad himself, of course; but then so was I. But I confess it flatters me to think that, in this my period of lunacy, I may have been a little useful to other lunatics.

V

NATIONALISM AND NOTTING HILL

At this point of the story I must for a moment go back in order to go on. In the previous pages I have said a good deal about Art, both in the home and the school; of the art I lost by my own fault or gained by my father's merit; of the gratitude I owe to the amateur and the apology I owe to the art master; of all I was taught without learning it, and all I learnt without anybody teaching it. But in a sketch of the period, this predominance of Art is rather out of proportion to the contemporary position of Science. It was true that I could never exactly be called a scientific character; and even as between the Classical and Modern sides of my old school, I should always have chosen rather to idle at Greek than to idle at Chemistry. But science was in the air of all that Victorian world, and children and boys were affected by the picturesque aspects of it. Several of my father's cronies were scientific either in their hobbies or their profession; one of them, a very delightful schoolmaster named Alexander Watherston, carried about with him a geological hammer, with which he would detach fossils from rocks or walls to my intense delight; so that the very name of a geological hammer still suggests something primal and poetic like the hammer of Thor. My mother's brother, Beaumont Grosjean, was an analytical chemist by calling, and a man stuffed with humour; I can recall how he professed to have proved by analysis the purity of one single product of current commerce; which was Nubian Blacking; I believe it no longer exists; so I can be neither reproached nor rewarded for the advertisement. But he was so captivated with this one case of commercial probity that he used the name as a moral term of eulogy, saying: "No man could have behaved in a more Nubian fashion," or, "Perhaps as Nubian an action as ever did honour to human nature." It was the same scientific uncle who told me various fairy-tales of science, which I regret to say that I believed much less than the fairy-tales of fairyland. Thus he told me that when I jumped off a chair, the earth jumped towards me. At the time I took it for granted that this was a lie; or at any rate a joke. What Einstein has done with it now is another story – or perhaps another joke. But I mention science and the scientific uncle for another reason here.

I am just old enough to remember in infancy the world before telephones. And I remember that my father and my uncle fitted up the first telephone I ever saw with their own metal and chemicals, a miniature telephone reaching from the top bedroom under the roof to the remote end of the garden. I was really impressed imaginatively by this; and I do not think I have ever been so much impressed since by any extension of it. The point is rather important in the whole theory of imagination. It did startle me that a voice should sound in the room when it was really as distant as the next street. It would hardly have startled me more if it had been as distant as the next town. It does not startle me any more if it is as distant as the next continent. The miracle is over. Thus I admired even the large scientific things most on a small scale. So I always found that I was much more attracted by the microscope than the telescope. I was not overwhelmed in childhood, by being told of remote stats which the sun never reached, any more than in manhood by being told of an empire on which the sun never set. I had no use for an empire that had no sunsets. But I was inspired and thrilled by looking through a little hole at a crystal like a pin's head; and seeing it change pattern and colour like a pigmy sunset.

I have already picked two quarrels with better men than myself, who were enthusiasts for childish romance, upon the reality of the romance of childhood. First, I disagree with them when they treat the infantile imagination as a sort of dream; whereas I remember it rather as a man dreaming might remember the world where he was awake. And second, I deny that children have suffered under a tyranny of moral tales. For I remember the time when it would have seemed the most hideous tyranny to take my moral tales away from me. And, in order to make this clear, I must contradict yet another common assumption in the romantic description of the dawn of life. The point is not very easy to explain; indeed I have spent the greater part of my life in an unsuccessful attempt to explain it. Upon the cart-loads of ill-constructed books in which I have completely failed to do so, I have no desire to dwell. But perhaps, as a general definition, this might be useful; or, if not as a definition, at least as a suggestion. From the first vaguely, and of late more and more clearly, I have felt that the world is conceiving liberty as something that merely works outwards. And I have always conceived it as something that works inwards.

The ordinary poetic description of the first dreams of life is a description of mere longing for larger and larger horizons. The imagination is supposed to work towards the infinite; though in that sense the infinite is the opposite of the imagination. For the imagination deals with an image. And an image is in its nature a thing that has an outline and therefore a limit. Now I will maintain, paradoxical as it may seem, that the child does not desire merely to fall out of the window, or even to fly through the air or to be drowned in the sea. When he wishes to go to other places, they are still places; even if nobody has ever been there. But in truth the case is much stronger than that. It is plain on the face of the facts that the child is positively in love with limits. He uses his imagination to invent imaginary limits. The nurse and the governess have never told him that it is his moral duty to step on alternate paving stones. He deliberately deprives this world of half its paving stones, in order to exult in a challenge that he has offered to himself. I played that kind of game with myself all over the mats and boards and carpets of the house; and, at the risk of being detained during His Majesty's pleasure, I will admit that I often play it still. In that sense I have constantly tried to cut down the actual space at my disposal; to divide and sub-divide, into these happy prisons, the house in which I was quite free to run wild. And I believe that there is in this psychological freak a truth without which the whole modern world is missing its main opportunity. If we look at the favourite nursery romances, or at least if we have the patience to look at them twice, we shall find that they all really support this view; even when they have largely been accepted as supporting the opposite view. The charm of Robinson Crusoe is not in the fact that he could find his way to a remote island; but in the fact that he could not find any way of getting away from it. It is that fact which gives an intensive interest and excitement to all the things that he had with him on the island; the axe and the parrot and the guns and the little hoard of grain. The tale of Treasure Island is not the record of a vague desire to go on a sea voyage for one's health. It ends where it began; and it began with Stevenson drawing a map of the island, with all its bays and capes cut out as clearly as fretwork. And the eternal interest of the Noah's Ark, considered as a toy, consists in its complete suggestion of compactness and isolation; of creatures so comically remote and fantastic being all locked up in one box; as if Noah had been told to pack up the sun and moon with his luggage. In other words, it is exactly the same game that I have played myself, by piling all the things I wanted on a sofa, and imagining that the carpet around me was the surrounding sea.

This game of self-limitation is one of the secret pleasures of life. As it says in the little manuals about such sports, the game is played in several forms. One very good way of playing it is to look at the nearest bookcase, and wonder whether you would find sufficient entertainment in that chance collection, even if you had no other books. But always it is dominated by this principle of division and restriction; which begins with the game played by the child with the paving stones. But I dwell upon it here because it must be understood as something real and rooted, so far as I am concerned, in order that the other views I have offered about these things may make any sort of sense. If anybody chooses to say that I have founded all my social philosophy on the antics of a baby, I am quite satisfied to bow and smile.

It is really relevant to insist that I do not know at what exact stage of my childhood or my youth the idea consolidated as a sort of local patriotism. A child has by the light of nature (or perhaps some better light) an idea of fortifying and defending things; of saying that he is the king of the castle, but of being rather glad than otherwise that it is such a small castle. But as it is my whole thesis that there is something very real behind all these first movements of the mind, I do not think I was ever surprised to find that this instinct corresponded to an idea. Only, by a rather curious coincidence in my life, it had only just developed as a private idea, when I found it clinched and supported by a public idea. If I have since gone back to public ideas, or to the outside of my existence, I have tried to explain that the most important part of it had long been in the inside of my life; perhaps a long time before I found it there.

I was one day wandering about the streets in part of North Kensington, telling myself stories of feudal sallies and sieges, in the manner of Walter Scott, and vaguely trying to apply them to the wilderness of bricks and mortar around me. I felt that London was already too large and loose a thing to be a city in the sense of a citadel. It seemed to me even larger and looser than the British Empire. And something irrationally arrested and pleased my eye about the look of one small block of little lighted shops, and I amused myself with the supposition that these alone were to be preserved and defended, like a hamlet in a desert. I found it quite exciting to count them and perceive that they contained the essentials of a civilisation, a chemist's shop, a bookshop, a provision merchant for food and a public-house for drink. Lastly, to my great delight, there was also an old curiosity shop bristling with swords and halberds; manifestly intended to arm the guard that was to fight for the sacred street. I wondered vaguely what they would attack or whither they would advance. And looking up, I saw grey with distance, but still seemingly immense in altitude, the tower of the Waterworks close to the street where I was born. It suddenly occurred to me that capturing the Waterworks might really mean the military stroke of flooding the valley; and with that torrent and cataract of visionary waters, the first fantastic notion of a tale called *The Napoleon of Notting Hill* rushed over my mind.

I have never taken my books seriously; but I take my opinions quite seriously. I do not mention my fortunately forgotten romance because I wish to emulate the academic seriousness of Mr Dodgson, who noted the exact conditions of time and landscape in which it first occurred to him that the Snark was after all a Boojum. But this detail of memory has to do with much more practical things. It happens to be the only way of explaining what was very soon to be my position in quite practical politics. It must first be clearly understood that contemporary politics, even in the common sense my own politics, were all driving or drifting exactly the other way. The two great movements during my youth and early manhood were Imperialism and Socialism. They were supposed to be fighting each other; and so doubtless they did, in the sense of waving Red Flags against Union Jacks. But as compared with those dim gropings in my own imagination, the two things were in union; at least as much in union as the Union Jack. Both believed in unification and centralisation on a large scale. Neither could have seen any meaning in my own fancy for having things on a smaller and smaller scale. That fancy itself was indeed too indistinct and instinctive as yet to suggest an alternative theory; and in some vague way I accepted the fashionable theories. I read Kipling and was attracted in many ways, though repelled in others. I called myself a Socialist; because the only alternative to being a Socialist was not being a Socialist. And not being a Socialist was a perfectly ghastly thing. It meant being a small-headed and sneering snob, who grumbled at the rates and the working-classes; or some hoary horrible old Darwinian who said the weakest must go to the wall. But in my heart I was a reluctant Socialist. I accepted the larger things as the lesser evil – or even the lesser good.

Rather in the sense in which I was a reluctant Socialist, I was even ready to be a reluctant Imperialist. It was rather as the Mr Burden of Mr Belloc was a reluctant Imperialist; for indeed I inherited the tradition of an older business world, not unlike Mr Burden's. All my instincts told me that I could not entirely lose hold of patriotism; neither then nor at any later time had I any liking for what is commonly connoted by pacifism. I was willing to accept colonial adventure if it was the only way of protecting my country; just as I was willing to accept collectivist organisation if it was the only way of protecting my poorer fellow-citizens. I was willing that Britain should boast of having an empire, if she really had nothing better to boast of. I was willing to let Mr Sidney Webb look after the poor, if nobody else would look after them, or if (as seemed to be assumed as an axiom of social science) it was quite impossible for them to look after themselves. But nothing of my heart or my imagination went with these wide generalisations; and something inside me was always subconsciously burrowing in the very opposite direction. I remained in this vague, but not entirely unhealthy state of mind, hung between an inward instinct I could not follow and an outward expansion I did not really wish to follow, until something happened in the outer world which not only woke me from my dreams like a thunder-clap, but like a lightning-flash revealed me to myself. In 1895 came the Jameson Raid, and a year or two afterwards the war with the two Republics of South Africa.

The nation seemed solid for the war. It was far more eager for the South African War than it was afterwards for the Great War. The latter was obviously much more crucial, and in my opinion much more just. But it did not produce that particular impression of a unanimous shout of applause such as marked the campaign for the extinction of President Kruger's Dutch state. Crowds would doubtless cry both against Kruger and Kaiser; but the Kaiser with his moustaches never became so popular a caricature as the President with his chin-beard. The name became indeed a general term for anything exotic and alien; and a too elegant poet with long curly hair and velvet knee-breeches would be hailed by the apt and descriptive cry of "Kruger!" But the apparent unity covered more influential and instructive groups. Journalism and politics were for the policy of Annexation. Most of the newspapers followed the *Daily Mail* in its morals if not in its manners. The Liberal Imperialists practically took the lead in the Liberal Party, so that even the opposition could hardly oppose. And it must always be remembered that these pro-war politicians were those who were later charged with moderation or (very absurdly) with anti-patriotism during the war of 1914; Asquith and Haldane and Grey. It seemed that all moderate men were on what was called the patriotic side. I knew little of politics then; and to me the unity seemed greater than it was; but it was very great. I saw all the public men and public bodies, the people in the street, my own middle-class and most of my family and friends, solid in favour of something that seemed inevitable and scientific and secure. And I suddenly realised that I hated it; that I hated the whole thing as I had never hated anything before.

What I hated about it was what a good many people liked about it. It was such a very cheerful war. I hated its confidence, its congratulatory anticipations, its optimism of the Stock Exchange. I hated its vile assurance of victory. It was regarded by many as an almost automatic process like the operation of a natural law; and I have always hated that sort of heathen notion of a natural law. As the war proceeded, indeed, it began to be dimly felt that it was proceeding and not progressing. When the British had many unexpected failures and the Boers many unexpected successes, there was a change in the public temper, and less of optimism and indeed little but obstinacy. But the note struck from the first was the note of the inevitable; a thing abhorrent to Christians and to lovers of liberty. The blows struck by the Boer nation at bay, the dash and dazzling evasions of De Wet, the capture of a British general at the very end of the campaign, sounded again and again the opposite note of defiance; of those who, as I wrote later in one of my first articles, "disregard the omens and disdain the stars." And all this swelled up within me into vague images of a modern resurrection of Marathon or

Thermopyl, and I saw again my recurring dream of the unscalable tower and the besieging citizens; and began to draw out the rude outlines of my little romance of London. But above all, perhaps, what began to repel me about the atmosphere of the adventure was something insincere about the most normal part of the national claim; the suggestion of something like a rescue of our exiled representatives, the commercial citizens of Johannesburg, who were commonly called the Outlanders. As this would have been the most sympathetic plea if it was genuine, it was the more repulsive if it was hypocritical.

For this was the best case for the war; that if the Boers were fighting for their country, the British were fighting for their countrymen. Only there was rather a queer look about some of the portraits of their countrymen. It was constantly asserted that an Englishman named Edgar had been murdered; but no portrait of Edgar was published, because it happened that he was entirely black. Other portraits were published; other Outlanders were paraded and they were of other tints and shades. We began to guess that the people the Boers called Outlanders were often people whom the British would call Outsiders. Their names were symbolic as their noses. I remember waiting with a Pro-Boer friend in the midst of a Jingo mob outside the celebrated Queen's Hall Meeting which ended in a free fight. My friend and I adopted a method of patriotic parody or *reductio ad absurdum*. We first proposed three cheers for Chamberlain, then three cheers for Rhodes, and then by degrees for more and more dubious and demi-naturalised patriots. We actually did get an innocent cheer for Beit. We got a more wavering cheer for Eckstein. But when it came to our impulsive appeal to the universal popularity of Albu, the irony of our intention was discovered; and the fight began. I found myself in a pugilistic encounter with an Imperialistic clerk, whose pugilism was at least no more scientific than my own. While this encounter (one of many other surrounding conflicts) was proceeding, another Imperialist must have abstracted my watch; the last I ever troubled to possess. He at any rate believed in the Policy of Annexation.

I was called a Pro-Boer and, unlike some Pro-Boers, I was very proud of the title. It expressed exactly what I meant much better than its idealistic synonyms. Some intellectuals indignantly repudiated the term, and said they were not Pro-Boers, but only lovers of peace or pacifists. But I emphatically was a Pro-Boer, and I emphatically was not a pacifist. My point was that the Boers were right in fighting; not that anybody must be wrong in fighting. I thought that their farmers were perfectly entitled to take to horse and rifle in defence of their farms, and their little farming commonwealth, when it was invaded by a more cosmopolitan empire at the command of very cosmopolitan financiers. As no less an authority than Mr Discobolus says in *Lear's Nonsense Rhymes*, I thought so then and I think so still. But this sort of militant sympathy naturally separated those who thought as I did from our colleagues who were mere anti-militarists. The consequence was not unimportant to me personally. It was that I found I belonged to a minority of a minority. Most of those who not unnaturally sympathised with the British, disapproved of us for sympathising with the Boers. Most of those who sympathised with the Boers disapproved of us for sympathising with them for the wrong reasons. Indeed, I do not know whether the Jingo or the Pacifist found us the more offensive and objectionable. It was in this rather quaint condition that I naturally gravitated towards a friendship which has since played so considerable a part in my life, public as well as private.

My friends had just come down from Oxford, Bentley from Merton and Oldershaw from "the House," where they had figured prominently in a group of young Liberals opposed in varying degrees to the current Imperialism; a group containing many names sufficiently famous afterwards; John Simon, now the well-known statesman and advocate, and Francis Hirst the economist. Soon after our reunion in London, I went to meet Lucian Oldershaw at a little restaurant in Soho. It was in the days before everybody had discovered the whereabouts of Soho; and these small French eating-houses were only valued by a few *gourmets* on the ground that they were still places where it was possible to eat. I have never been anything so refined as a *gourmet*; so I am happy to say that I am still quite capable of being a glutton. My ignorance of cookery is such that I can even eat the food in the most fashionable and expensive hotels in London. Sometimes, in those luxurious halls inhabited by the heroes and heroines of Oppenheim and Edgar Wallace, the food is just a shade too bad even for me. But those who really prefer eating good cutlets and omelettes to living on gilt plaster and pantomime footmen had already found their way to delightful little dens off Leicester Square, where in those days a man could get a half-bottle of perfectly good red wine for sixpence. To one of these I went to meet my friend, who entered the place followed by a sturdy man with a stiff straw hat of the period tilted over his eyes, which emphasised the peculiar length and strength of his chin. He had a high-shouldered way of wearing a coat so that it looked like a heavy overcoat, and instantly reminded me of the pictures of Napoleon; and, for some vague reason, especially of the pictures of Napoleon on horseback. But his eyes, not without anxiety, had that curious distant keenness that is seen in the eyes of sailors; and there was something about his walk that has even been compared to a sailor's roll. Long afterwards the words found their way into verse which expressed a certain consciousness of the combination, and of the blend of nations in his blood.

> Almighty God will surely say,
> St Michael, who is this that stands
> With Ireland in his doubtful eyes

NATIONALISM AND NOTTING HILL

> And Perigord between his hands,
> And on his arm the stirrup-thongs
> And in his gait the narrow seas
> And on his mouth Burgundian songs
> And in his heart the Pyrenees?

He sat down heavily on one of the benches and began to talk at once about some controversy or other; I gathered that the question was whether it could be reasonably maintained that King John was the best English king. He judicially decided in the negative; but, by the standards of Mrs Markham's *History of England* (to which he was much attached) he let the Plantagenet off lightly. After all, John had been a Regent, and no medieval Regent was a success. He went on talking, as he has, to my great pleasure and stimulation, gone on talking ever since. For this was Hilaire Belloc, already famous as an orator at Oxford, where he was always pitted against another brilliant speaker, named F E Smith. Belloc was supposed to represent Radicalism and Smith Toryism; but the contrast between them was more vital, and would have survived the reversing of the labels. Indeed the two characters and careers might stand as a study and problem in the meaning of failure and success.

As Belloc went on talking, he every now and then volleyed out very provocative parentheses on the subject of religion. He said that an important Californian lawyer was coming to England to call on his family, and had put up a great candle to St Christopher praying that he might be able to make the voyage. He declared that he, Belloc, was going to put up an even bigger candle in the hope that the visitor would not make the voyage. "People say what's the good of doing that?" he observed explosively. "I don't know what good it does. I know it's a thing that's done. Then they say it can't do any good – and there you have Dogma at once." All this amused me very much, but I was already conscious of a curious undercurrent of sympathy with him, which many of those who were equally amused did not feel. And when, on that night and many subsequent nights, we came to talking about the war, I found that the subconscious sympathy had something of a real significance. I have had occasion to say, somewhere or other, that I am an Anti-Vivisectionist and an Anti-Anti-Vivisectionist. Something of the same mystery united our minds; we were both Pro-Boers who hated Pro-Boers. Perhaps it would be truer to say that we hated a certain number of unimaginative, unhistorical anti-militarists who were too pedantic to call themselves Pro-Boers. Perhaps it would be truer still to say that it was they who hated us. But anyhow that was the first link in the alliance. Though his military imagination flung its battle-line far across history from the Roman Legions to the last details of the guns of Gravelotte, and mine was a parochial fancy of an impossible skirmish in Notting Hill, we knew that the moral of the fable and the facts was the same; and when I finished my Cockney fantasy, I dedicated it to him. It was from that dingy little Soho café, as from a cave of witchcraft, that there emerged the quadruped, the twiformed monster Mr Shaw has nicknamed the Chesterbelloc.

It would be grossly unjust to suggest that all or most of the anti-war party were like the prigs I have mentioned; though few of them of course were military in the Bellocian manner. And to one group of them I have a permanent gratitude; the Oxford group which I have already mentioned; and which included my own friends from Oxford. This group was just then enabled to achieve a very important work; which will probably be not without an ultimate effect on history. It managed to buy the old Radical weekly paper The Speaker and run it with admirable spirit and courage in rather a new mood of Radicalism; what some of its enemies might have called a romantic Radicalism. Its editor was Mr J L Hammond, who was afterwards, with his wife, to do so great an historical service as the author of studies on the English Labourer in the last few centuries. He certainly was the last man in the world to be accused of a smug materialism or a merely tame love of peace. No indignation could have been at once more fiery and more delicate, in the sense of discriminating. And I knew that he also understood the truth, when I heard him say the words which so many would have misunderstood: "Imperialism is worse than Jingoism. A Jingo is a noisy fellow, who may happen to make a noise on the right side. But the Imperialist is the direct enemy of liberty." That was exactly what I meant; the Boers might be making a noise (with Mauser rifles) but I thought it was a noise on the right side. It was at about the same time, and by the same connection, that I was able to begin making a very small noise on the right side myself. As I note elsewhere, the very first articles of mine to appear publicly were art reviews in the Bookman; and the original responsibility of letting me loose in the literary world lies with my friend the late Sir Ernest Hodder Williams. But the first connected series of articles, the first regular job in support of a regular cause, was made possible for me by Hammond and his friends of the new *Speaker*. It was there that I wrote, along with many pugnacious political articles, a series of casual essays afterwards republished as The Defendant. The name of Defendant is the only thing I cannot defend. It was certainly a quite incorrect and illogical use of language. The papers were in defence of various other things, such as Penny Dreadfuls and Skeletons. But a defendant does not properly mean a person defending other things. It means a person defending himself; and I should be the last to defend anything so indefensible.

It was by the same political connection that I was drawn still further into politics, as well as still further into journalism. The next turning-point of my journalistic fate was the purchase of the *Daily News* by the Pro-Boer Liberals; for it had belonged up to this moment, like practically every Liberal daily paper, to the Liberal Imperialists. A group of Liberals, of whom Mr George

Cadbury was the principal capitalist and the late Mr R C Lehmann the principal practical journalist, appointed as literary editor my friend Mr Archibald Marshall, who in his turn had the rashness to appoint me as a regular weekly contributor. Here I wrote an article every Saturday for many years; I was described, in the phrase of the time, as having a Saturday pulpit, rather like a Sunday pulpit. Whatever were the merits of the sermon, it is probable that I had a larger congregation than I have ever had before or since. And I occupied it until I gave it up long afterwards, at another political crisis, the story of which I shall have to tell on a later page.

I began to see a little of the leading politicians, though they seldom talked politics; and I imagine that politicians seldom do. I had already interviewed Lord Morley, when I was given the commission in the English Men of Letters which he edited; and I had been struck by something indescribable which has marked most public men of his profession. He was quite friendly and simple, and I am sure quite sincere; but he was in a manner cautious; and conscious of the possibility that his followers might lead him further than he wished to go. He spoke with a certain fatherly admiration of my friends of the Pro-Boer party, Hammond and Hirst and the rest; but he seemed to warn me that they were too fiery; and I did not want to be warned, being myself on fire. In short, he was a wise and good man; but he was not what numberless and nameless admirers would have thought him; he was not a clear intellectual fanatic; a foe of compromise; a sheer democrat called Honest John. He was a Front-Bench man, though a good one. The same applied to most of the Front-Bench men I have known; and I am glad to say I knew mostly the good ones. I had great joy out of the hearty humours of old Asquith, the late Lord Oxford; and though our conversations were light and even flippant, he was one who rose gloriously to flippancy. Once when he appeared in Court dress, on some superbly important occasion, an uncontrollable impulse of impertinence led me to ask whether the Court sword would really come out of its sheath. "Oh, yes," he said, shaking a shaggily frowning head at me, "do not provoke me." But he also had about the fundamentals of politics and ethics this curious quality of vagueness, which I have found so often in men holding high responsibilities. He did not mind answering a silly question about a sword; but if it had been a sensible question about a super-tax, he would have adopted, however genially, a fencing sort of swordsmanship. He would have faintly felt that he was being heckled, and almost been disposed to ask for notice of that question. I have a difficulty in not darkening the fine shade that I intend; he was very public, as public men go; but they all seem to become hazier as they mount higher. It is the young and unknown who have decisive doctrines and sharply declared intentions. I once expressed it by saying, I think with some truth, that politicians have no politics.

As a fact, the one Front-Bench man who seemed in the days of my youth still eternally young was for me, in those days, on the opposite Front-Bench. The wonderful thing about George Wyndham was that he had come through political life without losing his political opinions, or indeed any of his opinions. Precisely what gave him such a genius for friendship was that life had left in him so much of himself; so much of his youth; so much even of his childhood. He might never have been a Cabinet Minister; he might have been any common literary or artistic fellow, with a soul to save and some dim and secretive ideas about saving it. He was not always trying, like Charles Augustus Fortescue, "to take a judgment broad and wide;" he had prejudices and private dogmas for which he would fight like a private person. When once or twice the talk of Mr Asquith turned to religious matters, I found he was fully satisfied with that sort of broad idealism, that rather diluted "essence of Christianity" which is often sincere but seldom significant of any special social decision. But George Wyndham was an Anglo-Catholic as an individual, and would have practised his religion in any state of life. There was about him that edge, like the edge of a sword, which I cannot help preferring to being knocked down with a spiritual sandbag.

George Wyndham had all sorts of odd and original notions; and one of his eccentricities was to set a subject for conversation and ask for opinions all round, as if it were an examination or a game. One day I remember he sternly announced "Japan," and asked me to start with a few words. I said: "I distrust Japan because it is imitating us at our worst. If it had imitated the Middle Ages or the French Revolution, I could understand; but it is imitating factories and materialism. It is like looking in the mirror and seeing a monkey." He held up his hand like a master of the ceremonies, "That will do. That is enough;" and passed on to the next, who was I think Major, now General Seeley; who said he distrusted Japan for certain Imperial reasons connected with our Colonies and national defence. Then Mr Winston Churchill said that what amused him was that as long as Japan was beautiful and polite, people treated it as barbarous; and now it has become ugly and vulgar, it was treated with respect, or words to that effect. Then Charles Masterman, in his manner of luxuriant gloom, said the Japs were Huns who would sweep us off the earth; that they were much stronger and more skilful than we, and were also detestable. Then one or two others spoke, expressing the same negative view, and then Wyndham, in his whimsical way, wound up with one of his extraordinary historical theories (of which he had a large selection) and said the Hairy Ainu was the cousin of the European and had been conquered by these horrid Mongols. "I do think," he said gravely, "that we ought to come to the rescue of the Hairy Ainu." And then somebody said with simple wonder: "Look here; we've been all round the table; and every manjack of us, for some reason serious or otherwise, seems to hate the Japanese. Why are we not only allies of the Japanese, but forbidden to say a word against them in any of the newspapers? Why is it the fashion or convention to praise the Japs everywhere and all the time?" But at that, I think, Mr Churchill smiled the inscrutable smile of the statesman; and that veil of vagueness, of which I have spoken, seemed to descend upon everybody; and we never had an answer to the question, either then or since.

Charles Masterman, of whom I have just spoken, was a very remarkable man. He was also a very subtle and curious character; and many of my own best friends entirely misunderstood and underrated him. It is true that as he rose higher in politics, the veil of the politician began to descend a little on him also; but he became a politician from the noblest bitterness on behalf of the poor; and what was blamed in him was the fault of much more ignoble men. What was blamable, as distinct from what was blamed, in him was due to two things; he was a pessimistic official. He had had a dark Puritan upbringing and retained a sort of feeling of the perversity of the gods; he said to me, "I am the sort of man who goes under a hedge to eat an apple." But he was also an organiser and liked governing; only his pessimism made him think that government had always been bad, and was now no worse than usual. Therefore, to men on fire for reform, he came to seem an obstacle and an official apologist; but the last thing he really wanted was to apologise for anything. He had a startling insight into character, and a way of suddenly expressing it, so that it braced rather than hurt. As Oldershaw once said to me, "His candour is beautiful." But his melancholy made him contented, where happier men were discontented. His pessimism did the worst work of optimism. In person he was long, loose and lounging; and nearly as untidy as I was.

Apart from these various glimpses of various parties, my main work was on the *Daily News*, then practically controlled by Mr Cadbury with Mr A G Gardiner as its well-read and sympathetic editor; and I only dimly appreciated what I now see to have been the process by which the Press came to be run like a big business. I remember gazing blankly at the poky little entrance being replaced by a revolving door; then a novelty to me, though probably to nobody else. It reminded me vaguely of a cattle-gate, and I remember asking old Mr Cadbury whether it was meant to keep cows out of the office. He laughed immensely at this simple jest, having himself an attractive simplicity; but the incident is connected chiefly in my mind with a jest rather less arcadian. There was working in the office a very prominent journalist of the Nonconformist culture, who took himself so seriously that in any crowd of common men he was certain to be taken frivolously. I am ashamed to say that I circulated, about this bland and blameless publicist, a legend that the mechanical structure of the new door was the key to the mystery of his permanent presence in the office. Again and again he had been thrown out, but that with such ill-judged violence that the swinging portal swung him back again into the interior. The more unerring the aim, the more violent the energy, with which old Mr Cadbury flung him towards the front-steps, the more certain was his successful contributor to turn up smiling and be swept back to his office and his desk. Thus, I would say, having even then a tendency to moralise along such lines, every mechanical improvement brings a new problem with it. I do not demand faith in the fable, but I have not been discouraged in the moral, by seeing motoring lead to massacre, aviation destroy cities, and machines increase unemployment.

Generally, meanwhile, I began to see something of the political world, and especially that allied to our own wing of the Liberal Party; notably in the enjoyment of the hospitality which the late Mr Cadbury used to extend to large gatherings of his contributors and friends. It was an entertaining experience, especially when it illustrated, as it generally did, the very varied elements of which our party was made up. It was at one of these house-parties of the Cadburys that I first met a man for whom I had a very great regard, apart from the fact that his company was always amusing; I mean Will Crooks, for it always jarred against his whole solid personality to refer to him as Mr Crooks. I have known a great many Labour members, and liked most of them; quite as much at any rate as Liberal members. The Labour members I knew covered every type from frigid Cambridge dons to eccentric English and Scottish aristocrats. Will Crooks was the only Labour leader I ever knew who reminded me for a single moment of the English labouring classes. His humour really was the humour of an omnibus conductor or a railway porter; and that sort of humour is a much more powerful and real thing than most modern forms of education or eloquence. His criticism on beholding a company of advanced Socialist intellectuals was not that they gave too concentrated a power to the abstraction of the State, or that they followed an impossible ideal unsupported by self-interest, but that, as he put it, "They got no backs to their 'eads." His wife also was as representative as a Roman matron; and it is in connection with her that I specially recall the curious clash of types and cultures that went on even inside our own political party. I remember an ethereal little lady with pale blue eyes and pale green garments, who was the wife of a well-known Anti-War journalist. She had a touching timidity in advancing her ideals; but, when they were advanced, they were a very serious business indeed. I remember that Mr Noel Buxton, whose acquaintance I made about this time, was describing in an animated and amusing fashion the scurry and scamper of his life while contesting a seat at the election. In a dreadful hour, he happened to use the expression: "I just had time to snatch a cutlet – ;" and the prophetess in the green garments was goaded, by the god within her, to speak. When Buxton had left the room she did so.

"Do you think that was really necessary?" she said with a painful fixity, like one in a trance. "Man is no better for a cutlet. Man does not really need cutlets."

At this point she received hearty, one might almost say heavy support, from what was probably an unexpected quarter.

"No, my dear," said Mrs Crooks in resounding tones, "A man doesn't want a cutlet! What's the good of a cutlet? What a man wants is a good chump chop or a bit of the under-cut; and I'd see he got it."

The other lady sighed; it was not quite what she had meant; and she was obviously a little alarmed to advance again against her large and solid opponent and be felled to the earth with a mutton-bone. But that little comedy of cross-purposes has always remained in my memory, as a perfect parable of the two kinds of Simple Life, the false and the true.

The vegetarian lady was really a very charming lady; but a very serious lady. Almost immediately after the above incident, I had to take her into dinner. We passed through the conservatory, and merely in order to change the subject in a flippant fashion, I pointed to an insect-eating plant and said: "Don't you vegetarians feel remorse when you look at that? You live by devouring harmless plants; and here is a plant that actually devours animals. Surely it is a just judgment. It is the revenge of the vegetable world."

She looked at me with staring blue eyes that were absolutely grave and unsmiling. "Oh," she said, "but I don't approve of revenge."

This, I need hardly say, shattered and prostrated me altogether; I could only murmur in a vague and sullen manner that of course, if she didn't believe in revenge, what was Christianity coming to, or words to that effect. But she long lingered in my thoughts and her type of thinking has run through all my life and times, like a thread of pale green and blue.

I mixed myself in politics also in other ways; I can hardly say in more practical ways. For the politics were not very practical politics – at least, not when I practised them. Charles Masterman used to swear with derisive gusto that when we went canvassing together, he went all down one side of a street and up most of the other, and found me in the first house, still arguing the philosophy of government with the first householder. This was perhaps unduly darkened by a jovial pessimism which belonged to Charles Masterman. But it is perfectly true that I began electioneering under the extraordinary delusion that the object of canvassing is conversion. The object of canvassing is counting. The only real reason for people being pestered in their own houses by party agents is quite unconnected with the principles of the party (which are often a complete mystery to the agents): it is simply that the agents may discover from the words, manner, gesticulations, oaths, curses, kicks or blows of the householder, whether he is likely to vote for the party candidate, or not to vote at all. I learnt this lesson gradually myself; from a vast variety of human faces and gestures revealed by the opening of front-doors. My friend Oldershaw and I went down together to canvass for a Liberal candidate in the country. It seems strange now to remember that, in our innocence, we did not know anything about him except that he was a Liberal candidate. He was, so far as my knowledge goes, a perfectly worthy and respectable gentleman; but as we passed through that and many other political elections a curious and obscure feeling began to grow in my mind. At the time I was not even conscious of it; even now I do not know how to describe that cold and creeping suggestion of the subconsciousness. When it ultimately rose to the surface and shaped itself, long afterwards, in other campaigns, into a half articulate question, I think the question was, "Why is the candidate nearly always the worst duffer on his own platform?" To these elections and by-elections, to which I went in many places, many other speakers also went, always more eloquent and then at least much better known than I. There were on the platform men like John Simon and Belloc who spoke as well as it is possible to speak, probably better than they have ever spoken since. And all the time, as often as not, the man we were sending up specially to speak, in the supreme court of Parliament, could not speak at all. He was some solid and dressy tailor's dummy, with a single eye-glass or waxed moustaches, who repeated exactly the same dull formula at every separate meeting. There is something interesting, as a matter of psychology, in this unconfessed half-consciousness in the mind of youth that things are not really right, even while the will and the convictions are ready to shout with loyalty to their perfect and universal rightness. Looking back on it now, after those other political experiences of Marconi days, which I shall have to describe later, I know exactly what it was I felt; I also know exactly what it was I did not understand. I know that what runs modern politics is money; and that the superiority of the fool in the frock-coat over Belloc and Simon simply consisted in the fact that he was richer than they were. But I was then quite innocent of all these things; and especially in the case of the first Liberal candidate I worked for, I shouted with sustained enthusiasm and fidelity. The extraordinary thing, about the first candidate I worked for, is that he got in.

But though I fear I was not of much use to the electioneering, it was ultimately of some use to me; as I saw more of the country life than a Londoner like myself had yet imagined, and encountered not a few entertaining country types. I remember at another election a sturdy old woman of Somerset, with a somewhat menacing and almost malevolent stare, who informed me on her own doorstep that she was a Liberal and I could not see her husband, because he was still a Tory. She then informed me that she had been twice married before, and both her husbands had been Tories when they married her, but had become Liberals afterwards. She jerked her thumb over her shoulder towards the invisible Conservative within and said, "I'll have him ready by the 'lection." I was not permitted to penetrate further into this cavern of witchcraft, where she manufactured Liberals out of the most unpromising materials; and (it would appear) destroyed them afterwards. But she was only one of a number of such quaint and forcible rustics whom I encountered in my political travels. Nor indeed were they the only things that I encountered. For all this funny little fuss of politics was in this case spread out like a sprawling sham fight, or the manoeuvres on Salisbury Plain, over that enormous area of noble hills and valleys which had seen so many vaster struggles in the past, reaching back to that aboriginal struggle of the Pagans and the Christians which is the genesis of all our history. And such primitive things were probably already working their way to the surface of my own mind; things that I afterwards attempted to throw into very inadequate but at least more elemental and universal literary form. For I remember the faint and hazy inspiration that troubled me one evening on the road, as I looked beyond the little hamlet, patched so incongruously with a few election posters, and saw hung upon the hills, as if it were hung upon the heavens, remote as a pale cloud and archaic as a gigantic hieroglyph; the White Horse.

I only mention it here because there will be some misunderstanding even of my accidental and amateurish intervention in politics, if it is not understood that our political idealism, unpopular as it was, was felt inwardly as national and not as international. It was that which was a permanent source of irritation and misunderstanding, both within and without the political party. To us it seemed obvious that Patriotism and Imperialism were not only not the same thing, but very nearly opposite things. But it did not seem obvious, but very puzzling, to the great majority of healthy patriots and innocent imperialists. It seemed equally puzzling to a great many anti-patriots and anti-Imperialists. Towards the end of this period, we published a book intended to explain our rather peculiar position; it was called "England a Nation;" it was edited by Oldershaw and had contributions by Masterman and myself and others. One of the contributions came from an Irish Nationalist member, my friend Hugh Law; and it was about this time, naturally enough, that I began to see something of the Irish Nationalists and to feel a strong and special sympathy with Irish Nationalism. Of this I may say more in another place; it is sufficient to remark here that it is to me a considerable satisfaction to think that I have always felt it the first duty of a real English patriot to sympathise with the passionate patriotism of Ireland; that I expressed it through the worst times of her tragedy and have not lost it in her triumph.

Curiously enough, however, my sharpest memory of the puzzle of this patriotic paradox, and the difficulty of making others see what to me was so obvious, is not connected with Ireland or with England; but, of all places in the world, with Germany. Sometime after all these events, I had to visit Frankfurt, where I took on rather casually the task of lecturing on English literature to a congress of German schoolmasters. We discussed Walter Scott's *Marmion* and other metrical romances; we sang English songs over German beer, and had a very pleasant time. But there was already stirring, even among those mild and amiable Germans, something that was not so pleasant; and though they expressed it quite politely I suddenly found myself once more in the same difficulty about the national and the imperial notion. For, speaking to some of them at large about literature, as to a merely cosmopolitan world of culture, I touched on this preference of mine for what some consider a narrower national idea. I found that they also were puzzled; they assured me, with that gravity with which Germans alone can repeat what they regard as a platitude, that Imperialismus and Patriotismus were the same thing. When they discovered that I did not like Imperialismus, even for my own country, a very curious expression came into their eyes, and a still more curious notion seems to have come into their heads. They formed the extraordinary idea that I was an internationalist, indifferent, or even hostile, to English interests. Perhaps they thought Gilbert Keith Chesterton was an alias of Houston Stewart Chamberlain. Anyhow, they began to talk more openly, but still vaguely; and there grew gradually on my consciousness the conviction that these extraordinary people really thought that I might accept or approve, on some toshy ethnological or sociological ground or other, the extension of the Teutonic Race at the expense even of the impotence or absorption of my own land. It was a somewhat difficult situation; for they said nothing definite that I had any right to resent; it was merely that I felt in the atmosphere a pressure and a threat. It was *der tag*. After thinking a moment, I said, "Well, gentlemen, if it ever came to anything like that, I think I should have to refer you to the poem of Scott that we have been discussing." And I gravely repeated the answer of Marmion, when King James says that they may meet again in war as far south as Tamworth Castle.

> Much honour'd were my humble home,
> If in its halls King James should come;
> But Nottingham has archers good,
> And Yorkshire men are stern of mood;
> Northumbrian prickers wild and rude...
> And many a banner will be torn,
> And many a knight to earth be borne,
> And many a sheaf of arrows spent,
> 'Ere Scotland's King shall cross the Trent.

I looked at them and they at me, and I think they understood; and there rose up like an enormous shadow over that drinking-hall the terror of things to be.

VI

THE FANTASTIC SUBURB

When I was a young journalist on the *Daily News*, I wrote in some article or other the sentence, "Clapham, like every other city, is built on a volcano." When I opened the paper next day, I found the words confronting me, "Kensington, like every other city, is built on a volcano." It did not matter, of course, but I was a little puzzled and mentioned it to my immediate superior in the office, as if it were some freak of a fanciful compositor. But he glowered at me in a heavy and resentful manner, which would alone be a confession of guilt, if there were any guilt, and said rather sulkily, "Why should it be Clapham?" And then, as if throwing off the mask, "Well, I live at Clapham." And he, knowing that I lived at Kensington, had bitterly transferred to that royal borough what he imagined to be a taunt.

"But I was glorifying Clapham!" I cried pathetically, "I was showing it as epical and elemental and founded in the holy flame." "You think you're funny, don't you?" he said. "I think I'm right," I said, making that modest claim not for the last time; and then, not for the last but perhaps for the first time, the terrible truth dawned upon me.

If you said in a Basque village or a Bavarian town that the place was romantic, some might draw the dreadful deduction that you were an artist, and therefore possibly a madman; but nobody would have any particular reason to doubt that the madman meant what he said. But the citizen of Clapham *could* not believe that I meant what I said. The patriot of Clapham could not find it creditable or conceivable that *any* remark about Clapham could be anything but a sneer at Clapham. He could not even say the word so that the first syllable of "Clapham" sounded like the last syllable of "thunderclap." There was utterly veiled from his sight the visionary Clapham, the volcanic Clapham, what I may be allowed to put upon the cosmic map as Thunderclapham. I assured him again and again, almost with tears, that I was warmly sympathetic with any sensitive feelings he might have, if he was really proud of Clapham. But that was exactly the horrid secret. He was not proud of Clapham. The Clapham patriot was ashamed of Clapham.

The Clapham journalist, who glowered at me, has been the problem of my life. He has haunted me at every turn and corner like a shadow, as if he were a blackmailer or a murderer. It was against him that I marshalled the silly pantomime halberdiers of Notting Hill and all the rest. In other words, everything I have thought and done grew originally out of that problem which seemed to me a paradox. I shall have to refer to many problems in these pages, if they are to be truthful pages; and to glance at solutions with some of which the reader may agree, with some of which he may very violently disagree. But I will ask him to remember throughout that this was the primary problem for me, certainly in order of time and largely in order of logic. It was the problem of how men could be made to realise the wonder and splendour of being alive, in environments which their own daily criticism treated as dead-alive, and which their imagination had left for dead. It is normal for a man to boast if he can, or even when he can't, that he is a citizen of no mean city. But these men had really resigned themselves to being citizens of mean cities; and on every side of us the mean cities stretched far away beyond the horizon; mean in architecture, mean in costume, mean even in manners; but, what was the only thing that really mattered, mean in the imaginative conception of their own inhabitants. These mean cities were indeed supposed to be the component parts of a very great city; but in the thoughts of most modern people, the great city has become a journalistic generalisation, no longer imaginative and very nearly imaginary. On the other hand, the modern mode of life, only professing to be prosaic, pressed upon them day and night and was the real moulder of their minds. This, I say by way of preliminary guide or direction, was what originally led me into certain groups or movements and away from others.

What was called my medievalism was simply that I was very much interested in the historic meaning of Clapham Common. What was called my dislike of Imperialism was a dislike of making England an Empire, in the sense of something more like Clapham Junction. For my own visionary Clapham consisted of houses standing still; and not of trucks and trains rattling by; and I did not want England to be a sort of cloakroom or clearing-house for luggage labelled exports and imports. I wanted real English things that nobody else could import and that we enjoyed too much to export. And this was present even in the last and most disputed phase of change. I came to admit that some sort of universality, another sort of universality, would be needed before such places could really become shrines or sacred sites. In short, I eventually concluded, rightly or wrongly, that Clapham could not now be made mystical by the Clapham Sect. But I say it with the greatest respect for that old group of philanthropists, who devoted themselves to the cause of the remote negroes; the sect that did so much to liberate Africa; the Clapham Sect, that did so little to liberate Clapham.

Now it is essential to realise one fact following on the shadowy epic of Clapham and Kensington; that tale of two cities. It is necessary to insist that in those days, when Clapham was Clapham, London was Clapham; nay, Kensington was Clapham. I mean that, at this particular date, the general appearance of London was more plain and prosaic than it is now. There were indeed beautiful corners of Georgian and Regency architecture in many parts of London, and nowhere more than in Kensington. There are some still. But though there was some trace of the older movements in art, there was as yet no trace of the new ones. Morris had broken out here and there like a rash, in the form of wallpapers; but the very dullest phase of dead Victorianism was in most of the wallpapers and nearly all the walls. But London was already unthinkably large, in comparison with its few last relics of eighteenth-century elegance or its first faint signals of aesthetic revival. And that huge thing was a hideous thing, as a whole. The landscape of London was a thing of flat-chested houses, blank windows, ugly iron lamp-posts and vulgar vermilion pillar boxes; and as yet, of very little else.

If I have at all suggested the modest virtues of my own middle-class group and family, it will be obvious already, I hope, that we were as ugly as the railings and lamp-posts between which we walked. I mean that our dress and furniture were as yet untouched by anything 'arty,' in spite of a quite decently informed interest in art. We were even further from Bohemia than from Belgravia. When my mother said that we had never been respectable, she rather meant that we had never been dressy than that we had never been dowdy. By comparison with the aestheticism that has since crawled across London, we were all of us distinctly dowdy. It was the more so in my own family, because my father and my brother and I were negligent about externals we regarded as normal. We were careless in wearing careful clothes. The aesthetes were careful in wearing careless clothes. I wore an ordinary coat; it was due merely to undesigned friction or attrition if it became rather an extraordinary coat. The Bohemian wore a slouch-hat; but he did not slouch in it. I slouched in a top hat; a shocking bad hat, but not one designed to shock the bourgeois. I was myself, in that sense, entirely bourgeois. Sometimes that hat, or something like the ghost of it, makes a spectral reappearance still, and is extracted from the dustbin or the pawnshop or the British Museum, to figure at the King's Garden-Party. Of course, it may not be the same one. The great original was certainly more suited to a scarecrow in a kitchen-garden than to a guest in a king's garden. But the point is that we never thought about the fashions, or the conventions, sufficiently seriously either to fulfil them or to defy them. My father was in a hundred happy and fruitful ways an amateur; but in no way at all a dilettante. And as this memoir must concern his much less estimable descendant, who actually went to an art-school, he may at least be allowed to boast that, if he failed to be an artist, he never tried to be an aesthete.

In short, the reader (if any) must not be misled at this stage by that Falstaffian figure in a brigand's hat and cloak, which has appeared in many caricatures. That figure was a later work of art; though the artist was not merely the caricaturist; but a lady artist touched on as lightly as possible in this very Victorian narrative. That caricature merely commemorates what the female genius could do with the most unpromising materials. But when I was a boy or a bachelor, my dress and appearance were just like everybody else's, only worse. My madness, which was considerable, was wholly within. But that madness was more and more moving in the direction of some vague and visionary revolt against the prosaic flatness of a nineteenth-century city and civilisation; an imaginative impatience with the cylindrical hats and the rectangular houses; in short, that movement of the mind I have already associated with *Napoleon of Notting Hill* and the imperfect patriot of Clapham. I had perhaps got no further than the feeling that those imprisoned in these inhuman outlines were human beings; that it was a bad thing that living souls should be thus feebly and crudely represented by houses like ill-drawn diagrams of Euclid, or streets and railways like dingy sections of machinery. I remember speaking to Masterman, very early in our acquaintance, as we watched the harassed crowds pouring through the passages of the Underground to the iron and symbolic Inner Circle, and quoting the words of Kipling about the disabled battleship:

> For it is not meet that English stock
> Should bide in the heart of an eight-day clock
> The death they may not see.

But I always retained a dim sense of something sacred in English stock, or in human stock, which separated me from the mere pessimism of the period. I never doubted that the human beings inside the houses were themselves almost miraculous; like magic and talismanic dolls, in whatever ugly dolls'-houses. For me, those brown brick boxes were really Christmas boxes. For, after all, Christmas boxes often came tied up in brown paper; and the jerrybuilders' achievements in brown brick were often extremely like brown paper.

To sum up, I accepted my environment and the practical fact that all hats and houses were like our hats and houses; and that this Cockney cosmos, so far as a Cockney could see, stretched away to the ends of the earth. For this reason, it fell out, as a rather determining accident, that I first saw as from afar, the first fantastic signal of something new and as yet far from fashionable; something like a new purple patch on that grey stretch of streets. It would not be remarkable now, but it was remarkable then. In those days I had the habit of walking over very wide stretches and circles of London; I always walked to and from my first art-school in St John's Wood; and it will give some hint of how London has altered to say that I commonly walked from Kensington to St Paul's Cathedral, and for a great part of the way in the middle of the road. One day I had turned my aimless steps westward, through the tangle of Hammersmith Broadway and along the road that goes to Kew, when I turned for some reason, or more likely without a reason, into a side street and straggled across the dusty turf through which ran a railway, and across the railway one of those disproportionately high bridges which bestride such narrow railway-lines like stilts. By a culmination of futility, I climbed up to this high and practically unused bridge; it was evening, and I think it was then I saw in the distance of that grey landscape, like a ragged red cloud of sunset, the queer artificial village of Bedford Park.

It is difficult, as I have said, to explain how there was then something fanciful about what is now so familiar. That sort of manufactured quaintness is now hardly even quaint; but at that time it was even queer. Bedford Park did look like what it partially professed to be; a colony for artists who were almost aliens; a refuge for persecuted poets and painters hiding in their red-brick catacombs or dying behind their red-brick barricades, when the world should conquer Bedford Park. In that somewhat nonsensical sense, it is rather Bedford Park that has conquered the world. Today, model cottages, council houses and arty-crafty shops – tomorrow, for all I know, prisons and workhouses and madhouses may present (outside) that minimum of picturesqueness, which was then considered the preposterous pose of those addicted to painting pictures. Certainly, if the clerk in Clapham had then been actually presented with such a fantastic cottage, he might have thought that the fairytale house was really a madhouse. This aesthetic experiment was quite recent; it had some elements of real co-operative and corporative independence; its own stores and post-office and church and inn. But the whole was vaguely under the patronage of old Mr Comyns Carr, who was not only regarded as the patriarch or the oldest inhabitant, but in some sense as the founder and father of the republic. He was not really so very old; but then the republic was very new; much newer than the new republic of Mr Mallock, though filled with philosophical gossip of much the same sort, over which the patriarch benevolently beamed and brooded. At least, to quote a literary phrase then much quoted, he was older than the rocks which he sat among, or the roofs he sat under; and we might well have murmured another contemporary tag, a little vaguely perhaps, from memory:

> Match me this marvel, save where aesthetes are,
> A rose-red suburb half as old as Carr.

But though I think we all felt, if subconsciously, something dreamily theatrical about the thing, that it was partly a dream and partly a joke, it was not merely a fraud. Intelligent people will insinuate themselves even into an intelligentsia; and important people lived there quietly rather than importantly. Professor Yorke Powell, the distinguished historian, paraded there his long leonine beard and menacing and misleading eyebrows; and Dr Todhunter, the eminent Celtic scholar, represented the Irish colony in the battles of culture. And in the same connection, if it was a place of shadows it could hardly be called a place of shams, when it contained one who is still perhaps the greatest poet writing in our tongue. There is always something fanciful about the conjunction of the world that the poet sees and the place he lives in; the fancy that the great golden lions of Blake roared and roamed in a small court off the Strand, or that Camberwell may have been haunted by Sordello, couched like a lion and expressing himself rather like a sphinx. And it amuses me to think that under those toy trees and gimcrack gables there was already passing a pageant of strange gods and the head-dresses of forgotten priests and the horns of holy unicorns and the wrinkled sleep of Druidic vegetation, and all the emblems of a new heraldry of human imagination.

William Butler Yeats might seem as solitary as an eagle; but he had a nest. Wherever there is Ireland there is the Family; and it counts for a great deal. If the reader requires a test, let him ask why there is still a habit of calling this great and often grim genius "Willie Yeats." Nobody, to my knowledge, talks about "Jackie Masefield," or "Alfie Noyes," or (what might be misunderstood by the light-minded) "Ruddy Kipling." But in the case of Yeats, such familiarity might seem singularly incongruous with his tastes and temper; and analagous to talking of the great Gulliver as "Johnny Swift." His own tone and temper, in public as well as private expression, is of a fastidiousness the very reverse of such familiarity.

> There is no fool can call me friend
> And I may drink at the journey's end
> With Landor and with Donne.

I mention it merely as a point of impersonal description, without pronouncing on the problem; it takes all sorts to make a world. I dare say that there are a good many fools who can call me a friend and also (a more chastening thought) a good many friends who can call me a fool. But in Yeats that fastidiousness is not only sincere but essentially noble, being full of a finer anger against the victory of baser over better things, leading him to call the terrible words over the great grave in St Patrick's Cathedral, "the noblest epitaph in history." The reason why, in spite of all this, the largest possible assembly and assortment of fools is probably at this moment calling poor Yeats "Willie," at any rate behind his back, is to be found in the curious corporate stamp always left by the Irish family as a whole. The intensity and individualism of genius itself could never wash out of the world's memories the general impression of Willie and Lily and Lolly and Jack; names cast backwards and forwards in a unique sort of comedy of Irish wit, gossip, satire, family quarrels and family pride. I knew the family more or less as a whole in those days; and for long afterwards knew and admired those sisters of the poet who maintained in the Cuala industry a school of decoration and drapery not unworthy of the great lines about the heavens' embroidered cloths. W B is perhaps the best talker I ever met, except his old father who alas will talk no more in this earthly tavern, though I hope he is still talking in Paradise. Among twenty other qualities, he had that rare but very real thing, entirely spontaneous style. The words will not come pouring out, any more than the bricks that make a great building come pouring out; they are simply arranged like lightning; as if a man could build a cathedral as quickly as a conjurer builds a house of cards. A long and elaborately balanced sentence, with dependent clauses alternative or antithetical, would flow out of such talkers with every word falling into its place, quite as immediately and innocently as most people would say it was a fine day or a funny business in the papers. I can still remember old Yeats, that graceful greybeard, saying in an offhand way about the South African War, "Mr Joseph Chamberlain has the character, as he has the face, of the shrewish woman who ruins her husband by her extravagance; and Lord Salisbury has the character, as he has the face, of the man who is so ruined." That style, or swift construction of a complicated sentence, was the sign of a lucidity now largely lost. You will find it in the most spontaneous explosions of Dr Johnson. Since then some muddled notion has arisen that talking in that complete style is artificial; merely because the man knows what he means and means to say it. I know not from what nonsense world the notion first came; that there is some connection between being sincere and being semi-articulate. But it seems to be a notion that a man must mean what he says, because he breaks down even in trying to say it; or that he must be a marvel of power and decision, because he discovers in the middle of a sentence that he does not know what he was going to say. Hence the conversation of current comedy; and the pathetic belief that talk may be endless, so long as no statement is allowed to come to an end.

Yeats affected me strongly, but in two opposite ways; like the positive and negative poles of a magnet. It is necessary to explain what I mean, not so much for the sake of my own groping notions at this time, as for the sake of explaining the peculiarity of the period; about which most critics seem to be completely wrong at the present time. There was much in Victorian ideas that I dislike and much that I respect; but there was nothing whatever about Victorian ideas corresponding to what is now called Victorian. I am actually old enough to remember the Victorian Age; and it was almost a complete contrast to all that is now connoted by that word. It had all the vices that are now called virtues; religious doubt, intellectual unrest, a hungry credulity about new things, a complete lack of equilibrium. It also had all the virtues that are now called vices; a rich sense of romance, a passionate desire to make the love of man and woman once more what it was in Eden, a strong sense of the absolute necessity of some significance in human life. But everything that everybody tells me now about the Victorian atmosphere I feel instantly to be false, like a fog, which merely shuts out a vista. And in nothing is this more true than in the particular truth I must now try to describe.

The general background of all my boyhood was agnostic. My own parents were rather exceptional, among people so intelligent, in believing at all in a personal God or in personal immortality. I remember when my friend Lucian Oldershaw, who introduced me to this Bohemian colony, said to me suddenly, looking back on the tired lessons in the Greek Testament at St Paul's School, "Of course, you and I were taught our religion by agnostics;" and I, suddenly seeing the faces of all my schoolmasters, except one or two eccentric clergymen, knew that he was right. It was not specially our generation, it was much more the previous generation, that was agnostic after the fashion of Huxley. It was the period of which Mr H G Wells, a sportive but spiritual child of Huxley, wrote truly enough that it was "full of the ironical silences that follow great controversies;" and in that controversy, Huxley had been superficially successful. So successful, that Mr Wells, in the same passage, went so far as to say that the Bishops "socially so much in evidence, are intellectually in hiding."... How dear and distant it all seems! I have lived to see biological controversies, in which it is much truer to say that the official Darwinians are in hiding. The "silence" following on the first evolutionary controversy was a good deal more "ironical" than Mr Wells was then aware. But then certainly the silence seemed to be one of religion defeated; a desert of materialism. Men no more expected the myriad mystical reactions now moving all nations than the flat-chested mansions of Pimlico and Bloomsbury had expected to see spreading through the land the crested roofs and cranky chimneys of Bedford Park.

But it was not in *this* that Bedford Park was eccentric. There was nothing new or odd about not having a religion. Socialism, mostly upon the rather wallpaper pattern of Morris, was a relatively new thing. Socialism, in the style of Bernard Shaw and the Fabians, was a rising thing. But agnosticism was an established thing. We might almost say that agnosticism was an established church. There was a uniformity of unbelief, like the Elizabethan demand for uniformity of belief; not among eccentric people, but simply among educated people. And above all, among the educated people older than myself.

There were, indeed, fine fighting atheists. But they were mostly fighting something else besides theism. There could be no more virile or valiant type of them than my old friend Archie MacGregor, the artist, who was fighting the Boer War. As we agreed on this, we fell into a strong companionship; but even in those days, I realised that his atheism was not really revolutionary in the matter of morals. It was just the other way. It was not any "new morality," but very decidedly the "old morality" that he was defending against Imperialism, merely on the ground that it was murder and theft. He was defending against the new ethic of Nietzsche the old ethic of Naboth. This, Mr Wells and the Fabians saw with typical lucidity: that the sentimental Socialists were inconsistent, in saying that a peasant has no right to a field, but a peasantry has a right to an oilfield. Mr Wells is not really a pacifist any more than a militarist; but the only sort of war he thinks right is the only sort of war I think wrong. Anyhow, broadly speaking, it is a complete mistake to suppose that the rebels who denounced Church and Chapel were those who denounced Empire and Army. The divisions cut across; but they cut mainly the other way. A fighting Pro-Boer like MacGregor was in as much of a minority among atheists as among artists; even in Bedford Park. I soon discovered that, when I emerged into the larger world of artists and literary men. No two men could have been more opposite than Henley and Colvin; and I was later to be in some sense a witness to the duel they fought over the dead body of Stevenson. But they were both stubborn materialists and they were both stubborn militarists. The truth is that for most men about this time Imperialism, or at least patriotism, was a substitute for religion. Men believed in the British Empire precisely because they had nothing else to believe in. Those beacon-fires of an imperial insularity shot a momentary gleam even over the dark landscape of the Shropshire Lad; though I fear that many innocent patriots did not perceive the Voltairean sneer in the patriotic lines: "Get you the sons your fathers got, and God will save the Queen." My present prejudices would be satisfied by saying that the last decay of Protestantism took the form of Prussianism.

But I am here describing myself as I was, when pure and unpolluted by such prejudices. And what I wish to attest, merely as a witness to the fact, is that the background of all the world was not merely atheism, but atheist orthodoxy, and even atheist respectability. That was quite as common in Belgravia as in Bohemia. That was above all normal in Suburbia; and only for that reason in this particular eccentric suburb. In that suburb, the type of the time was not a man like Archie MacGregor but a man like St John Hankin. And the point is that a man like St John Hankin was not eccentric but centric. He was a pessimist, which is something more atheistic than an atheist; he was a fundamental sceptic, that is a man without fundamentals; he was one who disbelieved in Man much more than he did in God; he despised democracy even more than devotion; he was professedly without enthusiasms of any kind; but in all this he was centric. He was very near to the centre of the culture and philosophy of London at that time. He was a man of real talent; and the memory of some of his amusing literary travesties still remains. I did not dislike him, though many did; but I did in a sense despair of him, as he despaired of everything. But it is entirely typical of the time that his pessimism managed to appear in *Punch*; and that, almost alone amid those ragged or ridiculous or affected artistic costumes, he always wore evening dress. He had a low opinion of the world, but he was a man of the world; and especially of the world as it was then.

Now against this drab background of dreary modern materialism, Willie Yeats was calmly walking about as the Man Who Knew the Fairies. Yeats stood for enchantment; exactly where Hankin stood for disenchantment. But I very specially rejoiced in the fighting instinct which made the Irishman so firm and positive about it. He was the real original rationalist who said that the fairies stand to reason. He staggered the materialists by attacking their abstract materialism with a completely concrete mysticism; "Imagination!" he would say with withering contempt; "There wasn't much imagination when Farmer Hogan was dragged out of bed and thrashed like a sack of potatoes – that they did, they had 'um out;" the Irish accent warming with scorn; "they had 'um out and thumped 'um; and that's not the sort of thing that a man wants to imagine." But the concrete examples were not only a comedy; he used one argument which was sound, and I have never forgotten it. It is the fact that it is not abnormal men like artists, but normal men like peasants, who have borne witness a thousand times to such things; it is the farmers who see the fairies. It is the agricultural labourer who calls a spade a spade who also calls a spirit a spirit; it is the woodcutter with no axe to grind, except for woodcutting, who will say he saw a man hang on a gallows and afterwards hang round it as a ghost. It is all very well to say we ought not to believe in the ghost on an ignorant man's evidence. But we should hang the man on the gallows on the same man's evidence.

I was all for fighting for Willie Yeats and his fairies against materialism. I was especially for fighting for Willie Yeats and his farmers against the mechanical urban materialism. But already a further complication had arisen, which I must try to explain; not only to explain myself, but to explain the whole development of the poetry and the period. There had already appeared in that world the beginnings of a reaction against materialism; something analogous to what has since appeared in the form of Spiritualism. It has even taken the yet more defiant form of Christian Science, which denied the existence of the body merely because its enemies had denied the existence of the soul. But the form it took first, or most generally, in the world of which I speak, was the thing commonly called Theosophy; also sometimes called Esoteric Buddhism. It is probable that I must here allow at least for the allegation of a prejudice. If it existed, it was not an orthodox or a religious or even a pious prejudice. I was myself almost entirely Pagan and Pantheist. When I disliked Theosophy I had no Theology. Perhaps I did not dislike Theosophy, but only Theosophists. It is certainly true, I am afraid, whatever the failure in charity, that I did dislike some Theosophists. But I did not dislike them because they had erroneous doctrines, when I myself had no doctrines; or because they had no claim to be Christians, when in fact they would have claimed Christianity, among other things, much more confidently than I could myself. I disliked them because they had shiny pebbly eyes and patient smiles. Their patience mostly consisted of waiting for others to rise to the spiritual plane where they themselves already stood. It is a curious fact, that they never seemed to hope that *they* might evolve and reach the plane where their honest greengrocer already stood. They never wanted to hitch their own lumbering waggon to a soaring cabman; or see the soul of their charwoman like a star beacon to the spheres where the immortals are. Yet I suspect that I am unjust to these people in their real personalities. I fancy it was a combination of three things; Asia and Evolution and the English lady; and I think they would be nicer separate.

Now Yeats was not in the least like these Theosophical ladies; nor did he follow or seek out their special spiritual prophetess, Mrs Besant, who was a dignified, ladylike, sincere idealistic egoist. He sought out Madam Blavatsky, who was a coarse, witty, vigorous, scandalous old scallywag; and I admire his taste. But I do think that this particular Oriental twist led him a dance, when he followed the fakirs and not the fairies. I shall not be misunderstood if I say of that great man that he was bewitched; that is, that Madam Blavatsky was a witch.

For whether or no Yeats was bewitched, it is certain that Yeats was not deceived. He was not taken in by the theosophical smile; or all that shining, or rather shiny, surface of optimism. He, having a more penetrating mind, had already penetrated to the essential pessimism that lies behind that Asiatic placidity; and it is arguable that the pessimism was not so depressing as the optimism. Anyhow, while those highly refined English ladies were stepping from star to star, as from stair to stair, he knew enough of what was meant by the Sorrowful Wheel, to realise that this starry stairway was uncommonly like a treadmill. The more feverish of my friends, in this circle, used to go and sit in rooms full of images of Buddha to calm themselves; though I myself never needed any image of Buddha to encourage me to do nothing or to go to sleep. But Yeats knew something of the mind and not only the face of Buddha; and if he would never have used such Tennysonian terms, he knew that it meant for his own mind, if calm at all, if any calm, a calm despair. In the scheme of mysticism to which he more and more tended after his first more fortunate adventures among farmers and fairies, the ancient religions stood more and more for the idea that the secret of the sphinx is that she has no secret. The veil of Isis was more and more merely the veil of Maya; illusion, ending with the last illusion that the veil of Isis is rent; the last and worst illusion that we are really disillusioned. He said to me once, apropos of somebody's disappointment about something achieved, "You would not get out of your chair and walk across the room, if Nature had not her bag of illusions." Then he added, as if against a silent protest, "It isn't a very cheerful philosophy that everything is illusion." It was not. I cannot answer for the fairies, but I doubt whether the farmers accepted it; and there was something in one half-grown Cockney journalist which entirely refused to accept it. So that I found myself in this odd double attitude towards the poet, agreeing with him about the fairy-tales on which most people disagreed with him, and disagreeing with him about the philosophy on which most people agreed with him, though in a much muddier and more prosaic way. Thus, when I read that wonderful poetical play, *Land of Heart's Desire*, produced soon after at the Abbey Theatre, I was conscious of the sharp sensation, not so much that I disbelieved in the fairies, as that I disagreed with them. Though I had then no more notion of being a Catholic than of being a Cannibal, my sympathies were all for the Family against the Fairy. They were even then for the priest against the fairy. In all that magic burst of music, there was only one thing said by the fairy with which I fully and entirely sympathised; and that was the line: "I am tired of winds and waters and pale lights." I do not think I have anything to alter in the sentence of literary criticism that I wrote long after: "There is only one thing against the *Land of Heart's Desire*; the heart does not desire it." Yet I admired the play almost passionately as a play; and in the debates of mere literature, always defended it against stupid jokes about the Celtic Twilight uttered by those who preferred the London Fog. So, later on, when I was on the *Daily News*, I defended, against the dramatic critic, the dramatic merit of a later play, which is full of good things; the play called *Where There is Nothing There is God*. But I was all groping and groaning and travailing with an inchoate and half-baked philosophy of my own, which was very nearly the reverse of the remark that where there is nothing there is God. The truth presented itself to me, rather, in the form that where there is anything there is God. Neither statement is adequate in philosophy; but I should have been amazed to know how near in some ways was my Anything to the *Ens* of St Thomas Aquinas.

There was a debating-club in Bedford Park, on which I first tried my crude ideas with even cruder rhetoric. It deserved better treatment. It was frightful fun. It was called the "I D K"; and an awful seal of secrecy was supposed to attach to the true meaning of the initials. Perhaps the Theosophists did really believe that it meant India's Divine Karma. Possibly the Socialists did interpret it as "Individualists Deserve Kicking." But it was a strict rule of the club that its members should profess ignorance of the meaning of its name; in the manner of the Know-Nothing movement in American politics. The stranger, the mere intruder into the sacred village, would ask, "But what does I D K mean?" and the initiate was expected to shrug his shoulders and say, "I don't know," in an offhand manner; in the hope that it would not be realised that, in a seeming refusal to reply, he had in fact replied. I know not whether this motto was symbolic of the agnosticism of men like Hankin or the mysticism of men like Yeats. But both points of view were, of course, present; and I think they pretty well divided that intellectual world between them. Certainly I always preferred the Celtic Twilight to the materialistic midnight. I had more sympathy with the magician's cloak that clothed the man who believed in magic, or the dark elf-locks of the poet who had really something to tell us about elves, than with the black clothes and blank shirt-front of the sort of man who seemed to proclaim that the modern world, even when it is festive, is only the more funereal. What I did not realise was that there was a third angle, and a very acute angle, which was capable of piercing with the sharpness, and some would say the narrowness of a sword.

The secretary of this debating-club always proved her efficiency by entirely refusing to debate. She was one of a family of sisters, with one brother, whom I had grown to know through the offices of Oldershaw; and they had a cousin on the premises, who was engaged to a German professor and permanently fascinated by the subject of German fairy-tales. She was naturally attracted also to the Celtic fairy-tales that were loose in the neighbourhood; and one day she came back glowing with the news that Willie Yeats had cast her horoscope, or performed some such occult rite, and told her that she was especially under the influence of the moon. I happened to mention this to a sister of the secretary, who had only just returned to the family circle, and she told me in the most normal and unpretentious tone that she hated the moon.

I talked to the same lady several times afterwards; and found that this was a perfectly honest statement of the fact. Her attitude on this and other things might be called a prejudice; but it could not possibly be called a fad, still less an affectation. She really had an obstinate objection to all those natural forces that seemed to be sterile or aimless; she disliked loud winds that seemed to be going nowhere; she did not care much for the sea, a spectacle of which I was very fond; and by the same instinct she was up against the moon, which she said looked like an imbecile. On the other hand, she had a sort of hungry appetite for all the fruitful things like fields and gardens and anything connected with production; about which she was quite practical. She practised gardening; in that curious Cockney culture she would have been quite ready to practise farming; and on the same perverse principle, she actually practised a religion. This was something utterly unaccountable both to me and to the whole fussy culture in which she lived. Any number of people proclaimed religions, chiefly oriental religions, analysed or argued about them; but that anybody could regard religion as a practical thing like gardening was something quite new to me and, to her neighbours, new and incomprehensible. She had been, by an accident, brought up in the school of an Anglo-Catholic convent; and, to all that agnostic or mystic world, practising a religion was much more puzzling than professing it. She was a queer card. She wore a green velvet dress barred with grey fur, which I should have called artistic, but that she hated all the talk about art; and she had an attractive face, which I should have called elvish, but that she hated all the talk about elves. But what was arresting and almost blood-curdling about her, in that social atmosphere, was not so much that she hated it, as that she was entirely unaffected by it. She never knew what was meant by being "under the influence" of Yeats or Shaw or Tolstoy or anybody else. She was intelligent, with a great love of literature, and especially of Stevenson. But if Stevenson had walked into the room and explained his personal doubts about personal immortality, she would have regretted that he should be wrong upon the point; but would otherwise have been utterly unaffected. She was not at all like Robespierre, except in a taste for neatness in dress; and yet it is only in Mr Belloc's book on Robespierre that I have ever found any words that describe the unique quality that cut her off from the current culture and saved her from it. "God had given him in his mind a stone tabernacle in which certain great truths were preserved imperishable."

I saw a good deal of her later on, at various social occasions of the district; she was a witness to the grand and grotesque occasion on which I rode a bicycle for the first and last time; attired in the frock-coat and top hat of the period, on the tennis lawn at Bedford Park. Believe it or not (as the great newspapers say when they tell lies based on ignorance of the elements of history) but it is true that I rode round and round the tennis court with a complete natural balance, only disturbed by the intellectual problem of how I could possibly get off; eventually I fell off; I did not notice what happened to my hat, but then I seldom did. The image of that monstrous revolving ride has often recurred to me, as indicating that something odd must have happened to me about that time. The lady in question worked very hard as secretary of an educational society in London; and I formed the impression then, which I have not lost, that the worst of work nowadays is what happens to people when they cease working; the racketing of trains and trams and the slow return to remote homes. She was a very alert person, and normally quite the reverse of absent-minded; but she told me once with some remorse that she had been so tired as to leave her parasol in the waiting-room of a railway-station. We thought no more of it for the moment; but as I walked home that night, by my custom, from Bedford Park to Kensington, very nearly in the middle of the night, I happened to see the identical railway-station stand up black and bulky against the moonlight; and I committed my first and last crime; which was burglary, and very enjoyable. The station, or that part of the station, seemed to be entirely locked up; but I knew exactly the whereabouts of the waiting-room in question; and I found the shortest cut to it was to climb up the steep grassy embankment and crawl under the platform out upon the line; I then clambered on to the platform and recovered the parasol. As I returned by the same route (still in the battered top hat and the considerably deranged frock-coat) I stared up at the sky and found myself filled with all sorts of strange sensations. I felt as if I had just fallen from the moon, with the parasol for a parachute. Anyhow, as I looked back up the tilt of turf grey in the moonshine, like unearthly lunar grasses, I did not share the lady's impiety to the patroness of lunatics.

It was fortunate, however, that our next most important meeting was not under the sign of the moon but of the sun. She has often affirmed, during our later acquaintance, that if the sun had not been shining to her complete satisfaction on that day, the issue might have been quite different. It happened in St James's Park; where they keep the ducks and the little bridge, which has been mentioned in no less authoritative a work than Mr Belloc's Essay on Bridges, since I find myself quoting that author once more. I think he deals in some detail, in his best topographical manner, with various historic sites on the Continent; but later relapses into a larger manner, somewhat thus: "The time has now come to talk at large about Bridges. The longest bridge in the world is the Forth Bridge, and the shortest bridge in the world is a plank over a ditch in the village of Loudwater. The bridge that frightens you most is the Brooklyn Bridge, and the bridge that frightens you least is the bridge in St James's Park." I admit that I crossed that bridge in undeserved safety; and perhaps I was affected by my early romantic vision of the bridge leading to the princess' tower. But I can assure my friend the author that the bridge of St James's Park can frighten you a good deal.

VII

THE CRIME OF ORTHODOXY

I used to say that my autobiography ought to consist of a series of short stories like those about Sherlock Holmes; only that his were astonishing examples of observation, and mine astonishing examples of lack of observation. In short, they were to be "Adventures" concerned with my absence of mind, instead of his presence of mind. One, I remember, was called "The Adventure of the Pro-Boer's Corkscrew," and commemorated the fact that I once borrowed a corkscrew from Hammond and found myself trying to open my front-door with it, with my latch-key in the other hand. Few will believe my statement, but it is none the less true, that the incident came before and not after the more appropriate use of the corkscrew. I was perfectly sober; probably I should have been more vigilant if I had been drunk. Another anecdote, expanded into "The Adventure of the Astonished Clerk," accused me of having asked for a cup of coffee instead of a ticket at the booking-office of a railway station, and doubtless I went on to ask the waitress politely for a third single to Battersea. I am not particularly proud of this characteristic, for I think that presence of mind is far more really poetical than absence of mind. But I only mention it, at this stage, because it introduces a character who played a considerable part in the fortunes of my friends and myself; and who, in the absorbing narrative of "The Adventure of the Curate's Trousers" was cast for the important part of the curate.

I cannot remember exactly where my brother or I first met the Rev. Conrad Noel. I rather fancy it was at some strange club where somebody was lecturing on Nietzsche; and where the debaters (by a typical transition) passed from the gratifying thought that Nietzsche attacked Christianity to the natural inference that he was a True Christian. And I admired the common sense of a curate, with dark curly hair and a striking face, who got up and pointed out that Nietzsche would be even more opposed to True Christianity than to False Christianity, supposing there were any True Christianity to oppose. I learned that the curate's name was Noel, but in many ways his intervention was symbolic of my experience of that strange world. The Intelligentsia of the artistic and vaguely anarchic clubs was indeed a very strange world. And the strangest thing about it, I fancy, was that, while it thought a great deal about thinking, it did not think. Everything seemed to come at second or third hand; from Nietzsche or Tolstoy or Ibsen or Shaw; and there was a pleasant atmosphere of discussing all these things, without any particular sense of responsibility for coming to any conclusion on them. The company often included really clever people like Mr Edgar Jepson, who always seemed as if he had strayed out of Society to smile mysteriously in Bohemia. Here and there it would include a man who had not only cleverness but strong traditional beliefs, which he kept largely to himself; like my old friend Louis McQuilland, who was long content to appear as a modern of the club called the Moderns, dealing in detached epigrams of the Wilde and Whistler fashion; and guarding within him all the time a flame of pure Catholic faith and burning Irish Nationalism, which never appeared save when those sacred things were challenged. But I think it profoundly significant, as a matter of intellectual instincts, that he preferred the almost avowed nonsense of the Decadents to the more high-minded and heretical earnestness of the Fabians. He once said in his wrath, on the occasion of the hundredth eulogy on *Candida* or *Arms and the Man*, something which ran (if I remember right) in a Scriptural form, "Stay me with Hitchens, comfort me with Beerbohm; for I am sick of Shaw."

But a large section of the Intelligentsia seemed wholly devoid of Intelligence. As was perhaps natural, those who pontificated most pompously were often the most windy and hollow. I remember a man with a long beard and a deep booming voice who proclaimed at intervals: "What we need is Love," or "All we require is Love," like the detonations of a heavy gun. I remember another radiant little man who spread out his fingers and said: "Heaven is here! It is now!" which seemed a disturbing thought under the circumstances. There was an aged, aged man who seemed to live at one of these literary clubs; and who would hold up a large hand at intervals and preface some fairly ordinary observation by saying, "A Thought." One day Jepson, I think, goaded beyond endurance, is said to have exploded with the words, "But, good God man, you don't call that a thought, do you?" But that was what was the matter with not a few of these thinkers. A sort of Theosophist said to me, "Good and evil, truth and falsehood, folly and wisdom are only aspects of the same upward movement of the universe." Even at that stage it occurred to me to ask, "Supposing there is no difference between good and bad, or between false and true, what is the difference between up and down?"

Now there was one thing that I began to note, as I noted it on that minor occasion of the debate on Nietzsche. All that clique, in praising the Ibsenite and Shavian drama, was of course very contemptuous of the old Victorian drama. It sneered steadily at the stock types of old farces; at the drawling guardsmen and grotesque grocers of *Caste* or *Our Boys*. But there was one old farcical type that had become far more false; and that was the comic curate of *The Private Secretary*: the simpleton who "did not like London" and asked for a glass of milk and a Bath bun. And many of the sceptics in that highly scientific world had not, by any means, outgrown the Victorian joke about the curate. Having myself been trained, first on the farce about the curate, and then on the scepticism about the priest, I was quite ready to believe that a dying superstition was represented by such feeble persons. As a fact, I found that they were very often by far the ablest and most forcible persons. In debate after debate I noticed the same thing happen, that I have already noted in the debate on Nietzsche. It was the farcical curate, it was the feeble-minded clergyman, who got up and applied to the wandering discussion at least some sort of test of some sort of truth; who showed all the advantages of having been tolerably trained in some sort of system of thinking. Dreadful seeds of doubt began to be sown in my mind. I was almost tempted to question the accuracy of the anticlerical legend; nay, even the accuracy of the farce of *The Private Secretary*. It seemed to me that the despised curates were rather more intelligent than anybody else; that they, alone in that world of intellectualism, were trying to use their intellects. For that reason I begin such adventures with the Adventure of the Curate's Trousers. For that reason I mention first Mr Conrad Noel. He had no Bath bun. He did not confine himself to a glass of milk. Nobody, with the smallest knowledge of him, could truthfully say that he did not like London.

Conrad Noel, the son of a poet and the grandson of a peer, had all the incalculable elements of the eccentric aristocrat; the sort of eccentric aristocrat who so often figures as a particularly destructive democrat. That great gentleman, Cunninghame Graham, whom I knew more slightly but always respected profoundly, was the same sort of uncompromising rebel; but he had a sort of Scottish seriousness similar to Spanish seriousness; while Noel's humour was half English and half Irish but always mainly humorous. He delighted, of course, in shocking people and taking a rise out of them; I remember how he used to say, shaking his head with an air of brooding concentration: "Ah, how little people know about the work of a clergyman's life; such demands on him! Such distracting and different duties! All the afternoon behind the scenes at the Butterfly Theatre, talking to Poppy

Pimpernel; all the evening doing a pub-crawl with Jack Bootle; back to the club after dinner, etc." As a matter of fact, he occupied much of his time with things perhaps equally fantastic but more intellectual. He had a love of nosing out the head-quarters of incredible or insane sects; and wrote an amusing record of them called "Byways of Belief." He had a special affection for an old gentleman with long grey whiskers, living in the suburbs; whose name, it appeared, was King Solomon David Jesus. This prophet was not afraid to protest, as a prophet should, against what he considered the pomps and vanities of this world. He began the interview by coldly rebuking Conrad Noel for having sent in a visiting-card inscribed, "Rev. Conrad Noel;" since all such official titles were abolished in the New Dispensation. Conrad delicately insinuated, in self-defence, that there seemed to be something about calling oneself Solomon David Jesus, which might raise rather grave problems of identity and a somewhat formidable historical comparison. And anyhow, an old gentleman who called himself King could hardly insist on such severe republican simplicity. However, the monarch explained that his title had been given him by an actual voice speaking out of the sky; and the Rev. Conrad admitted that he could not claim that his visiting-card had been thus written at dictation.

Sometimes, instead of his visiting the New Religions, the New Religions visited him, which was rather more alarming. He and his wife, a very charming little lady whose demureness was perhaps a little deceptive, had gone out to a matinee and came back to find ten Doukhabors eating their tea. Doukhabors, it may be explained to those who have had no such happy visitations, are a sect of Russian Pacifists and practical Communists, who believe in living by mutual hospitality. It is a curious and mystifying circumstance, by the way, that while the Doukhabors lived in Russia and had differences with a foreign authority, they invariably behaved themselves like a band of saints and according to the highest pattern of primitive Christians; but when they crossed to Canada, and came under a British authority, they were strangely demoralised, and degenerated into dangerous fanatics who used to go about stealing horses out of carts and cows out of sheds, because they disapproved of the captivity of animals. Anyhow, Conrad Noel, who certainly would not have thought the worse of them for defying either the Russian or the British Empire, had met a member of this sect somewhere; and I suppose in some hazy and hearty fashion invited him to pay a call some day. He was there with nine others like unto himself, stowing away the muffins and macaroons; and explaining that they would be delighted to pay for so ample and sumptuous a meal; but unfortunately, they did not approve of money. "If, however;" explained the Primitive Christian, "there is any small form of service" – any domestic assistance they could offer in return, they would be delighted thus to discharge the debt. Then was a light of battle to be seen in the eye of Mrs

Conrad Noel, who proceeded in quiet tones to tell them all the things she would undoubtedly like done; there were a great many of them, more than I can recall; but I have a general impression that carrying the grand piano up five floors on to the roof, or carting the billiard table to the other end of the garden, were typical of the class of tasks to which the tottering and staggering Doukhabors were directed, by that gentle but vindictive lady. It is to be feared that none of them came to the house of that hospitable Christian Socialist again; except indeed one isolated Doukhabor, who struck out a line for himself; for the simple domestic toil with which he paid for his meal consisted in going into Noel's study and altering Noel's sermon; blacking out whole passages of it and inserting sentiments of a more unimpeachably Doukhabor tendency. In his case, I suspect that Mr Noel, as well as Mrs Noel, began to have doubts about the Doukhabor ideal.

But Mr Noel certainly never lost his belief in what may be called the Russian Communist ideal; though he would have been as astonished as anybody else if he had been told then of the fortunes that lay before Russian Communism. Here, however, I am chiefly concerned with him as an example of my preliminary prevailing impression of how stupid the anti-clericals were and how much more relatively intelligent the clerics were. From this time also, dates the first faint beginnings of my own divergence from the merely Communist to what is called the Distributist ideal. It was, after all, only the further sub-division of my Notting Hill romance from the street to the house; but it was solidified by Belloc, my Irish friends and my French holidays. But I fancy the first spark flew when a Theosophist, at a drawing-room meeting, was droning on about the immorality of Christians who believed in the Forgiveness of Sins; since there was only Karma, by which we reap what we sow. "If that window is broken," he said mournfully, "our host (Sir Richard Stapley) might pardon it; but the window will still be broken." Whereupon a spectacled baldish little curate, quite unknown to me, jumped up and said, "But it isn't wrong to break a window. It's only wrong because it's Stapley's window; and if he doesn't mind, why should anybody else?"

Anyhow, it was when I was staying with Conrad Noel, afterwards famous as the parson who flew the Red Flag from his church at Thaxted in Essex, that I happened to be dressing for dinner and made the (it seems to me) very excusable error of mistaking his black clerical trousers for my evening ones. I trust I violated no grave ecclesiastical law, relative to the unlawful assumption of priestly vestments; but Conrad Noel himself was always fairly casual in the matter of costume. The world thought him a very Bohemian sort of clergyman, as it now thinks him a very Bolshevist sort of clergyman. The world would be wiser if it realised that, in spite of this, he was and is a very unworldly sort of clergyman; and much too unworldly to be judged rightly by the world. I did not always agree with his attitude, and I do not now altogether agree with his politics; but I have always known that he glowed with conviction and the simplicity of the fighting spirit. But in those days his external eccentricity was more provocative than is a red rag to a bull or a red flag to a bully. He delighted in making the quaintest combinations of costume made up of the clerical, the artistic and the proletarian. He took great pleasure in appearing in correct clerical clothes, surmounted with a sort of hairy or furry cap, making him look like an aesthetic rat-catcher. I had the pleasure of walking with him, thus attired, right across the vast stretch of South London, starting from Blackfriars Bridge and going on till we saw the green hills beyond Croydon; a very interesting expedition too rarely undertaken by those from the richer side of the river. I also remember one occasion when I was walking away from some meeting with him and with Dr Percy Dearmer, then chiefly famous as an authority on the history of ritual and vestments. Dr Dearmer was in the habit of walking about in a cassock and biretta which he had carefully reconstructed as being of exactly the right pattern for an Anglican or Anglo-Catholic priest; and he was humorously grieved when its strictly traditional and national character was misunderstood by the little boys in the street. Somebody would call out, "No Popery," or "To hell with the Pope," or some other sentiment of larger and more liberal religion. And Percy Dearmer would sternly stop them and say, "Are you aware that this is the precise costume in which Latimer went to the stake?"

Meanwhile my own costume, however calamitous, was the result rather of accident than design; but this was sometime later and my wife had already disguised me as far as possible in the large hat and cloak familiar to caricaturists. But it was also at a sufficiently early date in English history for frock-coats to be worn on formal occasions. I had taken off the cloak and retained the frock-coat and wide hat; and I must have borne a more or less formless resemblance to a Boer missionary. Thus I walked innocently down the street, with the hairy cap of the aesthetic rat-catcher on one side and the ceremonial biretta and cassock of Bishop Latimer on the other. And Charles Masterman, who always wore conventional clothes in an unconventional manner, a top hat on the back of his head and an umbrella flourished with derisive gestures, walked behind and pointed at the three of us as we unconsciously filled the pavement and cried aloud, "Could you see three backs like that anywhere in God's creation?"

I mention this fringe of eccentricity, even of eccentricity in dress, upon the border of the Anglo-Catholic party in the Anglican Church, because it really had a great deal to do with the beginning of the process by which Bohemian journalists, like my brother and myself, were drawn towards the serious consideration of the theory of a Church. I was considerably influenced by Conrad Noel; and my brother, I think, even more so.

I have said very little of my brother so far, in spite of the great part he played in my boyhood and youth; and the omission has been due to anything in the world except oblivion. My brother was much too remarkable a person not to have a chapter to himself. And I have decided, not without thought, that he will be best presented at full length when the time comes to deal with his very vital effect on modern history, and the whole story of the campaign against political corruption. But it is relevant here to remark that he differed from me at the very beginning; and not least in beginning his questions at the beginning. I always retained a sort of lingering loyalty or vague sympathy with the traditions of the past; so that, even during the period when I practically believed in nothing, I believed in what some have called "the wish to believe." But my brother at the beginning did not even wish to believe; or at least did not wish to admit that he wished to believe. He adopted the extreme attitude of antagonism, and almost of anarchism; largely, no doubt, out of a reaction and as the result of our interminable arguments, or rather argument. For we really devoted all our boyhood to one long argument, unfortunately interrupted by meal-times, by school-times, by work hours and many such irritating and irrelevant frivolities. But though he was ready at first to take up the cudgels for anarchism or atheism or anything, he had the sort of mind in which anarchism or atheism could survive anything except the society of anarchists and atheists. He had far too lucid and lively a mind not to be bored with materialism as maintained by materialists. This negative reaction against negation, however, might not have carried him far, if the positive end of the magnet had not begun to attract him; in the person of personalities like Conrad Noel. It was certainly through that eccentric cleric that my brother began to cease to be anything so barren as a mere anti-clerical. I remember that, when conventional people complained of Noel's wild ways, or attributed to him worse things of which he certainly was not guilty, my brother Cecil answered them by quoting the words of the man healed of blindness in the Gospel; "Whether the man be a sinner or no, I know not; but this I know; that whereas I was blind, now I see."

The old High Church or Anglo-Catholic group, of which Conrad Noel represented the most revolutionary extreme and Percy Dearmer (at least at that time) the most historical and liturgical, was in fact a very fine body of men, to which I for one shall always feel a gratitude like that of my brother and the blind man in Scripture. Its leader, in so far as it had a leader among the higher branches of the Anglican system, was that most fascinating and memorable man, Henry Scott Holland, who moved among younger men like one much younger than they; unforgettable with his humorous frog's face and great stature and voice of bull-like bellowing; as if he were the frog that had conquered the fable and really turned into a bull. In an abstract intellectual sense, of course, their leader was rather Dr Gore; but anyone who knew his peculiar merits would expect him to seem a thinner and more shadowy figure in the background. Sometimes all of them assembled on one platform, especially on the platforms of the Christian Social Union, which I joined at a later date; and I hope that all who survive of those old friends, from whom I have been sundered in thought but never in sympathy, will forgive me if I recall here any of the follies that enlivened our friendship. I remember when about five or six of us addressed the astonished town of Nottingham, on what we considered to be its Christian duty towards the modern problem of industrial poverty. I remember the faces of the citizens of that great city while I spoke; and I regret to say that I recorded my impressions in some verses, supposed to represent the impressions of a Nottingham tradesman; they became something of a jest in out little circle and I quote them for the pleasure of recalling those old exhilarating days.

> The Christian Social Union here
> Was very much annoyed;
> It seems there is some duty
> Which we never should avoid,
> And so they sing a lot of hymns
> To help the Unemployed.
>
> Upon a platform at the end
> The speakers were displayed
> And Bishop Hoskins stood in front
> And hit a bell and said
> That Mr Carter was to pray,
> And Mr Carter prayed.
>
> Then Bishop Gore of Birmingham
> He stood upon one leg
> And said he would be happier
> If beggars didn't beg,
> And that if they pinched his palace
> It would take him down a peg.
>
> He said that Unemployment
> Was a horror and a blight,
> He said that charities produced
> Servility and spite,
> And stood upon the other leg
> And said it wasn't right.

And then a man named Chesterton
Got up and played with water,
He seemed to say that principles
Were nice and led to slaughter
And how we always compromised
And how we didn't orter.

Then Canon Holland fired ahead
Like fifty cannons firing,
We tried to find out what he meant
With infinite enquiring
But the way he made the windows jump
We couldn't help admiring.

He said the human soul should be
Ashamed of every sham,
He said a man should constantly
Ejaculate "I am"
…when he had done, I went outside
And got into a tram.

I rather prided myself on these lines, merely because they are, in the main, a very accurate report of the speeches: or of what the speeches probably appeared to be to the audience. And I also disinter them from their dustbin because they remind me of a characteristic expression of Scott Holland, which I have since found to be a characteristic problem of human life. There was one verse of my doggerel verses which I have omitted, because it would certainly be misunderstood, as Scott Holland himself was misunderstood. He was a man of great clearness and great fairness of mind, and what he said always meant something and was a result of the unpopular sport of thinking. But he was also a man with a natural surge of laughter within him, so that this broad strong mouth seemed always to be shut down on it in a grimace of restraint. I remember that on this occasion he was urging what is probably the best argument for State intervention, tending in the general direction of State Socialism, which was common in the Christian Social Union and pronounced in the definite and defiant Christian Socialists, like Conrad Noel. He said that the Commonwealth, the social authority, was worthy of being regarded in a positive and not merely in a negative light; that we ought to be able to trust the things it did, and not to think only of the things it punished us for doing. The politician should be more than the policeman; he should produce and construct and not merely punish. At this point his immense internal enjoyment of a joke bubbled to the surface and he said, waving his hand to the rigid and respectable Nottingham audience, "Punishment is an exceptional instrument. After all, it is only occasionally that you and I feel that tap on the shoulder, and that gruff recommendation to 'Come along quietly.' It is not every day of our lives that we are put in the dock and sentenced to some term of imprisonment. Most of our relations to Government are peaceable and friendly. Why, I suppose that even in this room there are quite half a dozen people who have never been in jail at all." A ghastly stare was fixed on all the faces of the audience; and I have ever since seen it in my own dreams; for it has constituted a considerable part of my own problem.

I have never understood, from that day to this, any more than he did, why a solid argument is any less solid because you make the illustrations as entertaining as you can. What Holland was saying was perfectly sensible and philosophical. It was that the State exists to provide lamp-posts and schools, as well as gibbets and jails. But I strongly suspect that many, who were sufficiently intelligent not to imagine that he was mad, did imagine that he was flippant. And I myself have made in the course of a less useful life the same curious discovery. if you say that two sheep added to two sheep make four sheep, your audience will accept it patiently – like sheep. But if you say it of two monkeys, or two kangaroos, or two sea-green griffins, people will refuse to believe that two and two make four. They seem to imagine that you must have made up the arithmetic, just as you have made up the illustration of the arithmetic. And though they would actually know that what you say is sense, if they thought about it sensibly, they cannot believe that anything decorated by an incidental joke can be sensible. Perhaps it explains why so many successful men are so dull – or why so many dull men are successful.

But I have also dwelt for a moment on such a meeting and such a group, because I am only too glad, in the light of after events, to testify to the pleasure with which I recall it. When people of many different parties talked of all High Churchmen as high and dry, when they used to talk of the dehumanised detachment of Charles Gore or the despairing depression of Charles Masterman, I had every motive to remember much better and brighter things; and to leave some little record here of how uproariously encouraging was the pessimism of Masterman, how subtly sympathetic the detachment of Dr Gore. Good friends and very gay companions... *O anima humana naturaliter Christiana*, whither were you marching so gallantly, that you could not find the natural way?

But I have been carried far ahead of my narrative by these memories of the Anglo-Catholic group, and all the names that naturally follow the mention of the first name of Noel. When Noel first appeared on the horizon of my brother and myself, my brother was frankly anti-religious and I had no religion except the very haziest religiosity. And it is necessary in this chapter to say something of the tendencies by which I shifted nearer and nearer to the orthodox side; and eventually found myself, as I have described, in the very heart of a clerical group of canons and curates. My first introduction, in Sydney Smith's phrase, came through very wild curates. Conrad Noel might have been the incarnate fulfilment of Sydney Smith's vision or fancy; and indeed it so happened that, in his case, while the wild curate was in every sense singular, the wild curates were also in the plural. My old friend the Rev. A L Lilley now a Canon of Hereford, was then the vicar of a parish in Paddington Green; and his large and genial sympathies expressed themselves in the marked eccentricity of his assistant clergy. For he was one of the two or three Broad Churchmen I have known who were actually broad. His curates were a group which we irreverently referred to at one time as a menagerie; one, I remember, was of gigantic stature with fierce grey hair, eyebrows and moustaches very like Mark Twain. Another was a Syrian and actually, I believe, a runaway monk from some monastery in the desert. The third was Conrad Noel. I have sometimes thought it must have been rather amusing to be a faithful parishioner of Paddington Green.

But the question here is of the intellectual approach, even to so eccentric a borderland of orthodoxy. And the reader must once more reconcile himself, with a groan, to some brief references to real beliefs, and the thing which some call theory, and I call thought. In the purely religious sense, I was brought up among people who were Unitarians and Universalists, but who were well aware that a great many people around them were becoming agnostics or even atheists. Indeed there were two tendencies in what was called the emancipation of faith from the creeds and dogmas of the past. The two tendencies were in flatly contrary directions; and it is thoroughly typical of the world that they were both called by the same name. Both were supposed to be liberal theology or the religion of all sensible men. But, in fact, one half of the sensible men were more and more arguing that, because God was in His heaven, all must be right with the world; with this world or with the next. The other half of them were specially bent on showing that it was very doubtful if there was any God in any heaven, and that it was so certain to the scientific eye that all is not right with the world, that it would be nearer the truth to say that all is wrong with the world. One of these movements of progress led into the glorious fairyland of George Macdonald, the other led into the stark and hollowed hills of Thomas Hardy. The one school was specially insisting that God must be supremely perfect if He exists; the other that, if He exists, He must be grossly imperfect. And by the time I passed from boyhood to manhood, the pessimistic doubt had considerably clouded the optimistic dogma.

Now I think the first thing that struck me as startling was exactly this; that these two schools, which were logically in contradiction, were practically in combination. The idealistic theists and the realistic atheists were allies –

against what? It has taken me about two-thirds of my life to find out the answer to that question. But when I first noticed it, the question seemed quite unanswerable; and, what was queerer still, to the people themselves it did not seem even questionable. I myself had sat at the feet of that large-hearted and poetic orator, Stopford Brooke, and I long accepted the sort of optimistic theism that he taught; it was substantially the same as that which I had learnt since childhood under the glamorous mysticism of George Macdonald. It was a full and substantial faith in the Fatherhood of God, and little could be said against it, even in theological theory, except that it rather ignored the free-will of man. Its Universalism was a sort of optimistic Calvinism. But, anyhow, that was my first faith, before anything that could really be called my first doubt. But what struck me as extraordinary, even at first, was that these optimists seemed to be in the same camp as the pessimists. To my simple mind, it seemed that there could be no connection except contradiction, between the man whose whole faith was in the Fatherhood of God, and the man who said there was no God or the man who said that God was no Father. I pointed out something of the sort, long afterwards, when liberal literary critics were supposed to class together the philosophies of Meredith and Hardy. It seemed to me obvious that Meredith maintains on the whole that Nature is to be trusted, and Hardy that Nature is not to be trusted. To my innocent mind, these two ideas seemed a little inconsistent. I had not yet discovered the higher synthesis which connects them. For the higher synthesis which connects them consists in wearing liberty ties and curiously shaped beards and hats, and meeting in cultured clubs where they drink coffee, or (in darker and more disreputable dens) cocoa. That is the only connection there is between the ideas; but it took me a long time to find it out. These sceptical doctrinaires do not recognise each other by the doctrines. They recognise each other by the beard or the clothes, as the lower animals know each other by the fur or the smell.

I suppose I have got a dogmatic mind. Anyhow, even when I did not believe in any of the things called dogmas, I assumed that people were sorted out into solid groups by the dogmas they believed or disbelieved. I supposed that the Theosophists all sat in the same hall because they all believed in Theosophy. I supposed the Theistic Church believed in Theism. I supposed that the atheists all combined because they disbelieved in Theism. I imagined that the Ethical Societies consisted entirely of people who believed in Ethics but not in theology or even religion. I have come to the conclusion that I was largely mistaken in this idea. I believe now that the congregations of these semi-secular chapels consist largely of one vast and vague sea of wandering doubters, with their wandering doubts, who may be found one Sunday seeking a solution from the Theists and another Sunday from the Theosophists. They may be scattered among many such chapels; they are only connected by the convention of unconventionality, which is connoted by "not going to church." I will give two incidents as examples of what I mean; though they are separated by a long interval of years. In the very early days of which I am now speaking, before I ever dreamed of being myself attached to any formal system of faith, I used to wander about to many assemblies giving lectures, or what were politely called lectures. I may remark that my suspicion was confirmed, by the fact that I very often saw the same people in quite different congregations; especially a worried-looking man with dark anxious eyes, and a very aged Jew with a long white beard and a smile carved immutably, like that of an Egyptian image.

On one occasion I had been lecturing to an Ethical Society, when I happened to see on the wall a portrait of Priestley, the great Unitarian of a hundred years ago. I remarked that it was a very fine engraving; and one of the faithful, to whom I was speaking, replied that it had probably been hung there because the place was quite recently a Unitarian chapel; I think he said only a few years before. I was considerably intrigued, knowing that the old Unitarians were as dogmatic as Moslems on the one point of the One God, and that the ethical group were as undogmatic as any agnostics upon that particular dogma. "That is very interesting," I said, "May I ask whether the whole of your society abandoned Theism all at once and in a body?"

"Well, no," he replied rather hazily, "I don't fancy it was exactly like that. I rather think the fact was that our leaders wanted very much to have Dr Stanton Coit as a preacher, and he wouldn't come unless the thing was simply an Ethical Society."

Of course I cannot answer for the accuracy of what the gentleman said, as I did not know him from Adam; but in any case my point here concerns the cloudy condition of the mind of the ordinary audiences, and not of the actual lecturers or leaders. Dr Stanton Coit himself, for instance, had a perfectly clear idea of an ethic unsupported by theology. But, taking this typical member of the movement, there is something rather extraordinary about what had actually happened, or what he seriously supposed had actually happened. By this theory, God Almighty had been dropped out of the whole business, as a concession to Dr Stanton Coit. It was generally felt, apparently, that it would be really rather churlish not to meet him on a little thing like that. Now it happened that, years afterwards, a friend of mine enquired after the fortunes of this particular Ethical Society, and was informed that its congregation was somewhat diminished. The reason given was that the distinguished ethical lecturer could hardly be expected to be so active as he had been in earlier days; and that in consequence a number of his followers had now "gone off to listen to Maude Royden." Now Miss Maude Royden, whatever may be counted controversial in her position, certainly professes to be enough of an orthodox Christian to play the part of a loyal Anglican, and even of an Anglican parson. So that the truly astonishing history of this school of thought, if we regard it as a school of thought, was more or less as follows. They began by believing in the Creation but not the Incarnation. For the sake of Dr Coit they ceased to believe in the Creation. And for the sake of Miss Royden they agreed to believe in the Creation and the Incarnation as well. The truth of the matter is, I imagine, that these particular people never did believe or disbelieve in anything. They liked to go and hear stimulating lecturers; and they had a vague preference, almost impossible to reduce to any definable thesis, for those lecturers who were supposed to be in some way heterodox and unconventional. And having since had longer and larger opportunities of watching the general drift of such people, and having seen the dark-eyed doubter and the patriarchal Jew in more and more motley and incongruous assemblies, I have come to the conclusion that there never were any large schools of thought, so separate and so static as I innocently imagined in my youth. I have been granted, as it were, a sort of general view or vision of all that field of negation and groping and curiosity. And I saw pretty much what it all really meant. There was no Theistic Church; there was no Theosophical Brotherhood; there were no Ethical Societies; there were no New Religions. But I saw Israel scattered on the hills as sheep that have not a shepherd; and I saw a large number of the sheep run about bleating eagerly in whatever neighbourhood it was supposed that a shepherd might be found.

Amid all this scattered thinking, sometimes not unfairly to be called scatter-brained thinking, I began to piece together the fragments of the old religious scheme; mainly by the various gaps that denoted its disappearance. And the more I saw of real human nature, the more I came to suspect that it was really rather bad for all these people that it had disappeared. Many of them held, and still hold, very noble and necessary truths in the social and secular area. But even these it seemed to me they held less firmly than they might have done, if there had been anything like a fundamental principle of morals and metaphysics to support them. Men who believed ardently in altruism were yet troubled by the necessity of believing with even more religious reverence in Darwinism, and even in the deductions from Darwinism about a ruthless struggle as the rule of life. Men who naturally accepted the moral equality of mankind yet did so, in a manner, shrinkingly, under the gigantic shadow of the Superman of Nietzsche and Shaw. Their hearts were in the right place; but their heads were emphatically in the wrong place, being generally poked or plunged into vast volumes of materialism and scepticism, crabbed, barren, servile and without any light of liberty or of hope.

I began to examine more exactly the general Christian theology which many execrated and few examined. I soon found that it did in fact correspond to many of these experiences of life; that even its paradoxes corresponded to the paradoxes of life. Long afterwards Father Waggett (to mention another very able man of the old Anglo-Catholic group), once said to me, as we stood on the Mount of Olives in view of Gethsemane and Aceldama, "Well, anyhow, it must be obvious to anybody that the doctrine of the Fall is the only *cheerful* view of human life." It is indeed obvious to me; but the thought passed over me at the moment, that a very large proportion of that old world of sceptical sects and cliques, to which I had once belonged, would find it a much more puzzling paradox than the paradoxes of Oscar Wilde and Bernard Shaw. I will not develop the argument here, which I have so often developed elsewhere; I merely mention it to suggest my general sense, even at this stage, that the old theological theory seemed more or less to fit into experience, while the new and negative theories did not fit into anything, least of all into each other. It was about this time that I had published some studies on contemporary writers, such as Kipling and Shaw and Wells; and feeling that each of them erred through an ultimate or religious error, I gave the book the title of *Heretics*. It was reviewed by Mr G S Street, the very delightful essayist, who casually used the expression that he was not going to bother about his theology until I had really stated mine. With all the solemnity of youth, I accepted this as a challenge; and wrote an outline of my own reasons for believing that the Christian theory, as summarised in the Apostles' Creed, would be found to be a better criticism of life than any of those that I had criticised. I called it Orthodoxy, but even at the time I was very much dissatisfied with the title. It sounded a thinnish sort of thing to be defending through thick and thin. Even then I fancy I had a dim foreshadowing that I should have to find some better name for it before I died. As it was, the only interesting effect of the title, or the book, that I ever heard of, occurred on the frontiers of Russia. There I believe the Censor, under the old Russian regime, destroyed the book without reading it. From its being called "Orthodoxy," he naturally inferred that it must be a book on the Greek Church. And from its being a book on the Greek Church, he naturally inferred that it must be an attack on it.

But there did remain one rather vague virtue about the title, from my point of view; that it was provocative. And it is an exact test of that extraordinary modern society that it really was provocative. I had begun to discover that, in all that welter of inconsistent and incompatible heresies, the one and only really unpardonable heresy was orthodoxy. A serious defence of orthodoxy was far more startling to the English critic than a serious attack on orthodoxy was to the Russian censor. And through this experience I learned two very interesting things, which serve to divide all this part of my life into two distinct periods. Very nearly everybody, in the ordinary literary and journalistic world, began by taking it for granted that my faith in the Christian creed was a pose or a paradox. The more cynical supposed that it was only a stunt. The more generous and loyal warmly maintained that it was only a joke. It was not until long afterwards that the full horror of the truth burst upon them; the disgraceful truth that I really thought the thing was true. And I have found, as I say, that this represents a real transition or border-line in the life of the apologists. Critics were almost entirely complimentary to what they were pleased to call my brilliant paradoxes; *until* they discovered that I really meant what I said. Since then they have been more combative; and I do not blame them.

I first made this discovery at a dinner-party, in connection with another controversy, which must be mentioned because it is relevant here. I think it was a dinner given by the staff of the *Clarion*, the important and popular Socialist paper of the period, then edited by Mr Robert Blatchford; a veteran whom I pause to salute across the ages, hoping he will not count me less friendly if I recall these battles of the distant past. As I shall explain in a moment, I had just had a very pugnacious public argument with Mr Blatchford, which, as I was then a comparatively young though relatively rising journalist, was naturally a landmark in my life. But I remember that there was, sitting next to me at this dinner, one of those very refined and rather academic gentlemen from Cambridge who seemed to form so considerable a section of the rugged stalwarts of Labour. There was a cloud on his brow, as if he were beginning to be puzzled about something; and he said suddenly, with abrupt civility, "Excuse my asking, Mr Chesterton, of course I shall quite understand if you prefer not to answer, and I shan't think any the worse of it, you know, even if it's true. But I suppose I'm right in thinking you don't really *believe* in those things you're defending against Blatchford?" I informed him with adamantine gravity that I did most definitely believe in those things I was defending against Blatchford. His cold and refined face did not move a visible muscle; and yet I knew in some fashion it had completely altered. "Oh, you do," he said, "I beg your pardon. Thank you. That's all I wanted to know." And he went on eating his (probably vegetarian) meal. But I was sure that for the rest of the evening, despite his calm, he felt as if he were sitting next to a fabulous griffin.

That this stage may be understood, it must be realised what the things I was defending against Blatchford were. It was not a question of some abstract theological thesis, like the definition of the Trinity or the dogmas of Election or Effectual Grace. I was not yet so far gone in orthodoxy as to be so theological as all that. What I was defending seemed to me a plain matter of ordinary human morals. Indeed it seemed to me to raise the question of the very possibility of any morals. It was the question of Responsibility, sometimes called the question of Free Will, which Mr Blatchford had attacked in a series of vigorous and even violent proclamations of Determinism; all apparently founded on having read a little book or pamphlet by Professor Haeckel. The question had a great many amusing or arresting aspects; but the point of it in this place is what I have already suggested. It was not that I began by believing in supernormal things. It was that the unbelievers began by disbelieving even in normal things. It was the secularists who drove me to theological ethics, by themselves destroying any sane or rational possibility of secular ethics. I might myself have been a secularist, so long as it meant that I could be merely responsible to secular society. It was the Determinist who told me, at the top of his voice, that I could not be responsible at all. And as I rather like being treated as a responsible being, and not as a lunatic let out for the day, I began to look around for some spiritual asylum that was not merely a lunatic asylum.

On that day, in short, I escaped from an error which still entangles many better men than myself. There is still a notion that the agnostic can remain secure of this world, so long as he does not wish to be what is called "other-worldly." He can be content with common sense about men and women, so long as he is not curious of mysteries about angels and archangels. It is not true. The questions of the sceptic strike direct at the heart of this our human life; they disturb this world, quite apart from the other world; and it is exactly common sense that they disturb most. There could not be a better example than this queer appearance, in my youth, of the determinist as a demagogue; shouting to a mob of millions that no man ought to be blamed for anything he did, because it was all heredity and environment. Logically, it would stop a man in the act of saying "Thank you" to somebody for passing the mustard. For how could he be praised for passing the mustard, if he could not be blamed for not passing the mustard? I know it can be maintained that fatalism makes no difference to the facts of our life. Some say that fatalists can still go on punishing or blaming. Some say (professing, with no little humour, to be humanitarian) that they can leave off blaming but still go on punishing. But if determinism made no difference, why should Blatchford thunder furiously from a pulpit about the difference it made? The explanation was to be found in Blatchford himself. He was a very normal man to have come by so abnormal a heresy; an old soldier with brown Italian eyes and a walrus moustache and full of the very sentiments that soldiers have and Socialists generally have not. He was a firm patriot and not a little of a Tory; certainly very much of a Protectionist. But this Determinism appealed to him through another very normal sentiment; the sentiment of undiluted compassion. He called his book of Determinist pamphlets a plea "for the Underdog." And it was obvious that he thought throughout of the sort of poor and disreputable and often oppressed person who can really be called the underdog. To him, and to many other men of healthy but vague modern sentiment, the notion of a sinner really connected itself entirely with the notion of a drunkard or a thieving tramp or some sort of scalawag at war with society. In the grossly unjust social system we suffer, it is probable enough that many of these really are punishable unjustly; that some ought not to be punished at all; that some, perhaps, are really not responsible at all. And Blatchford, seeing them driven to prison in droves, felt neither more nor less than a pity for the weak and the unfortunate; which was, at the worst, a slightly lopsided exaggeration of Christian charity. He was so anxious to forgive that he denied the need of forgiveness.

And I awaken from all these dreams of the past, suddenly, and with something like a shout of laughter. For the next episode in my life was one of helping certain friends and reformers to fix the terrible truth called Responsibility, not on tramps or drunkards, but on the rulers of the State and the richest men in the Empire. I was trying to put a chain and collar of Responsibility, not on the Underdog, but on the Top-dog. And the next thing that I was to hear about Blatchford was that he also, bursting with indignation, was demanding justice, punishment, vengeance almost without pardon, upon other strong tyrants who had trampled on the weak; and was fiercely nailing the arrogant princes of Prussia with Responsibility for the invasion of Belgium. So do paper sophistries go up in a great fire.

VIII

FIGURES IN FLEET STREET

The profound problem of how I ever managed to fall on my feet in Fleet Street is a mystery; at least it is still a mystery to me. It used to be said by critics that falling on my fet was only a preliminary to standing on my head. But in fact Fleet Street, not to mention my head, was a rather sea-sick and earthquaky sort of thing to stand on. On the whole, I think I owe my success (as the millionaires say) to having listened respectfully and rather bashfully to the very best advice, given by all the best journalists who had achieved the best sort of success in journalism; and then going away and doing the exact opposite. For what they all told me was that the secret of success in journalism was to study the particular journal and write what was suitable to it. And, partly by accident and ignorance and partly through the real rabid certainties of youth, I cannot remember that I ever wrote any article that was at all suitable to any paper.

On the contrary, I think I became a sort of comic success by contrast. I have a notion that the real advice I could give to a young journalist, now that I am myself an old journalist, is simply this: to write an article for the *Sporting Times* and another for the *Church Times*, and put them into the wrong envelopes. Then, if the articles were accepted and were reasonably intelligent, all the sporting men would go about saying to each other, "Great mistake to suppose there isn't a good case for us; really brainy fellows say so;" and all the clergymen would go about saying to each other, "Rattling good writing on some of our religious papers; very witty fellow." This is perhaps a little faint and fantastic as a theory; but it is the only theory upon which I can explain my own undeserved survival in the journalistic squabble on the old Fleet Street. I wrote on a Nonconformist organ like the old *Daily News* and told them all about French cafés and Catholic cathedrals; and they loved it, because they had never heard of them before. I wrote on a robust Labour organ like the old *Clarion* and defended medieval theology and all the things readers had never heard of; and their readers did not mind me a bit. What is really the matter, with almost every paper, is that it is much too full of things suitable to the paper. But in these later days of the solidification of journalism, like everything else, into trusts and monopolies, there seems to be even less likelihood of anyone repeating my rare and reckless and unscrupulous manoeuvre; of anyone waking up to find himself famous as the only funny man on the *Methodist Monthly*; or the only serious man on *Cocktail Comics*.

Anyhow, all will agree that I was an accident in Fleet Street. Some will say a fatal accident, such as is proclaimed on the placards of Fleet Street. But Fleet Street itself was full of such accidents; it might have been called the Street of Accident, as a man whom I am proud to have first met there afterwards called it the Street of Adventure. Philip Gibbs himself accentuated that intellectual incongruity which was the comedy of the place; he carried a curious air of being the right man in the wrong place. His fine falcon face, with its almost unearthly refinement, seemed set in a sort of fastidious despair about ever making it the right place. This was long before he gained his great distinctions as a war correspondent; but he dealt in the same detached way with the other great wars of the past. He had been studying the struggle between the great men of the French Revolution; and had concentrated on what seemed to me an unbalanced yet delicate detestation of Camille Desmoulins. He summoned him before a tribunal of earnest talk, in my presence; and all the time he was talking, I thought how like he looked to those high-minded, hatchet-faced, hard humanitarian idealists among the great revolutionists whom he criticised. David should have painted his profile. I begin with that impression of Gibbs precisely because his figure did seem so detached and clean cut against the background. But I myself was only the background; it was lightly alleged that I could by myself have constituted a back scene. In other words, I belonged to the old Bohemian life of Fleet Street; which has since been destroyed, not by the idealism of detachment, but by the materialism of machinery. A newspaper proprietor in later years assured me that it was a slander on journalism to tell all these tales about taverns and ragged pressmen and work and recreation coming at random at all hours of the night. "A newspaper office is now exactly like any other place of business," he said with a radiant smile; and I agreed with a groan. The very name of Bohemia has faded from the map of London as it has faded from the map of Europe. I have never understood why the new diplomacy abandoned that old and noble national name, which was among the things that were not lost on Mohacs Field; but it would seem that in both cases the best things are lost in victory and not in defeat. At least I know that I should have been annoyed if, in order to gain with doubtful judgment another strip of territory, I had been suddenly asked to talk about England as West Saxony; and that is what has happened to the long epic of Serbia, now described as North Slavia. I remember when it was announced that Bohemia was to cease to exist, at the very moment when it came into existence. It was to be called Czechoslovakia; and I went about asking people in Fleet Street whether this change was to be applied to the metaphorical Bohemia of our own romantic youth. When the wild son disturbed the respectable household was it to be said, "I wish Tom would get out of his Czechoslovakian ways," or, when Fleet Street grew riotous, "I hate these rowdy Czechoslovakian parties." But the question is merely fanciful; for there is very little left in Fleet Street that its worst enemies could call Czechoslovakian. The newspaper proprietor was perfectly right in his facts; journalism is now conducted like any other business. It is conducted as quietly, as soberly, as sensibly as the office of any successful moneylender or moderately fraudulent financier. To such persons, it will indeed seem idle if I recall that the old taverns in which men drank, or the old courts in which they starved, were often full of starving poets and drunken scholars; and all sorts of perverse personalities who sometimes even tried to tell the truth; men of the type of old Crosland, that queer cantankerous man, who hated so many things (including me) but who had often justified his great farewell, in which he said bitterly that he had:

> ...trod the path to hell,
> But there were many things he might have sold
> And did not sell.

For one thing, it was always said of him that he nearly died of hunger in Fleet Street with a volume of Shakespeare's Sonnets in his pocket.

A man of that impossible sort, of finer spiritual culture, and, therefore, of less fame or success, was Johnston Stephen, who was, I am proud to say, my friend. He was of the great Scottish family, of Leslie Stephen and of "J K S"; and he was quite as wise as the one and as witty as the other. But he had a certain distinction very difficult to define; the world with which he dealt simplified it by saying he was mad. I should prefer to say that he could not completely digest anything; he refused things of which he thoroughly approved at the last moment, with a movement like that of a bucking horse. Sometimes his objection was profound enough, and always illuminated by an idea; but he lacked the power of final adherence. He once made to me the very sensible remark, "The only little difficulty that I have about joining the Catholic Church is that I do not think I believe in God. All the rest of the Catholic system is so obviously right and so obviously superior to anything else, that I cannot imagine anyone having any doubt about it." And I remember that he was grimly gratified when I told him, at a later stage of my own beliefs, that real Catholics are intelligent enough to have this difficulty; and that St Thomas Aquinas practically begins his whole argument by saying, "Is there a God? Apparently not." But, I added, it was my experience that entering into the system even socially brought an ever-increasing certitude upon the original question. For the rest, while a fierily patriotic Scotsman, he had too much of such sympathy to be popular with many Scots. I remember when he was asked whether the Church was not corrupt and crying out for the Reformation, he answered with disconcerting warmth, "Who can doubt it? How horrible must have been the corruption which could have tolerated for so long three Catholic priests like John Knox and John Calvin and Martin Luther."

Somebody ought to have written a life of Stephen or collected his literary remains; which were left to vanish as journalistic remains. I once had a notion of doing it myself; it is one of the many duties I have neglected. There was an essay on Burns in my brother's paper, the *New Witness*, which was so much better than most essays on Burns, or essays on anything, that it might have made a man's name if the man had been on the make. He remains to me as a great monument of the futility of the present condition of fame, which is merely fashion. He had indeed violent freaks of temperament; but these did not in the old days extinguish a man like Swift or a man like Landor. If he is remembered in no better way, it is well that I should dedicate this passing note to his memory. He has long since discovered the answer to his only religious difficulty.

All these extremes were too extreme to be typical; the fine fanatic who said what he liked and died; the mere snob or sneak who said what he was told to say and lived, if you can call it living. But it is only fair to Fleet Street to say that there were some who kept their intellectual independence, and yet kept their connection with the working machine of journalism; mostly by having a wide range of variety in their work, and because monopoly was not yet so uniform as to prevent them having some choice of masters; even if it were already a choice of tyrants. Perhaps the most brilliant of these, who might without exaggeration be called the Queen of Fleet Street, was a lady with whom I have the great honour to be connected; I mean the wife of my brother Cecil. She has always managed to remain a free-lance or the Joan of Arc of a whole company of free-lances, though there is one field especially in which her banner has now been displayed to all. She always had a hundred irons in the fire; though only one of her fires is now so big as to be a bonfire and a beacon. Everyone has heard of the Cecil Houses, in which homeless women find that real hospitality, human and humorous, which was incredibly absent from the previous priggish philanthropy; and nearly everyone has read about their origin, in her own astounding book which records her own astounding adventure. She went out without a penny to live among the penniless; and brought back our only authoritative account of such a life. But not everybody understands that flame of angry charity which resents the poor being pestered even more than their being neglected; hating the selfishness of the sweater, but hating more the spiritual pride peculiar to the spy. She has sympathy with Communists, as I have, and perhaps points of agreement I have not. But I know that she stands, first, for the privacy of the poor who are allowed no privacy. She fights after all, as I do, for the private property of those who have none.

It marked a sort of sublimation of the Fleet Street spirit in my sister-in-law that, within healthy limits, she not only could do everything, but she would do anything. Her work was patchwork of the wildest and most bizarre description; and she was almost continuously in a state of hilarious irony in contemplation of its contrast. She would turn easily from a direct and demagogic, though quite tragically sincere appeal in a Sunday paper against official oppression of poor mothers to an almost cynical modern criticism of the most sophisticated modern plays. She would finish a hard controversial comment on the Marconi Case, full of facts and figures, for the *Eye-Witness*, and lightly turn to the next chapter in a shamelessly melodramatic and Victorian serial, full of innocent heroines and infamous villains, for "Fireside Romances," or "Wedding Bells." It was of her that the story was told that, having driven whole teams of plotters and counter-plotters successfully through a serious Scotch newspaper, she was pursuing one of the side-plots for a few chapters, when she received a telegram from the editor, "You have left your hero and heroine tied up in a cavern under the Thames for a week, and they are not married."

It was in connection with this last line of journalistic adventure that an incident occurred of greater public, indeed of a certain historic importance. It is not only a landmark in the history of the law, but it throws a lurid light on that curious lawlessness which, in many modern matters, seems to be the principal effect of law. My sister-in-law was contributing to a Sunday paper in serial form one of these bravely, not to say brazenly, romantic romances. In this case something brazen, in the sense of something theatrical and even pantomimic, was perfectly appropriate to the theme, for the villain on whom the tale revolved was represented as a theatrical producer on a colossal scale like that of Cochran or Reinhardt. He was represented as doing various unscrupulous things, as is the humble duty of a bad man in what is only meant to be a good story; but not otherwise of any extraordinary depravity, and even adorned with something of the magnanimity suitable to melodrama. I fear I have forgotten his name; perhaps, as the sequel will prove, it is just as well. But let us suppose, for the sake of argument or narrative, that his name in the story was Arthur Mandeville. Now it so happened that there floated about somewhere in the great dust cloud of atoms drifting round theatrical circles and occasionally or indirectly connected with theatrical or semi-theatrical enterprises, utterly unknown to anybody connected with the serial or the Sunday paper, a private individual whose name actually was Arthur Mandeville. He was not even an actor in any sense of an actor in action; he was certainly not a manager in any ordinary sense of having any theatre to manage; he was no mote in any position remotely resembling that of the man in the story than he was the Sultan or the President of the United States. But he was a man who had once, in a series of other small enterprises, paid salaries to some small company of performers and given some small show somewhere. This man brought an action for heavy damages against the paper, on the ground of a malicious and vindictive blasting of his private reputation; and he won it.

The extraordinary thing was that nobody, from first to last, pretended that there had been any attack upon this man at all. The judge, in giving his judgment in the man's favour, upon the law of the matter, repeatedly declared that it had been proved up to the hilt that the lady who wrote the story had never even heard of the gentleman whom she was supposed to have pursued with her envenomed darts. But the judge was none the less convinced that, as the law stood, the two coincidences of the name and of some shadowy and temporary point of contact with a similar profession, were enough to constitute a case of libel. A considerable section of the literary world awoke to this state of affairs in a condition of not unnatural alarm. It looked as if the trade of the novelist might well be classed among the dangerous trades, if he could not casually call the drunken sailor by the name of Jack Robinson, without some danger of being fined and sold up by all the Jack Robinsons who may happen to be sailing, or to have sailed, all the seas of the world. The ancient question of what should be done with the drunken sailor, if he invariably took a fancy to avenging himself legally upon anybody who should say "Jack Robinson," gave rise to some considerable literary and journalistic discussion at the time.

I remember, in the course of the controversy, that I suggested that we should have to fall back on some alternative to names, such as numbers, in describing the ringing repartees leading up to the duel in which the subtle and crafty 7991 died upon the sword of the too impetuous 3893; or the vows breathed by the passionate lips of 771 in the ear of 707. But another way of evading the difficulty, to which I was much more attached, was that of equipping all the characters with names so extraordinary that it was practically impossible that they could be the real names of any real people anywhere; and by way of illustration I wrote a moving love-scene between Bunchusa Blutterspangle and Splitcat Chintzibobs. Fortunately, for general journalistic convenience, my proposals were not accepted; and a much more practical proposal, invented by my sister-in-law, was carried out with complete success. She republished the whole story in book form; and before doing so went round to a number of the leading literary men of the day, especially those she knew best, and obtained their permission to use their names for all the characters in the book; retaining her own name, as a graceful acknowledgement, as the name of the original villain. Anyone curious enough to look up that curiosity of literature, will find the most famous persons figuring on every other page in the humblest or most improbable capacities; a dear old stage-door keeper of the name of Bernard Shaw, a cabman known to his comrades in the cab-shelter as Barry Pain, and many others whom I forget. Some little time afterwards, I think, this extraordinary condition of the law was altered, in a typically English manner; that is, not by anything so logical and pedantic as a new law, but simply by another judge saying that the law meant the exact opposite of what the first judge had said it meant. But this queer little affair has some relevance to more real problems that arose, when we found ourselves more seriously engaged in the same strange field of modern British legalism.

There is no Law of Libel. That is why everybody is so much afraid of it. That is why it is so tremendously and tragically and comically typical of a certain spirit that now fills all our social life and institutions; a spirit at once ingenious and evasive. Strange as it will sound, this is the English way of maintaining a Terror. The Latins, when they do it, do it by rigidity; but we actually do it by laxity. In plain words, we increase the terror of law by adding to it all the terrors of lawlessness. The machine is felt to be dangerous, not so much because it strikes by rule, as because it strikes at random. Or, at any rate, so far as any opponent looking for logical protection from it can calculate, it strikes at random. This is more true of almost all our laws than of any other laws in Christendom. But even lawyers would almost admit that it has come to be very like the truth about the law of libel. Some definitions of libel are so strict that nobody could really apply them; other parallel definitions are so loose that nobody could imagine to whom they could apply. The result is that libel, if nothing else, has become a mere weapon to crush any criticism of the powers that now rule the State.

All this must be kept in mind when we come to mote crucial and exciting events in connection with the *Eye-Witness*; I only mention this incident here to indicate the lively manner in which the lady in question conducted the endless comedy of Fleet Street. In connection with the paper above mentioned, of which my brother was first the sub-editor and then the editor, there were a hundred such anecdotes and amusing episodes. I fancy I can trace the lady's hand, as well as the editor's, in one of the most admirably absurd correspondences I have ever seen in the columns of journalism. It all began, if I remember right, with my brother writing something about the meeting between H G Wells and Booker Washington, the famous negro publicist in America, in which some doubt was thrown on how far Mr Wells understood the difficulties of Mr Washington, and by inference those of the White South in which he worked. This view was enforced and exaggerated in a letter dated from Bexley, which warned everybody of the real dangers of racial admixture and intermarriage; it was signed "White Man." This produced a fiery letter from Mr Wells, humorously headed, "The White Man of Bexley," as if the man were a sort of monster. Mr Wells said he did not know what life was like "among the pure whites of Bexley," but that elsewhere meeting people did not always mean marrying them; "The etiquette is calmer." Then, I think, a real negro intervened in the debate about his nature and destiny; and signed his letter, "Black Man." Then came a more detached query, I should guess from some Brahmin or Parsee student at some college, pointing out that the racial problem was not confined to the races of Africa; and asking what view was taken of intermarriage with the races of Asia. He signed his letter "Brown Man." Finally, there appeared a letter, of which I remember almost every word; for it was short and simple and touching in its appeal to larger and more tolerant ideals. It ran, I think, as follows:

"Sir, May I express my regret that you should continue a correspondence which causes considerable pain to many innocent persons, who, by no fault of their own, but by the iron laws of nature, inherit a complexion uncommon among their fellow-creatures and attractive only to the elite. Surely we can forget all these differences; and, whatever our race or colour, work hand in hand for the broadening of the brotherhood of humanity.

Yours faithfully,

Mauve Man with Green Spots."

This correspondence then ceased.

There were indeed other correspondences which seemed as if they would never cease. To few correspondents was given such power as that of the Mauve Man to paralyse all others with a sense that it was impossible to say or do any more. Some of these controversies are referred to in other connections in this book; some of them, like my own intermittent controversy with Mr Bernard Shaw, have been going on at intervals for the greater part of our lives. But the controversy to which my sister-in-law was most deeply and warmly committed, as being connected with the work that has since made her so deservedly famous, was the protection of the homes of the poor, especially against an interference more insulting than indifference: the great uniting indignation of our otherwise often diverse group.

She was married to my brother just before he went to the War, in a little Roman Catholic church off Fleet Street; for he was already of that communion. He was twice invalided home; he volunteered three times for the Front and the third time he met his death. In another chapter I shall deal with him more individually, and especially with that rarer sort of courage which he showed in politics, under instant threats of imprisonment and ruin. While in the trenches he wrote an excellent History of America and a bacchanalian ballade addressed to his fellow-soldiers, and having the refrain, "It was in Fleet Street that I learnt to drink." Even his Bohemian loyalty to the legend of the Street of Adventure would hardly have stretched itself to saying, "It was in Fleet Street that I learnt to think." For indeed he learnt to think in the nursery; and he was one of those who carry a sort of innocence of intellectual intensity through all things in life, whether they are Fleet Street or the Front. And my thoughts go back to poor Stephen and many noble madmen I knew, who had that quality, when I recall those lines one of our friends wrote about the Fanatic, or the man who wanted to keep his word; "That great word that every man gave God before his life began;" and who also, it will be remembered, "Had two witnesses to swear he kept it once in Berkeley Square; where hardly anything survives." For though my brother was the most good-humoured person I ever knew, and could live in good fellowship with absolutely anybody, not only the merely dirty, but the really vulgar, what was really deepest in him was a steep and even staggering obstinacy.

> He kept his word as none but he
> Could keep it; and as did not we,
> And round him while he kept his word
> Today's diseased and faithless herd,
> A moment loud, a moment strong,
> But foul for ever, rolled along.

IX

THE CASE AGAINST CORRUPTION

My brother, Cecil Edward Chesterton, was born when I was about five years old; and, after a brief pause, began to argue. He continued to argue to the end; for I am sure that he argued energetically with the soldiers among whom he died, in the last glory of the Great War. It is reported of me that when I was told that I possessed a brother, my first thought went to my own interminable taste for reciting verses, and that I said: "That's all right; now I shall always have an audience." If I did say this, I was in error. My brother was by no means disposed to be merely an audience; and frequently forced the function of an audience upon me. More frequently still, perhaps, it was a case of there being simultaneously two orators and no audience. We argued throughout our boyhood and youth until we became the pest of our whole social circle. We shouted at each other across the table, on the subject of Parnell or Puritanism or Charles the First's head, until out nearest and dearest fled at our approach, and we had a desert around us. And though it is not a matter of undiluted pleasure to recall having been so horrible a nuisance, I am rather glad in other ways that we did so early thrash out our own thoughts on almost all the subjects in the world. I am glad to think that through all those years we never stopped arguing; and we never once quarrelled.

Perhaps the principal objection to a quarrel is that it interrupts an argument. Anyhow, our argument was never interrupted until it began to reach its conclusion in the proper form; which is conviction. I do not say that at any particular moment either of us would have admitted being in error; but as a matter of fact, it was through that incessant process of disagreement that we came at last to agree. He began as a more mutinous sort of Pagan, a special enemy of the Puritan, a defender of Bohemian enjoyments, sociable but entirely secular. I began with more disposition to defend in a vague way the Victorian idealism, and even to say a word for Puritan religion, chiefly from a dim subconscious sympathy with any sort of religion. But in fact, by a process of elimination, we came more and more to think that the same sort of non-Puritan religion was the more plausible and promising; and to end eventually, but quite independently, in the same Church. I think it was a good thing that we had tested every link of logic by mutual hammering. I will even add something that sounds too like a boast; though it is meant to be a tribute. I will say that the man who had got used to arguing with Cecil Chesterton has never since had any reason to fear an argument with anybody.

The editor of the *New Statesman*, an acute critic of quite a different school from ours, said to me a little while ago: "Your brother was the very finest *debater* I have ever heard or heard of;" and such editors, of course, had known all the politicians and popular speakers. The qualities of his speaking were those of logic and lucidity combined with a sort of violent and startling courage. Indeed, he illustrated what I think is a common error on the subject of logic. The logician is too often presented as a prig; as a thin and frigid person of a pallid complexion. Both in experience and history, I have generally found that it was very full-blooded and warm-hearted people who had that gift of clear and connected thought. Charles Fox was like that; Danton was like that; and Cecil Chesterton was certainly like that. He had all that I have described as the Chesterton simplicity and steadiness in his personal relations; his affections were particularly fixed and tranquil; but in battle he had a sort of bull-necked pugnacity and intolerance. He did not seem to wish to live and leave a fallacy alive; he certainly could not leave a fallacy alone. The development of his political ideas was for a time decidedly divergent from my own. When I went to work with the Pro-Boers of the *Daily News*, and generally upheld the Liberal cause, though rather more romantically than many Liberals, he gravitated to a sort of practical Tory Democracy, which was more and more permeated by the Socialism of Sidney Webb and Bernard Shaw. He eventually became an active and effective member of the Fabian Executive. But what was much more important, he had within him a living and most menacing sort of intolerance; a hatred of the real corruptions and hypocrisies of modern politics and an extraordinary idea of telling the truth.

I have already indicated that I myself, though I believed in Liberalism, was finding it dimly difficult to believe in Liberals. It would be truer, perhaps, to say that I was finding it difficult to believe in politics; because the reality seemed almost unreal, as compared with the reputation or the report. I could give twenty instances to indicate what I mean; but they would be no more than indications, because the doubt itself was doubtful. I remember going to a great Liberal club, and walking about in a large crowded room, somewhere at the end of which a bald gentleman with a beard was reading something from a manuscript in a low voice. It was hardly unreasonable that we did not listen to him, because we could not in any case have heard; but I think a very large number of us did not even see him. We shifted and shunted about and collided with each other; I met various friends of mine and exchanged a few words; Bentley and Belloc and Hammond and the rest. We talked in an ordinary fashion; it is possible, though not certain, that one or other of us asked carelessly what was supposed to be happening in the other corner of the large hall. Then we drifted away together, talking about important things, or things which seemed to us important.

Next morning I saw across the front of my Liberal paper in gigantic headlines the phrase: "Lord Spencer Unfurls the Banner." Under this were other remarks, also in large letters, about how he had blown the trumpet for Free Trade and how the blast would ring through England and rally all the Free-Traders. It did appear, on careful examination, that the inaudible remarks which the old gentleman had read from the manuscript were concerned with economic arguments for Free Trade; and very excellent arguments too, for all I know. But the contrast between what that orator was to the people who heard him, and what he was to the thousands of newspaper-readers who did not hear him, was so huge a hiatus and disproportion that I do not think I ever quite got over it. I knew henceforward what was meant, or what might be meant, by a Scene in the House, or a Challenge from the Platform, or any of those sensational events which take place in the newspapers and nowhere else.

This sense of unreality in the party struggle, which was gradually growing upon me, grew much more swiftly on my brother and my friend Belloc; because they were by temperament of a more rapid and resolute sort. They entered into a sort of partnership for the study of the question; and the outcome of that partnership was a book which had a considerable effect; though at that time, of course, it was mostly an effect of irritation or incredulity. They collaborated in a work called *The Party System*, of which the general thesis was that there were really no Parties, though there certainly was a system. The system, according to this view, was essentially one of rotation; but of rotation revolving on a central group, which really consisted of the leading politicians on both sides; or, as they were called for convenience in the book, "The Front Benches." An unreal conflict was kept up for the benefit of the public, and to a certain extent with the innocent assistance of the rank and file; but the Leader of the House was more truly in partnership with the Leader of the Opposition than either of them were with their own followers, let alone their own constituents. This was the thesis maintained in the book; and for the moment its immediate importance in this narrative is not so much concerned with its truth or falsehood as with the personal results arising from the alliance of its two authors. For the point of view attracted sufficient attention to lead a few supporters to launch a weekly paper; of which Belloc was the editor and Cecil Chesterton the sub-editor; and to which I contributed first an occasional and eventually a weekly article.

There had never been anything like the *Eye-Witness* in England before; certainly not within the memory of the oldest men then living. Nor indeed has there ever been anything like it in England since. But its novelty and originality cannot be measured by those who can only compare it with what has happened in England since. It is a paradox palpably true that an original thing cannot at once be successful and still seem original. We can never appreciate how startling it might sound to be told that the earth was round, if we had really and invariably thought it was flat. By this time, so to speak, its roundness has become more flat than its flatness. It has become a dull platitude and only the denial of it would disturb us. So it is with political revolutions; and so it was with the considerable revolution introduced by the *Eye-Witness* in English journalism. Nobody can measure the change who was not brought up, as I was, in the ordinary newspaper-reading middle-class of the Victorian Age. We need not argue here about all that may be said for and against the idealism, or the optimism, or the sentimentalism, or the hypocrisy, or the virtue of the Victorian Age. It is enough to say that it rested solidly on some social convictions, that were not only conventions. One of them was the belief that English politics were not only free from political corruption, but almost entirely free from personal motives about money. It was a point of patriotic pride that set a limit to the fiercest movements of party anger. I can remember that old Tories like my grandfather would actually pause in the full sweep of their denunciations of the demoniac conduct of Mr Gladstone, to wave away the faintest suggestion that there could be any fiends tending the souls of our statesmen less erected, as Milton says, than the fiends of ambition or jealousy; "Heaven forbid that I should suggest that any English Prime Minister..." No; Frenchmen might have discovered the negotiable value of coins of the realm; Italians and Austrians might think it well worth while to double their income; the statesmen of Bulgaria or Bolivia might have some notion of the meaning of money; but English politicians passed their lives in an absent-minded trance, like that of Mr Skimpole; kept their eyes fixed on the fixed stars, never enquired whether politics had made them richer or poorer; and received their salaries with a start of surprise.

Well, for good or evil, that is all dead. And what killed it was primarily the journalistic explosion called the *Eye-Witness*; and especially its dealings with the Marconi Case and the question of the Sale of Peerages. In one sense indeed, as I shall suggest in a moment, the world fell far short of following up the lead of those particular leaders; and there has been nothing since recalling their pointed and personal denunciations. But the general tone has entirely altered. Everybody is familiar with jeers against politicians, jokes about political payments, journalistic allusions to the sale of honours or the Secret Party Fund; above all, nobody is now shocked by them. Perhaps it would be better if they were shocked, or in other words shamed by them. If they were ashamed of them, they might possibly make some attempt to alter them. For that is the weak side of the ultimate result of the revelations. The object of the *Eye-Witness* was to make the English public know and care about the peril of political corruption. It is now certain that the public does know. It is not so certain that the public does care. And we may well warn the more cynical and realistic generation around us not to be too confident in its superiority to the hoodwinked and humbug-ridden nineteenth century. I know that my Victorian uncles did not know how England is really governed. But I have a strong suspicion that if my Victorian uncles had known, they would have been horrified and not amused; and they would have put a stop to it somehow. Nobody is trying to put a stop to it now.

It is the fashion to divide recent history into Pre-War and Post-War conditions. I believe it is almost as essential to divide them into the Pre-Marconi and Post-Marconi days. It was during the agitations upon that affair that the ordinary English citizen lost his invincible ignorance; or, in ordinary language, his innocence. And as I happened to play a part, secondary indeed, but definite, in the quarrel about this affair, and as in any case anything that my brother did was of considerable importance to me and my affairs, it will be well to pause for a moment upon this peculiar business; which was at the time, of course, systematically misrepresented and which is still very widely misunderstood. I think it probable that centuries will pass before it is seen clearly and in its right perspective; and that then it will be seen as one of the turning-points in the whole history of England and the world.

There are various legends about it. One is, for instance, the legend that we denounced certain Cabinet Ministers because they gambled on the Stock Exchange. It is likely enough that we did make fun of a man like Mr Lloyd George, who made himself the mouthpiece of the Nonconformist Conscience and called on all the chapels to show forth the old fighting Puritan spirit, when he appeared in a transaction uncommonly like a gamble; just as we should denounce a politician who drank champagne and tried to start a campaign of Prohibition. But we should not denounce him for drinking champagne, but for prohibiting champagne. Similarly, we should not denounce a Puritan politician for gambling, so much as for talking as if nobody could ever gamble. My brother, I need not say, was not likely to be shocked at anybody indulging in a bet or a wager; though he might possibly have recommended him to do a flutter on the Derby or the Oaks rather than on the Stock Exchange. But, as a fact, the whole notion that the question was one of merely doing a flutter is a fiction. It is a fiction, which was put up by

131

the politicians at the time, as a mask for the fact. The charge against the Marconi Ministers was that they received a tip, or were "let in on the ground-floor," as the financial phrase goes, by a Government contractor whose contract was at the time being considered or accepted by the Government. In fact, on the face of it, at any rate, there were all the conditions that go to make up what is commonly called "a secret commission." Whether the acceptance of the tip did or did not affect the acceptance of the contract might be argued; but the question at issue was one of a contract and a tip, and not of an ordinary little flutter in stocks and shares. The pivotal fact of the position, of course, was that the Government contractor was the brother of one of these members of the Government. The very extraordinary monopoly which the Government then granted to the Marconi Company was in fact granted to its managing director, Mr Godfrey Isaacs, the brother of Sir Rufus Isaacs, then the Attorney General. These facts alone justified at least enquiry; and the first efforts of all the politicians were directed to preventing any enquiry at all.

Until the editor of the *Eye-Witness* forced the politicians to reveal something, the politicians had begun by protesting that there was nothing whatever to reveal. Mr Lloyd George spoke of mere rumours, by implication of baseless rumours, "passing from one foul lip to another." The particular Samuel who happened to be doing a Ministerial job at the moment got up and gratuitously asserted that none of his colleagues had ever had any financial connection with this company; alluding in a distant manner to the Marconi Company. Sir Rufus Isaacs made the same distant denial in almost the same words; in fact he drew quite a quaint picture of the far-off, the almost frigid relations between himself and Mr Godfrey Isaacs; and spoke of having once met his brother "at a family function," and heard for the first time of the success of his Government contract. Meanwhile, my brother, who had succeeded to the full editorship of the paper and renamed it the *New Witness*, continued a confessedly violent, not to say abusive attack on the Isaacses, but latterly and largely on the previous career of Mr Godfrey Isaacs as a promoter of ephemeral companies. Eventually, Mr Godfrey Isaacs prosecuted my brother for the personal libel on himself; much to my brother's delight. It is a rather remarkable fact that on the very day that my brother's reply was received, announcing that he intended to justify or prove his statement, the politicians took the first step towards telling some of the truth. The step may at first sight seem odd. It consisted of prosecuting for libel a French paper called *Le Matin*.

It seems odd; because there were some very conspicuous English papers to be prosecuted. There was the *New Witness*, roaring aloud week after week to be prosecuted. There was the *Morning Post*, which said many things nearly as strong; there was Mr Maxse, in the *National Review*, who said things quite as strong. I was myself so much amused with the inconsequence of this foreign diversion that I published some verses in the *New Witness* beginning:

> I am so swift to seize affronts
> My spirit is so high
> Whoever has insulted me
> Some foreigner must die.
> I made a claim for damage
> (For *The Times* has called me "thief")
> Against a paper in Alsace
> A paper called "Le Juif."
> And when the *Morning Post* unearthed
> Some murders I'd devised
> A Polish organ of finance
> At once apologised.
> …I know it sounds confusing
> But, as Mr Lammie said,
> The anger of a gentleman
> Is boiling in my head.

The actual method, of course, is by this time familiar enough. Some fool who has got the facts wrong is always prosecuted, instead of the serious critics who have got the facts right. And, in the case of *Le Matin*, the occasion was merely used as an opportunity for the Ministers involved to give their own version of the real facts before it was too late. To the profound astonishment and distress of many, they admitted that, in spite of the reassuring remarks in Parliament, they had in fact received a large number of shares from the American branch of the Marconi Company. Most of the loyal Liberals who followed them were rather flabbergasted; but in the ordinary Party press the matter was duly whitewashed. Of course, the ordinary Tory press would have done exactly the same with an ordinary Tory scandal, of which there were quite as many. But I should like to name and record here, *honoris causa* and for the credit of himself and the true Radical creed, the name of the late H W Massingham, the editor of *The Nation*, who alone in such a crisis spoke and acted like a man. He was as devoted to the Party of Peace, Retrenchment and Reform, as any of the others; but his devotion took the form of an instant appreciation of its moral danger. He came home from the *Matin* explanation, shaken and horror-stricken, and he printed in his paper the words, "Political corruption is the Achilles heel of Liberalism."

Attempts were made afterwards to justify all this inconsistency and contradiction, by explaining that the shares had been taken in the American branch of the enterprise and that the Parliamentary explanations had only referred to "this Company." I must confess that I should feel very much more charity towards the fiction if it were not for the explanation. I might easily forget and forgive, after all these years, if the politicians said they had lied as schoolboys lie, out of loyalty to their own class or club; and under certain conventions of Parliamentary self-defence; I might even think that this conventional fidelity was not so much merely dishonourable as a perverted form of honour. But if they say that a statement of that sort was not fiction, because the word "American" was suppressed, then (I grieve to say) I could only conclude that they did not know the meaning of truth. The test is perfectly simple. Suppose they had got up and told the whole simple truth, saying: "These Ministers have shares in American but not in English Marconis," the result would have been a shock; which they meant to avoid and did avoid. In other words, on their own theory of their own action, they meant to deceive and did deceive. That they deceived by a verbal equivocation of the double sense of "this Company" does not make it better, but worse. However, all their moral ideas were in such confusion that we need not necessarily even believe their explanation of their explanation. Their real reason may even have been better than their false excuse; and their lie may have been more loyal than they had the courage to confess.

Another legend about the Marconi Case, floating about like a cloud and obscuring its true outline, is this notion that my brother being convicted and fined the rather nominal sum of £100 was a legal answer to the attack on the Marconi Ministers. This is, as the lawyers say, a question of law as well as fact; and in both it is quite false. Mr Justice Phillimore, who was opposed to our case in a degree rather beyond the limits of the judicial, was nevertheless a very lucid and precise lawyer; and he left no doubt on this point whatever. In his summing up he said most emphatically that the jury had nothing whatever to do with the question of whether the politicians had improperly dabbled in Marconis; that their verdict was not to answer that political question one way or the other; that they were concerned solely with whether the individual Godfrey Isaacs, in his career as a company-promoter previous to the Marconi Case, had been unfairly described by the individual Cecil Chesterton. The jury were strongly instructed to find, and did find, that the description of the company-promoter was wrong. But the jury did not find, and were expressly told that they were not competent to find, that the conduct of the Marconi Ministers was right.

Whatever Godfrey Isaacs was really like, he is dead now; and I certainly am not going back to dig up the poor fellow's defunct companies. There are perhaps only two things to be added to that personal part of the story; and I think they are both worth adding. One is that it is supremely characteristic of my brother that, while he undoubtedly used all the violent vocabulary of Cobbett in attacking Godfrey Isaacs and the rest, he had not in fact the faintest grain of malice, or even irritation. He always spoke of the brothers Isaacs and their set, in private conversation, with perfect good-humour and charity; allowing for their Jewish virtues of family loyalty and the rest, and even finding excuses for the other politicians; though it is extremely typical of the real attitude of our group, which was accused of fanatical Anti-Semitism, that he was always more ready to excuse the Jews than the Gentiles. That is another of the legends about the Marconi Case; that it was an attack on Jews. As Mr Belloc said, in giving evidence, anybody less like a Jew than Mr Lloyd George it would be difficult to imagine. And there is to be added to this a curious and ironic conclusion of the matter; for many years after my brother received the Last Sacraments and died in a hospital in France, his old enemy, Godfrey Isaacs, died very shortly after having been converted to the same universal Catholic Church. No one would have rejoiced more than my brother; or with less bitterness or with more simplicity. It is the only reconciliation; and it can reconcile anybody. *Requiescant in pace.*

Finally, it may be worth noting that the last and least worthy of the legends about the Marconi Case was a notion, which I found floating about at one time, that my brother and Mr Belloc had parted company on the matter, because Mr Belloc in his evidence had referred the examiners to my brother as responsible editor of the later issues of the paper. As one who was inside all the councils, and was naturally prejudiced if anything on my brother's side, I may testify that there was never a word of truth in this supposed division or desertion. The policy of my brother, claiming to answer all questions himself, may have been wise or unwise; I myself had my doubts about its wisdom. But such as it was, it was adopted by him in consultation with Mr Belloc, as a part of their common policy; and on my suggestion, my brother afterwards inserted a note in the paper explaining this simple fact. The result was simple and significant. The Commission never dared to call him at all. For the rest, the political scandal was treated like all other political scandals. A Parliamentary Commission was appointed and reported that everything was very nice; a Minority Report was issued which reported that some things were not quite so nice; and political life (if you can call it life) went on as before. But what makes me laugh is the thought of the poor puzzled, honest and indignant Tories, who read the *Morning Post* and imagined that a Tory chivalry was storming the fortress of corrupt Radicalism, when they read the Parliamentary Debates on the subject; and especially the passage in which Arthur Balfour said that they must judge men like Lloyd George (whom they knew so well and loved so much) more leniently than they would judge a common outsider. The poor Primrose League must have been horribly mystified by the problem of this mildness on the Front Benches. They would have found the answer to the problem in a book called *The Party System.*

Soon after the affair had concluded, as such affairs always conclude in modern England, with a formal verdict and a white-washing committee, all our politics and practical life were turned upside down by the external earthquake of the Great War. There was not so complete a disconnection as some suppose; for Prussia was partly encouraged to attack by a gross exaggeration of the seriousness, I will not say of the Orangeman, but certainly of the seriousness with which the Englishman really regards the Orangeman. And that threat of civil war from Northern Ireland was very largely lashed into extravagance, as an expedient for proving that the Party System did mean something after all. For a very long time past, the Irish Question had been the only life in the English Parliament. It was alive because it was concerned with religion, or with two religions; and when the Irish Question was withdrawn, the English Parliamentary Party System visibly fell to pieces. But there were other ways in which the issue of corruption continued to affect the country in war-time; not least in the Dope Scandal and in the fact that firms did brazenly continue to trade with the enemy. But in truth, the evil connection went back further than that. As a fact, it goes back to the very beginning of the War, though few people even began to understand it until long afterwards.

If I were asked who produced or precipitated the Great War (in the instant sense that he prevented it being prevented), I should give an answer that would surprise nearly all sections of opinion, and almost certainly surprise the man himself. I should not say the Kaiser; for that simplification was only one of the series of British bogeys like Kruger before or Mussolini afterwards; though I am quite certain the evil originally arose with the power of Prussia. Still less should I say the Czar of Russia or some Slavonic fanatic who committed a crime at Sarajevo. Long after the acts and attitudes of all these people were recognised, it would have been perfectly possible to avoid the War; and nearly everybody wanted to avoid it. I should say that the fire-eater, who precipitated it when others might have prevented it, was some sort of worthy Quaker of the type of old Mr Cadbury, whom I knew and served in my youth.

And it all arose out of the existence of the Party System; or rather, in a sense, out of the non-existence of the Party System. When the public theory of a thing is different from the practical reality of that thing, there is always a convention of silence that cannot be broken; there are things that must not be said in public. The fact concealed in this case exactly illustrated the thesis of the book called *The Party System*; that there were not two real parties ruling alternately, but one real group, "the Front Benches," ruling all the time. The fact here was that the foreign policy of Asquith and Grey did not vitally differ from that which would have been pursued by Balfour and Bonar Law. All were patriots upon this point; all were, in my personal opinion, right; but anyhow, all thought that England would have to intervene if Germany threatened

France. They all thought so; and if they had all said so, and said so months before, Germany would never have challenged the power of such an alliance. My brother and many millions more would be walking about alive.

The Liberal leaders could not say so; not for fear of the Liberal Party, let alone the people; but for fear of the particular and powerful forces which supported the Liberal Party; and therefore supported the Party System. And under the conditions of our party politics, a party is supported not so much by fighting as by funds. They are called, heaven knows why, in a most extraordinary metaphor, "the sinews of war." They are provided by the sale of peerages to rich men and all sorts of ignominious methods; but there is no question of such methods here. Many such party supporters, and certainly Mr Cadbury, were in complete good faith, especially about supporting Peace. But very many of them were Quakers, simply because the Quakers happened to possess a minority of millionaires, a group much smaller but much richer than the Liberal Party as a whole. And the very constitution of modern party politics is such that a government has to placate such supporters, and profess to represent their ideals or prejudices, or whatever we happen to think them. In short, the whole thing was and is a plutocracy; but it was not specially in this case the fault of this group of plutocrats.

That increasing number of intellectuals, who are content to say that Democracy has been a failure, miss the point of the far more disastrous calamity that Plutocracy has been a success. I mean it has been the only sort of success it could be; for Plutocracy has no philosophy or morals or even meaning; it can only be a material success, that is, a base success. Plutocracy can only mean the success of plutocrats in being plutocrats. But this they enjoyed until a short time ago, when an economic judgment shook them like an earthquake. With Democracy the case is exactly the reverse. We may say, with some truth, that Democracy has failed; but we shall only mean that Democracy has failed to exist. It is nonsense to say that the complicated but centralised Capitalist States of the last hundred years have suffered from an extravagant sense of the equality of men or the simplicity of manhood. At most we might say that the civic theory has provided a sort of legal fiction, behind which a rich man could rule a civilisation where he could once rule a city; or a usurer throw his net over six nations, where he once threw it over one village. But there is no stronger proof of the fact that it emphatically is plutocracy, and most emphatically is not democracy, that has caused popular institutions to become unpopular, than this example of the pull of the Pacifists upon the Liberal Government just before the Great War. It is only necessary to ask exactly how much such extreme Pacifists counted in the Party Fund, and how much they counted in the Party.

For no electioneering agent, however active and anxious, would have got into an abnormal panic about the votes of the Quakers. He would have given them the normal attention that he would give to the *votes* of the Plymouth Brethren or the Peculiar People, who would very probably have the habit of voting Liberal. There are not enough individual Quakers to create a landslide of votes at a General Election. By the nature of modern politics, and nobody's fault in particular, the whole point and pivot of the situation was not the large proportion of men who were Quakers, but the large proportion of Quakers who were millionaires. And since this situation is bad at its best, as with Quakers who were sincere in their Pacifism, we can hardly think too badly of so bad a situation at its worst. At its worst it meant that the worst sort of traitors could and did trade with the enemy throughout the War, that the worst sort of profiteers could and did blackmail their own country for bloodsucking profits in the worst hour of her peril, that the worst sort of politicians could play any game they liked with the honour of England and the happiness of Europe, if they were backed and boomed by some vulgar monopolist millionaire; and these insolent interests nearly brought us to a crash in the supreme crisis of our history; because Parliament had come to mean only a secret government by the rich.

So ended the last considerable attempt to purge Parliament, or the ancient institution of the English. Some years before a similar attempt had been made in France, inspired by the chivalry of Déroulède, who acted much in the military and Christian spirit of Belloc and my brother. That also had failed; and Parliaments continued to prosper; that is they continued to rot. We have lived to see the last phase; when the revolt against that rot in representative institutions broke out further south, in the very gates of Rome; and it did not fail. But it has brought with it changes not wholly comforting to one who loves liberty and the ancient English conception of a Free Parliament. I am proud to have been among those who tried to save it, even if it was too late.

X

FRIENDSHIP AND FOOLERY

There are some who complain of a man for doing nothing; there are some, still more mysterious and amazing, who complain of having nothing to do. When actually presented with some beautiful blank hours or days, they will grumble at their blankness. When given the gift of loneliness, which is the gift of liberty, they will cast it away; they will destroy it deliberately with some dreadful game with cards or a little ball. I speak only for myself; I know it takes all sorts to make a world; but I cannot repress a shudder when I see them throwing away their hard-won holidays by doing something. For my own part, I never can get enough Nothing to do. I feel as if I had never had leisure to unpack a tenth part of the luggage of my life and thoughts. I need not say that there is nothing particularly misanthropic in my desire for isolation; quite the other way. In my morbid boyhood, as I have said, I was sometimes, in quite a horrible sense, solitary in society. But in my manhood, I have never felt more sociable than I do in solitude.

I have already figured here as a lunatic; and have now only to add that I have occasionally been a happy lunatic as well as an unhappy one. And as I have mentioned the joy of solitude, it will be suitably erratic to proceed at once to the joy of many jokes with many companions; and above all, it will be well to begin with the best of all my companionships. I am not going to describe my honeymoon, at some of the more comic incidents of which I have already glanced. After we were married, my wife and I lived for about a year in Kensington, the place of my childhood; but I think we both knew that it was not to be the real place of our abode. I remember that we strolled out one day, for a sort of second honeymoon, and went upon a journey into the void, a voyage deliberately objectless. I saw a passing omnibus labelled "Hanwell," and, feeling this to be an appropriate omen, we boarded it and left it somewhere at a stray station, which I entered and asked the man in the ticket-office where the next train went to. He uttered the pedantic reply: "Where do you want to go to?" And I uttered the profound and philosophical rejoinder, "Wherever the next train goes to." It seemed that it went to Slough; which may seem to be singular taste, even in a train. However, we went to Slough, and from there set out walking with even less notion of where we were going. And in that fashion we passed through the large and quiet cross-roads of a sort of village, and stayed at an inn called the White Hart. We asked the name of the place and were told that it was called Beaconsfield (I mean of course that it was called Beconsfield and not Beaconsfield), and we said to each other: "This is the sort of place where some day we will make our home."

The things that come back to me in my memory, as most worth doing and worth remembering, are all sorts of absurd interludes and escapades with my companions; full of their conversation and coloured with their characters. Belloc still awaits a Boswell. His vivacious and awakening personality has shown all the continuity of Dr Johnson's; and though he has had personal sorrow and in later years not a little solitude, he was fully entitled to say, like the man in his own song:

> For you that took the all in all, the things you left were three,
> A loud voice for singing and clear eyes to see
> And a spouting fount of life within that never yet has dried.

Bentley or Conrad Noel were characters who could have been put into any comedy; and the levities of Maurice Baring were worthy of some fantastic macaroni or *incroyable* of the eighteenth century.

Among the memories that are blown back to me, as by a wind over the Downs, is that of the winter day when Belloc dragged us through Sussex to find the source of the Arun. The company included his wife and mine; none of us had been long married, and perhaps we knew less than we do now of the diversity of human temperaments, not to say temperatures. He and I were fond of cold weather; my wife and his wife, who was a very charming Californian, were not. We did find the place where the Arun rose in the hills; and it was indeed, of all the sights I have seen, one of the most beautiful; I might almost say the most classical. For it rose in a (partly frozen) pool in a small grove of slender trees, silver with the frost, that looked somehow like the pale and delicate pillars of a temple. But I think the ladies, though both of them sensitive to scenery, looked on that cold paradise with something of a cold eye. When this began to be discovered, Belloc instantly proposed the remedy of hot rum, in large tumblers at an adjoining inn; and we were puzzled by the fact that the remedy was regarded with almost as much distaste as the disease. However, we ourselves, who did not feel the cold, heartily consumed the rum; and Belloc, who has always had a trick of repeating scraps of recently discovered verse which happened to please him, would volley out at intervals the lines of Miss Coleridge:

> We were young, we were merry, we were very very wise,
> And the doors stood open at our feast;
> When there passed us a woman with the west in her eyes
> And a man with his back to the east.

There is no doubt, so far as we were concerned, that we were young and were merry; but I have sometimes doubted since whether we were very very wise.

We then returned to Belloc's house; where he rather neutralised the effects of the restoring warmth, by continually flinging open the door and rushing out to a telescope in the garden (it was already a frosty starlight) and loudly hallooing to the ladies to come and see God making energy. His wife declined, in terms of not a little humour; to which he retorted cheerfully;

> We were young, we were merry, we were very very wise,
> And the doors stood open at our feast;
> When there passed us a woman with the west in her eyes
> And a man with his back to the east.

Needless to say, however, his hospitality terminated with a magnificent feast of wine, and all ended in a glow of gaiety; but there lingers a sort of legend of that day in winter, when some of us were so much more interested in the barometer than the telescope. The feminine aspect of the story was afterwards embodied in an echo of the everlasting refrain:

> We were cold, we were bitter, we were very nearly dead,
> And the doors stood open by desire,
> And there faced us a woman with a cold in her head
> And a man with his back to the fire.

Those are the sort of silly things that come back to me in memory; and a real life of anybody would almost entirely consist of them. But a real life of anybody is a very difficult thing to write; and as I have failed two or three times in trying to do it to other people, I am under no illusion that I can really do it to myself.

I remember another rather ridiculous private incident which had more of what is called public interest. For it involved the meeting of Belloc and a very famous and distinguished author; and I think the meeting was the most comic comedy of cross-purposes that ever happened in the world. One could write books about its significance, social, national, international and historic. It had in it all sorts of things; including the outside and the inside of England. And yet as an anecdote it would probably seem pointless, so subtle and penetrating is the point.

One summer we took a house at Rye, that wonderful inland island, crowned with a town as with a citadel, like a hill in a medieval picture. It happened that the house next to us was the old oak-panelled mansion which had attracted, one might almost say across the Atlantic, the fine aquiline eye of Henry James. For Henry James, of course, was an American who had reacted against America; and steeped his sensitive psychology in everything that seemed most antiquatedly and aristocratically English. In his search for the finest shades among the shadows of the past, one might have guessed that he would pick out that town from all towns and that house from all houses. It had been the seat of a considerable patrician family of the neighbourhood, which had long ago decayed and disappeared. It had, I believe, rows of family portraits, which Henry James treated as reverently as family ghosts. I think in a way he really regarded himself as a sort of steward or custodian of the mysteries and secrets of a great house, where ghosts might have walked with all possible propriety. The legend says (I never learned for certain if it was true) that he had actually traced that dead family-tree until he found that there was far away in some manufacturing town, one unconscious descendant of the family, who was a cheerful and commonplace commercial clerk. And it is said that Henry James would ask this youth down to his dark ancestral house, and receive him with funereal hospitality, and I am sure with comments of a quite excruciating tact and delicacy. Henry James always spoke with an air which I can only call gracefully groping; that is not so much groping in the dark in blindness as groping in the light in bewilderment, through seeing too many avenues and obstacles. I would not compare it, in the unkind phrase of Mr H G Wells, to an elephant trying to pick up a pea. But I agree that it was like something with a very sensitive and flexible proboscis, feeling its way through a forest of facts; to us often invisible facts. It is said, I say, that these thin straws of sympathy and subtlety were duly split for the benefit of the astonished commercial gentleman, while Henry James, with his bowed domelike head, drooped with unfathomable apologies and rendered a sort of silent account of his stewardship. It is also said that the commercial gentleman thought the visit a great bore and the ancestral home a hell of a place; and probably fidgeted about with a longing to go out for a B and S and the *Pink'Un*.

Whether this tale be true or not, it is certain that Henry James inhabited the house with all the gravity and loyalty of the family ghosts; not without something of the oppressive delicacy of a highly cultured family butler. He was in point of fact a very stately and courteous old gentleman; and, in some social aspects especially, rather uniquely gracious. He proved in one point that there was a truth in his cult of tact. He was serious with children. I saw a little boy gravely present him with a crushed and dirty dandelion. He bowed; but he did not smile. That restraint was a better proof of the understanding of children than the writing of *What Maisie Knew*. But in all relations of life he erred, if he erred, on the side of solemnity and slowness; and it was this, I suppose, that got at last upon the too lively nerves of Mr Wells; who used, even in those days, to make irreverent darts and dashes through the sombre house and the sacred garden and drop notes to me over the garden wall. I shall have more to say of Mr H G Wells and his notes later; here we are halted at the moment when Mr Henry James heard of our arrival in Rye and proceeded (after exactly the correct interval) to pay his call in state.

Needless to say, it was a very stately call of state; and James seemed to fill worthily the formal frock-coat of those far-off days. As no man is so dreadfully well-dressed as a well-dressed American, so no man is so terribly well-mannered as a well-mannered American. He brought his brother William with him, the famous American philosopher; and though William James was breezier than his brother when you knew him, there was something finally ceremonial about this idea of the whole family on the march. We talked about the best literature of the day; James a little tactfully, myself a little nervously. I found he was more strict than I had imagined about the rules of artistic arrangement; he deplored rather than depreciated Bernard Shaw, because plays like *Getting Married* were practically formless. He said something complimentary about something of mine; but represented himself as respectfully wondering how I wrote all I did. I suspected him of meaning why rather than how. We then proceeded to consider gravely the work of Hugh Walpole, with many delicate degrees of appreciation and doubt; when I heard from the front garden a loud bellowing noise resembling that of an impatient fog-horn. I knew, however, that it was not a fog-horn; because it was roaring out, "Gilbert! Gilbert!" and was like only one voice in the world; as rousing as that recalled in one of its former phrases, of those who

> Heard Ney shouting to the guns to unlimber
> And hold the Beresina Bridge at night.

I knew it was Belloc, probably shouting for bacon and beer; but even I had no notion of the form or guise under which he would present himself.

I had every reason to believe that he was a hundred miles away in France. And so, apparently, he had been; walking with a friend of his in the Foreign Office, a co-religionist of one of the old Catholic families; and by some miscalculation they had found themselves in the middle of their travels entirely without money. Belloc is legitimately proud of having on occasion lived, and being able to live, the life of the poor. One of the Ballades of the *Eye-Witness*, which was never published, described tramping abroad in this fashion:

> To sleep and smell the incense of the tar,
> To wake and watch Italian dawns aglow
> And underneath the branch a single star,
> Good Lord, how little wealthy people know.

In this spirit they started to get home practically without money. Their clothes collapsed and they managed to get into some workmen's slops. They had no razors and could not afford a shave. They must have saved their last penny to recross the sea; and then they started walking from Dover to Rye; where they knew their nearest friend for the moment resided. They arrived, roaring for food and drink and derisively accusing each other of having secretly washed, in violation of an implied contract between tramps. In this fashion they burst in upon the balanced tea-cup and tentative sentence of Mr Henry James.

Henry James had a name for being subtle; but I think that situation was too subtle for him. I doubt to this day whether he, of all men, did not miss the irony of the best comedy in which he ever played a part. He left America because he loved Europe, and all that was meant by England or France; the gentry, the gallantry, the traditions of lineage and locality, the life that had been lived beneath old portraits in oak-panelled rooms. And there, on the other side of the tea-table, was Europe, was the old thing that made France and England, the posterity of the English squires and the French soldiers; ragged, unshaven, shouting for beer, shameless above all shades of poverty and wealth; sprawling, indifferent, secure. And what looked across at it was still the Puritan refinement of Boston; and the space it looked across was wider than the Atlantic.

It is only fair to say that my two friends were at the moment so disreputable that even an English innkeeper was faintly at fault in his unfailing nose for gentlemen. He knew they were not tramps; but he had to rally his powers of belief to become completely convinced that they were a Member of Parliament and an official at the Foreign Office. But, though he was a simple and even stupid man, I am not sure that he did not know more about it than Henry James. The fact that one of my friends insisted on having a bottle of port decanted and carrying it through the streets of Rye, like a part of a religious procession, completely restored his confidence in the class to which such lunatics belonged. I have always been haunted by the contradictions of that comedy; and if I could ever express all that was involved in it, I should write a great book on international affairs. I do not say I should become the champion of an Anglo-American Alliance; for any fool can do that, and indeed generally does. But I should begin to suggest something which is often named and has never been even remotely approached: an Anglo-American Understanding.

In those days down at Rye, as I have said, I saw something of Mr H G Wells, and learnt to appreciate that in him which I think made him rebel against the atmosphere of Henry James; though Henry James did really appreciate that quality in Wells. Indeed, Henry James expressed it as well as it could be expressed by saying, "Whatever Wells writes is not only alive, but kicking." It seems rather unfortunate that, after this, it should have been Henry James who was kicked. But I can sympathise in some ways with H G's mutiny against the oak panelling and the ghosts. What I have always liked about Wells is his vigorous and unaffected readiness for a lark. He was one of the best men in the world with whom to start a standing joke; though perhaps he did not like it to stand too long after it was started. I remember we worked a toy theatre together with a pantomime about Sidney Webb. I also remember that it was we who invented the well-known and widespread national game of Gype. All sorts of variations and complications were invented in connection with Gype. There was Land Gype and Water Gype. I myself cut out and coloured pieces of cardboard of mysterious and significant shapes, the instruments of Table Gype; a game for the little ones. It was even duly settled what disease threatened the over-assiduous player; he tended to suffer from Gyper's Ear. My friends and I introduced allusions to the fashionable sport in our articles; Bentley successfully passed one through the *Daily News* and I through some other paper. Everything was in order and going forward; except the game itself, which has not yet been invented.

I can understand a man like Wells feeling that Henry James would show a certain frigidity towards Gype; and for the sacred memory of Gype I can excuse his reaction; but I have always thought that he reacted too swiftly to everything; possibly as a part of the swiftness of his natural genius. I have never ceased to admire and sympathise; but I think he has always been too much in a state of reaction. To use the name which would probably annoy him most, I think he is a permanent reactionary. Whenever I met him, he seemed to be coming from somewhere, rather than going anywhere. He always had been a Liberal, or had been a Fabian, or had been a friend of Henry James or Bernard Shaw. And he was so often nearly right, that his movements irritated me like the sight of somebody's hat being perpetually washed up by the sea and never touching the shore. But I think he thought that the object of opening the mind is simply opening the mind. Whereas I am incurably convinced that the object of opening the mind, as of opening the mouth, is to shut it again on something solid.

The name of Mr H G Wells has already inevitably suggested the name of Mr Bernard Shaw; and it is a mere accident of the arrangement of this book that he has not figured in it fairly prominently from the first. As I have explained on an earlier page, I myself began with an acceptance of Socialism; simply because it seemed at the time the only alternative to the dismal acceptance of Capitalism. I have also noted that my brother, who took Socialism more seriously or at least more scientifically, became a recognised influence in the Fabian Society and was at that time much more familiar with G B S than I. He was also, by the nature of the case, much more in agreement with him. My principal experience, from first to last, has been in argument with him. And it is worth remarking that I have learned to have a warmer admiration and affection out of all that argument than most people get out of agreement. Bernard Shaw, unlike some whom I have had to consider here, is seen at his best when he is antagonistic. I might say that he is seen at his best when he is wrong. I might also add that he generally is wrong. Or rather, everything is wrong about him except himself.

I began arguing with Mr Bernard Shaw in print almost as early as I began doing anything. It was about my Pro-Boer sympathies in the South African War. Those who do not understand what the Fabian political philosophy was may not realise that the leading Fabians were nearly all Imperialists. Mr and Mrs Sidney Webb were in that matter strong Imperialists; Hubert Bland was a still stronger Imperialist; my brother was as strong an Imperialist as Hubert Bland. And even Bernard Shaw, though retaining a certain liberty to chaff everybody, was quite definitely an Imperialist, as compared with myself and my friends the Pro-Boers. Since then a legend has arisen, especially among his stupidest opponents, that Mr Bernard Shaw is an impudent Irish revolutionary who has always been Anti-British. The truth is that Mr Bernard Shaw has always been a great deal too Pro-British. The play of *John Bull's Other Island* is a great deal too Pro-British. It makes the Other Island a great deal too much John Bull's. It credits the English businessman with a success in Ireland that he has never had. It suggests, indeed, that the success is almost due to the stupidity. But in fact the attempts of men like Balfour and Birrell and Wyndham and Morley to rule Ireland might be much more truly described as a brilliant failure than a stupid success. The point was not that stupid men made something out of it, but that clever men made nothing. So it was in this old and determining crisis of the war with the Dutch Republic. As compared with Belloc or myself, Bernard Shaw was definitely in favour of the South African War. At any rate, he was very definitely in favour of the South African Peace, the particular Pax Britannica that was aimed at by the South African War. It was the same, for that matter, with Mr H G Wells; then a sort of semi-detached Fabian. He went out of his way to scoff at the indignation of the Pro-Boers against the Concentration Camps. Indeed, he still maintains, while holding all wars indefensible, that this is the only sort of war to be defended. He says that great wars between great powers are absurd, but that it might be necessary, in policing the planet, to force backward peoples to open their resources to cosmopolitan commerce. In other words, he defends the only sort of war I thoroughly despise, the bullying of small states for their oil or gold; and he despises the only sort of war that I really defend, a war of civilisations and religions, to determine the moral destiny of mankind.

I say this as a compliment to the Fabians. I say it as a compliment to their consistency, as well as contradiction of their controversial views. They were and are quite right, holding their views about centralisation, to be on the side of the Big Battalions and the Big Businesses. It is the sentimental Socialists (as Mr Wells quite truly points out) who are inconsistent, in saying that a peasant has no right to a cornfield, but a peasantry has a right to an oil-field. It is they who are the more nebulous thinkers when they defend small nationalities but not small properties; more nebulous, but sometimes much nicer. There is only a thin sheet of paper between the Imperialist and the Internationalist; and the first Fabians had the lucidity to see the fact. Most of the other Socialists have preferred sheets of paper, and they have grown thinner and thinner sheets.

In the same way Mr Bernard Shaw has been highly flattered by the false charges brought against him; especially the general charge of being a sort of Irish rebel. Anyone who remembers those old times knows that he was, if anything, the very reverse. It was a part of the Fabian cult of common sense to regard Irish nationalism as a narrow sentimentalism, distracting men from the main business of socialising the resources of the whole world. But I only note this error here to emphasise the fact that my controversy with G B S, both logically and chronologically, is from the beginning. Since then I have argued with him on almost every subject in the world; and we have always been on opposite sides, without affectation or animosity. I have defended the institution of the family against his Platonist fancies about the State. I have defended the institutions of Beef and Beer against his hygienic severity of vegetarianism and total abstinence. I have defended the old Liberal notion of nationalism against the new Socialist notion of internationalism. I have defended the cause of the Allies against the perverse sympathy felt by pacifists for the militarism of the Central Empires. I have defended what I regard as the sacred limitations of Man against what he regards as the soaring illimitability of Superman. Indeed, it was in this last matter of Man and Superman that I felt the difference to become most clear and acute; and we had many discussions upon it with all sides. It was my friend Lucian

Oldershaw who announced his intention of writing an answer to *Man and Superman*, called "Shaw and Oldershaw."

For in fact all these differences come back to a religious difference; indeed I think all differences do. I did not know myself, at the beginning, what the religious difference was; still less what the religion was. But the difference is this; that the Shavians believe in evolution exactly as the old Imperialists believed in expansion. They believe in a great growing and groping thing like a tree; but I believe in the flower and the fruit; and the flower is often small. The fruit is final and in that sense finite; it has a form and therefore a limit. There has been stamped upon it an image, which is the crown and consummation of an aim; and the medieval mystics used the same metaphor and called it Fruition. And as applied to man, it means this; that man has been made more sacred than any superman or super-monkey; that his very limitations have already become holy and like a home; because of that sunken chamber in the rocks, where God became very small.

I have dwelt on this long duel that I may end with the right salute to the duellist. It is not easy to dispute violently with a man for twenty years, about sex, about sin, about sacraments, about personal points of honour, about all the most sacred or delicate essentials of existence, without sometimes being irritated or feeling that he hits unfair blows or employs discreditable ingenuities. And I can testify that I have never read a reply by Bernard Shaw that did not leave me in a better and not a worse temper or frame of mind; which did not seem to come out of inexhaustible fountains of fair-mindedness and intellectual geniality; which did not savour somehow of that native largeness which the philosopher attributed to the Magnanimous Man. It is necessary to disagree with him as much as I do, in order to admire him as much as I do; and I am proud of him as a foe even more than as a friend.

Thus it happened that, while there are few of my contemporaries I like better, we have met more in public than in private; and generally upon platforms; especially upon platforms where we were put up to fight each other, like two knock-about comedians. And indeed he has his eccentricities, rather perhaps to be called consistencies, which often hamper conventional conviviality. Even hostesses, let alone hosts, are sometimes puzzled by a gentleman who has rather more horror of tea than of wine or beer. When I have met him among my more festive friends, he has always stood up starkly for his negative ideals, sometimes to the point of defiance. Among the more joyful of the memories that I am stirring in this chapter were many of the moonstruck banquets given by Mr Maurice Baring; who in such matters might well have a chapter to himself. The trouble is that I fear the chapter would be found incredible and cast discredit on the rest of this laborious but reliable narrative. It is not for me to do justice here to the godlike joy of life that induced a gentleman to celebrate his fiftieth birthday in a Brighton hotel at midnight by dancing a Russian dance with inconceivable contortions and then plunging into the sea in evening dress. It were not wholly wise perhaps to tell the whole story of that great supper-party in a vast tent in a garden in Westminster; after which eggs were boiled in Sir Herbert Tree's hat (because it was the most chic and shining of the hats of the company); and I remember indulging in a wild fencing match with real swords against a gentleman who was, fortunately, more intoxicated than I. The whole of that great occasion was actually recorded in cold blood, of all places in the world, in a French newspaper. The reason was that a little French journalist, after making a placid and witty speech full of compliments, had then indulged for the rest of the evening in the treacherous Gallic trick of strict temperance. I remember that his article (which was highly unreliable), began with the words, " 'I denounce Shaw. He is sober.' Who said these words? These were the words of George Wells;" and continued in an equally personal vein. But it is really true, and I know that Shaw would think it merely consistent and creditable, that he himself got up and sternly protested and then stalked out of the room, as a seventeenth-century Puritan might have left a tavern full of Cavaliers.

But even the most sincere seventeenth-century Puritan was in error in supposing that Cavaliers could not be sincere, and even serious. He may often have classed with mere roysterers men of the quality of Donne or Herbert or Sir Thomas Browne. There was a great deal of wisdom as well as wit over the nuts and wine in those riots of my youth; and not only outstanding wisdom, but outstanding virtue. It is a coincidence that I have already symbolised such virtue in the surname of Herbert. Maurice Baring himself has recorded in a noble elegy the virtues of the Herbert of his own generation; the second Auberon Herbert, son of the eccentric Individualist, who afterwards inherited the title of Lord Lucas. He was assuredly the good cavalier. Every man was the better for meeting him, in however Bacchanalian an environment; courage and frankness and the love of freedom stood out of him like staring signals, though he was entirely modest and natural; and the battered party name of Liberal meant something so long as he was alive. His courage was of the queerest quality; casual and as it were, in a quiet way, crazy. He had a wooden leg or foot, having lost the use of one limb in the South African War; and I have known him climb out of the window at the top of a dizzy tower of flats and crawl somehow like a fly to the next window, without railing or balcony or any apparent foothold; and having re-entered by the next window, climb out again by the next, so weaving a sort of winding pattern round the top of the building. This story is strictly true; but there were a great many legends in that circle, the growth of which it was amusing to watch. I once smashed an ordinary tumbler at Herbert's table, and an ever-blossoming tradition sprang up that it had been a vessel of inconceivable artistic and monetary value, its price perpetually mounting into millions and its form and colour taking on

149

the glories of the Arabian Nights. From this incident (and from the joyful manner in which Baring trampled like an elephant among the fragments of the crystal) arose a catchword used by many of us in many subsequent controversies, in defence of romantic and revolutionary things; the expression: "I like the noise of breaking glass." I made it the refrain of a ballade which began:

> Prince, when I took your goblet tall
> And smashed it with inebriate care,
> I knew not how from Rome and Gaul
> You gained it; I was unaware
> It stood by Charlemagne's great chair
> And served St Peter at High Mass.
> ...I'm sorry if the thing was rare;
> I like the noise of breaking glass.

It is only just to our happy company to say that we did not confine ourselves to saying or singing out own lyrics; though Belloc was generally ready to oblige; and the loud and roaring but none the less pathetic song with the chorus:

> And the Gates of Heaven are opening wide
> To let poor Hilary in.

was first heard, I think, at one of these quiet evenings for mutual edification and culture. But we must have sung a vast number of the finest songs in the English language, by poets ancient and modern; and a legend persists that, when Herbert had rooms not far from Buckingham Palace, we sang "Drake's Drum" with such passionate patriotism that King Edward the Seventh sent in a request for the noise to stop.

I was mainly led to the mention of these idle though agreeable memories, by remarking that his quite unaffected aversion to this sort of thing marked the Puritanic element in Bernard Shaw. He is probably still regarded by many as a buffoon; as a fact he has far too little sympathy with mere buffoonery. His austerity in such things is so much a part of his personality and purity of aim, that one can hardly wish it altered; but the truth remains that the Puritan cannot understand the morality and religion of the Cavalier. In most matters I have found myself rather more in sympathy with Mr Bernard Shaw than with Mr H G Wells, the other genius of the Fabians, warmly as I admire them both. But, in this matter, Wells was more of my sort than Shaw. Wells does understand the glow and body of good spirits, even when they are animal spirits; and he understands the Saturnalia in which the senator can sometimes relax like the slave. Even here, however, there is a distinction. Shaw has plenty of appetite for adventure; but in his case it would be most welcome as open air adventure. He would not see the fun of cellars or smugglers' caves; but require a levity in some sense celestial in the literal sense of being *sub divo*. To put it shortly, Wells would understand larking; but Shaw would only understand skylarking.

I was destined to see some of his skylarking on one occasion at least; and to be privileged to play the fool with him far from the political platform, if not so very far from the theatrical stage. It began by Bernard Shaw coming down to my house in Beaconsfield, in the heartiest spirits and proposing that we should appear together, disguised as Cowboys, in a film of some sort projected by Sir James Barrie. I will not describe the purpose or character of the performance; because nobody ever discovered it; presumably with the exception of Sir James Barrie. But throughout the proceedings, even Barrie had rather the appearance of concealing his secret from himself. All I could gather was that two other well-known persons, Lord Howard de Walden and Mr William Archer, the grave Scottish critic and translator of Ibsen, had also consented to be Cowboys. "Well," I said, after a somewhat blank pause of reflection. "God forbid that anyone should say I did not see a joke, if William Archer could see it." Then, after a pause, I asked: "But what is the joke?" Shaw replied with hilarious vagueness that nobody knew what the joke was. That was the joke.

I found that the mysterious proceeding practically divided itself into two parts. Both were pleasantly conspiratorial in the manner of Mr Oppenheim or Mr Edgar Wallace. One consisted of an appointment in a sort of abandoned brickfield somewhere in the wilds of Essex; in which spot, it was alleged, our cow-punching costumes were already concealed. The other consisted of an invitation to supper at the Savoy, to "talk things over" with Barrie and Granville Barker. I kept both these melodramatic assignations; and though neither of them threw any light upon what we were supposed to be doing, they were both very amusing in their way and rather different from what might have been expected. We went down to the waste land in Essex and found our Wild West equipment. But considerable indignation was felt against William Archer; who, with true Scottish foresight, arrived there first and put on the best pair of trousers. They were indeed a magnificent pair of fur trousers; while the other three riders of the prairie had to be content with canvas trousers. A running commentary upon this piece of individualism continued throughout the afternoon; while we were being rolled in barrels, roped over faked precipices and eventually turned loose in a field to lasso wild ponies, which were so tame that they ran after us instead of our running after them, and nosed in our pockets for pieces of sugar. Whatever may be the strain on credulity, it is also a fact that we all got on to the same motor-bicycle;

the wheels of which were spun round under us to produce the illusion of hurtling like a thunderbolt down the mountain-pass. When the rest finally vanished over the cliffs, clinging to the rope, they left me behind as a necessary weight to secure it; and Granville Barker kept on calling out to me to Register Self-Sacrifice and Register Resignation, which I did with such wild and sweeping gestures as occurred to me; not, I am proud to say, without general applause. And all this time Barrie, with his little figure behind his large pipe, was standing about in an impenetrable manner; and nothing could extract from him the faintest indication of why we were being put through these ordeals. Never had the silencing effects of the Arcadia Mixture appeared to me more powerful or more unscrupulous. It was as if the smoke that rose from that pipe was a vapour not only of magic, but of black magic.

But the other half of the mystery was, if possible, more mysterious. It was all the more mysterious because it was public, not to say crowded. I went to the Savoy supper under the impression that Barrie and Barker would explain to a small party some small part of the scheme. Instead of that I found the stage of the Savoy Theatre thronged with nearly everybody in London, as the Society papers say when they mean everybody in Society. From the Prime Minister, Mr Asquith, to the yellowest and most cryptic Oriental attaché, they were all there, dining at little tables and talking about everything but the matter in hand. At least they were all there except Sir James Barrie; who on this occasion made himself almost completely invisible. Towards the end of the meal, Sir Edward Elgar casually remarked to my wife: "I suppose you know you're being filmed all this time."

From what I know of the lady, it is unlikely that she was brandishing a champagne-bottle or otherwise attracting social attention; but some of them were throwing bread about and showing marked relaxation from the cares of State. Then the Original Four, whom destiny had selected for a wild western life, were approached with private instructions, which worked out in public as follows. The stage was cleared and the company adjourned to the auditorium, where Bernard Shaw harangued them in a furious speech, with savage gesticulations denouncing Barker and Barrie and finally drawing an enormous sword. The other three of us rose at this signal, also brandishing swords, and stormed the stage, going out through the back scenery. And there We (whoever We were) disappear for ever from the record and reasonable understanding of mankind; for never from that day to this has the faintest light been thrown on the reasons of our remarkable behaviour. I have since heard in a remote and roundabout way certain vague suggestions, to the effect that there was some symbolical notion of our vanishing from real life and being captured or caught up into the film world of romance; being engaged through all the rest of the play in struggling to fight our way back to reality. Whether this was the idea I have never known for certain; I only know that I received immediately afterwards a friendly and apologetic note from Sir James Barrie, saying that the whole scheme was going to be dropped.

I do not know; but I have often wondered. And I have sometimes fancied that there was another sense, darker than my own fancy, in which the secret put in Barrie's pipe had ended in smoke. There had really been a sort of unearthly unreality in all the levity of those last hours; like something high and shrill that might crack; and it did crack. I have sometimes wondered whether it was felt that this fantasy of fashionable London would appear incongruous with something that happened some days later. For what happened then was that a certain Ultimatum went out from the Austrian Government against Serbia. I rang up Maurice Baring at a further stage of that rapidly developing business; and I can remember the tones of his voice when he said: "We've got to fight. They've all got to fight. I don't see how anybody can help it."

If the Cowboys were indeed struggling to find the road back to Reality, they found it all right.

XI

THE SHADOW OF THE SWORD

I had been living, already for a long time, in the town of Beaconsfield in the County of Bucks; the town which some Colonials imagine to have been named after Lord Beaconsfield the politician. It is rather as if they thought that England had been named after Mr England the pirate. I am almost tempted to add that I say it with an apology to pirates. I do not know for certain why Disraeli took his title from Beaconsfield, which he scarcely ever visited, rather than from Hughenden, where he lived. But I was told by old Lord Burnham, the founder of the Daily Telegraph, that (as the story ran) he had chosen the title originally intended for Burke, who did live at Beaconsfield and whose legend still clings in many ways to the place. Mr Garvin, the editor of the Observer, lives in what was once the house of Burke's agent and the oak-tree in my own garden was one of the line of trees that marked the limit of his land. I am glad that Mr Garvin fits into that political landscape much better than I do; for I admire Burke in many things while disagreeing with him in nearly everything. But Mr Garvin strikes me as being rather like Burke; in his Irish origin, in his English Conservatism, in his eloquence and gravity and something that can only be called urgency of mind. I once suggested to him that he should appear at a local festival as Burke and I as Fox; a part to which I have no claim except in circumference. But I hope there will never come a dark and difficult hour when political differences become personal, and Mr Garvin begins to throw daggers about and say that our friendship is at an end.

I have lived in Beaconsfield from the time when it was almost a village to the time when, as the enemy profanely says, it is almost a suburb. It would be truer to say that the two things in some sense still exist side by side; and the popular instinct has recognised the division by actually talking about the Old Town and the New Town. I once planned a massive and exhaustive sociological work, in several volumes, which was to be called "The Two Barbers of Beaconsfield," and based entirely upon the talk of the two excellent citizens to whom I went to get shaved. For those two shops do indeed belong to two different civilisations. The hairdresser of the New Town belongs to the new world and has the spotlessness of the specialist; the other has what may be called the ambidexterity of the peasant, shaving (so to speak) with one hand while he stuffs squirrels or sells tobacco with the other. The latter tells me from his own recollection what happened in Old Beaconsfield; the former, or his assistants, tell me from the *Daily Mail* what has not happened in a wider world. But I suggest this comparison merely as an introduction to a parallel matter of local interest; which happens to embody, better perhaps than any other emblem, all those larger matters that are more than local. If I wanted to write a book about the whole of this great passage in the history of England, including the Great War and many other changes almost as great, I should write it in the form of a History of the Beaconsfield War Memorial.

The plain primary proposal was that a cross should be set up at the cross-roads. Before the discussion was half over there had entered into it the following subjects of debate: (1) The Position of Woman in the Modern World; (2) Prohibition and the Drink Question; (3) The Excellence or Exaggeration of the Cult of Athletics; (4) The Problem of Unemployment, Especially in Relation to Ex-Service Men; (5) The Question of Support for Hospitals and the General Claims of Surgery and Medicine; (6) The Justice of the War; (7) Above all, or rather under all, for it was in many ways masked or symbolically suggested, the great war of religion which has never ceased to divide mankind, especially since that sign was set up among them. Those who debated the matter were a little group of the inhabitants of a little country town; the rector and the doctor and the bank manager and the respectable tradesmen of the place, with a few hangers-on like myself, of the more disreputable professions of journalism or the arts. But the powers that were present there in the spirit came out of all the ages and all the battlefields of history; Mahomet was there and the Iconoclasts, who came riding out of the East to ruin the statues of Italy, and Calvin and Rousseau and the Russian anarchs and all the older England that is buried under Puritanism; and Henry the Third ordering the little images for Westminster and Henry the Fifth, after Agincourt, on his knees before the shrines of Paris. If one could really write that little story of that little place, it would be the greatest of historical monographs.

The first thing to note, as typical of the modern tone, is a certain effect of toleration which actually results in timidity. Religious liberty might be supposed to mean that everybody is free to discuss religion. In practice it means that hardly anybody is allowed to mention it. There is a further qualification of some interest; that in this, as in many things, there is an immense intellectual superiority in the poor, and even in the ignorant. The cottagers of the Old Town either liked the Cross because it was Christian and said so, or else disliked the Cross because it was Popish and said so. But the leaders of the No-Popery Party were ashamed to talk No-Popery. They did not say in so many words that they thought a Crucifix a wicked thing; but they said, in any number of words, that they thought a parish pump or a public fountain or a municipal motor-bus a good thing. But the greater number of them tended to the proposal of a Club Building, especially for ex-service men; where the latter could have refreshment (that is where the Drink Question came in) or play games (that is where the Athletic Question came in) or possibly even share the Club on equal terms with their wives and women-folk (that is where the Wrongs of Women came in) and generally, in fact, enjoy all that we should desire ex-soldiers to enjoy, if there were really any chance of letting them do so. The scheme was in that sense admirable; but, as it proceeded, it became almost too admirable, in the original Latin sense of astonishing. Those who had propounded it called themselves, I need hardly say, the Practical Party. They justly condemned us of the other group as dreamers and mystical visionaries. They set to work to draw up their plans for the Club; and they were certainly plans of the most magnificent completeness. There were to be cricket-fields and football fields and swimming baths and golf courses, for all I know. The incident has a primary moral, with reference to that strange modern notion about what is practical and constructive, which seems merely to mean what is large and largely advertised. By the end of the controversy the plan of the Practical Party had swelled to the ends of the earth and taken on the dimensions of Aladdin's Palace. There was not the remotest chance of collecting subscriptions for such a scheme; at the rate it was developing it might run to millions. Meanwhile, the vision of the mere visionaries could be realised easily for a few hundred pounds.

And the second moral to the story is this; that the modern mind finds it very difficult to understand the idea of an aim or object. When I was speaking on behalf of the simple stone monument at the cross-roads, I quoted the excellent saying of Mr Bingley in *Pride and Prejudice*, when his sister asks him, just before the ball, whether it would not be much more rational if conversation at a ball took the place of dancing; and he answers: "Much more rational, but not half so like a ball." I pointed out that a parish-pump might seem to some more rational than a Cross, but it was not half so like a War Memorial. A club, or a hospital ward, or anything having its own practical purpose, policy and future, would not really be a War Memorial at all; it would not be in practice a memory of the War. If people thought it wrong to have a memory of the War, let them say so. If they did not approve of wasting money on a War Memorial, let us scrap the War Memorial and save the money. But to do something totally different which we wanted to do, on pretence of doing something else that we did not do, was unworthy of *Homo sapiens* and the dignity of that poor old anthropoid. I got some converts to my view; but I think that many still thought I was not practical; though in fact I was very specially practical, for those who understand what is really meant by a Pragma. The most practical test of the problem of unmemorial memorials was offered by the Rector of Beaconsfield, who simply got up and said: "We already have a ward in the Wycombe Hospital which was supposed to commemorate something. Can anybody here tell me what it commemorates?"

Anyhow, the Cross was the crux; and it is no pun but a plain truth to put it so. But the curious point is that few of those who found the Cross crucial would admit in so many words that it was crucial because it was the Cross. They advanced all sorts of alternative objections or made all sorts of alternative proposals. One lady wished to have a statue of a soldier, and I shuddered inwardly, knowing what such statues can be; fortunately another lady, with a nephew in the Navy, called out indignantly, "What about the sailors?" Whereupon the first lady said with hasty but hearty apology, "Oh, yes; and a sailor as well." Whereupon a third lady, with a brother in the Air Force, proposed that this also should be included in the group; and the first lady with large and generous gestures accepted all and every addition of the kind; so that this magnificent sculptural monument was soon towering into tanks and toppling with aeroplanes. It seemed a little dangerous; but it was safer than a market-cross. Other objections to the latter symbol were adduced, probably to cover the real objection; such as the monument as an obstacle to traffic. The local doctor, an admirable physician but a sceptic of rather a schoolboy sort, observed warmly, "If you do stick up a thing like this, I hope you'll stick a light on it, or all our cars will smash into it in the dark." Whereupon my wife, who was then an ardent Anglo-Catholic, observed with an appearance of dreamy rapture, "Oh, yes! How beautiful! A lamp continually burning before the Cross!" Which was not exactly what the man of science had proposed; but it could not have been more warmly seconded.

Lastly, the most significant part of this social episode was the end of it. If anyone fails to realise how lasting, or lingering, in spite of everything, are the old social forms of England and its structure as an ancient aristocratic state, he could not do better than consider the last quiet and ironic ending of the great battle of the Beaconsfield War Memorial. There was a huge paper plebiscite in which hardly anybody knew what he was voting for, but which turned up somehow with a narrow numerical majority for the building of the Club. The Club, for which the practical majority had voted, was never built.

The Cross, for which the more mystical minority had largely forgotten to vote, was built. When the whole fuss of papers and public meetings was over, and everybody was thinking about other things, the rector of the parish raised a quiet subscription of his own among his own co-religionists and sympathisers; got enough money to put up a Cross and put it up. Meanwhile Lord Burnham, the chief landlord of the neighbourhood, equally casually informed the Ex-Service Men and their sympathisers that they could use a hall, which was his property, for their Club if they liked. They appeared to be perfectly contented; and so far from demanding any other Club, seemed to have become fairly indifferent about the use of this one. So did the Great War pass over Beaconsfield, making the world safe for Democracy and the holding of any number of public meetings full of the revolutionary hopes of the Modern World; and so in the end the whole matter was decided at the private discretion of the Squire and Parson, as it was in the days of old.

There was a sequel, however, involving more serious things. A renewed shock went through the anti-clerical party on finding that the Cross was a Crucifix. This represented, to many amiable and professedly moderate Nonconformists and other Protestants, exactly that extra touch that they could not tolerate. The distinction is all the more clearly to be kept in mind because it is, on the face of it, an entirely irrational distinction. The sort of Evangelical who demands what he calls a Living Christ must surely find it difficult to reconcile with his religion an indifference to a Dying Christ; but anyhow one would think he would prefer it to a Dead Cross. To salute the Cross in that sense is literally to bow down to wood and stone; since it is only an image in stone of something that was made of wood. It is surely less idolatrous to salute the Incarnate God or His image; and the case is further complicated by the relation of the image to the other object. If a man were ready to wreck every statue of Julius Caesar, but also ready to kiss the sword that killed him, he would be liable to be misunderstood as an ardent admirer of Caesar. If a man hated to have a portrait of Charles the First, but rubbed his hands with joy at the sight of the axe that beheaded him, he would have himself to blame if he were regarded rather as a Roundhead than a Royalist. And to permit a picture of the engine of execution, while forbidding a picture of the victim, is just as strange and sinister in the case of Christ as in that of Caesar. And this illustrates something about the whole situation, which grew clearer and clearer to me about this time and initiated the next step of my life.

Of that revolution in my life I shall write more fully later. But for the moment, in the particular connection under consideration, I will say this. The fact that, after all these alarums and excursions, and as the almost inconsequent outcome of so much fuss and turmoil, a carved crucifix does now actually stand in the heart of the little town that is my home, is naturally a source of intense and somewhat ironic joy to me. But, with quite undiminished sympathy and respect for my friends and neighbours who did actually set it up, there is a certain quality in the way in which it came, and the way in which it was accepted, that is not to me entirely acceptable. I do not want the crucifix to be a compromise, or a concession to the weaker brethren, or a makeweight or a by-product. I want it to be a blazon and a boast. I want there to be no more doubt about our all glorying in it than there would have been in any body of old Crusaders pitting the Cross against the Crescent. And if anyone wants to know my feelings about a point on which I touch rarely and with reluctance: the relation of the Church I left to the Church I joined, there is the answer as compact and concrete as a stone image. I do not want to be in a religion in which I am allowed to have a crucifix. I feel the same about the much more controversial question of the honour paid to the Blessed Virgin. If people do not like that cult, they are quite right not to be Catholics. But in people who are Catholics, or call themselves Catholics, I want the idea not only liked but loved and loved ardently, and above all proudly proclaimed. I want it to be what the Protestants are perfectly right in calling it; the badge and sign of a Papist. I want to be allowed to be enthusiastic about the existence of the enthusiasm; not to have my chief enthusiasm coldly tolerated as an eccentricity of myself. And that is why, with all the good will in the world, I cannot feel the crucifix at one end of the town as a substitute for the little Roman Catholic Church at the other.

But I have here introduced the War Memorial in connection with the other matter of the War. I have purposely approached the episode of the War from the wrong end. I have spoken first of certain problems that arose when it was all over; because it happens to illustrate certain peculiarities in my own position and experience. There are certain things to be said that can hardly be said except as by one regarding the War in retrospect; the problem involved had hardly arisen when we only saw it in prospect; and yet, unless I pass on to some such summary, all that I say on this subject may be much misunderstood; especially in the atmosphere that has been spreading during the last ten or twelve years.

I have always suffered from the disadvantage, among my solid and sturdy British countrymen, of not altering my opinions quickly enough. I have generally attempted, in a modest way, to have reasons for my opinions; and I have never been able to see why the opinions should change until the reasons change. If I were really a sturdy and stolid Briton, it would, of course, be enough for me that the fashions change. For that sort of sturdy Briton does not want to be consistent with himself; he only wants to be consistent with everybody else. But having what I am pleased to suppose a sort of political philosophy, I have in many matters retained my political opinions. I thought in the first days of the Home Rule quarrel that Ireland ought to be governed by Irish ideas. And I still think so, even when my fellow Liberals have made the shocking discovery that Irish ideas are ordinary ideas. I thought that England's action in the South African War was wrong; and I still think it was wrong. I thought that England's action in the Great War was right; and I still think it was right. I did not learn my politics in the first case from the *Daily Mail*, and I do not propose to learn any others in the second case from the *Daily Express*. In the first case, I thought and think that Jewish financial power should not dominate England. In the second case, I thought and think that Prussian militarism and materialism should not dominate Europe. Until I alter my view of those two principles, I can see no reason for altering my view of the practical applications of them. Obstinacy of this sort, founded on a cold insensibility to the fluctuations of the market and to all the weight which attaches to the opinions of the two or three men who own all the newspapers, has on the face of it all sorts of disadvantages in dividing an individual from his contemporaries. But it has some advantages; and one advantage is that the man can look, without division of heart or disturbance of mind, at the War Memorial of Beaconsfield.

For the whole point at issue is really there. The Memorial was set up, like the Monument after the Great Fire, to commemorate the fact that something had been saved out of the Great War. What was saved was Beaconsfield; just as what was saved was Britain; not an ideal Beaconsfield, not a perfect or perfectly progressing Beaconsfield, not a New Beaconsfield with gates of gold and pearl descending out of heaven from God; but Beaconsfield. A certain social balance, a certain mode of life, a certain tradition of morals and manners, some parts of which I regret, some parts of which I value, was in fact menaced by the fate of falling into a complete and perhaps permanent inferiority and impotence, as compared with another tradition and mode of life. It is all nonsense to say that in such a struggle defeat would not have been destruction, merely because it probably would not have been what is legally called annexation. States so defeated become vassal-states, retaining a merely formal independence, and in every vital matter steered by the diplomacy and penetrated by the culture of the conqueror. The men whose names are written on the Beaconsfield War Memorial died to prevent Beaconsfield being so immediately overshadowed by Berlin that all its reforms would be modelled on Berlin, all its products used for the international purposes of Berlin, even if the King of Prussia were not called in so many words the Suzerain of the King of England. They died to prevent it and they did prevent it. Let those who enjoy the thought insist that they died in vain.

Conflict came to a head in Europe because the Prussian was insufferable. What would he have been like if he, who was already insufferable, had been shown to be insuperable? What would the Kaiser, with his Mailed Fist and his boasts of being Attila and the leader of the Huns, even in time of peace, have been like if he had issued completely victorious out of a universal war? Yet there is the common sense question to be asked, if we are asking whether it was worth while for men to fight and go on fighting. It is not the point to put wild and visionary questions about whether the world has been vastly improved by the War; whether Utopia or the New Jerusalem have come out of the War; to ask in that apocalyptic fashion what has come out of the War. We have come out of the War, and come out alive; England and Europe have come out of the War, with all their sins on their heads, confused, corrupted, degraded; but not dead. The only defensible war is a war of defence. And a war of defence, by its very definition and nature, is one from which a man comes back battered and bleeding and only boasting that he is not dead.

Those who now think too little of the Allied Cause are those who once thought too much of it. Those who are disappointed with the great defence of civilisation are those who expected too much of it. A rather unstable genius like Mr H G Wells is typical of the whole contradiction. He began by calling the Allied effort, The War That Will End War. He has ended by saying, through his rather equivocal mask of Mr Clissold, that it was no better than a forest fire and that it settled nothing. It is hard to say which of the two statements is the more absurd. It settled exactly what it set out to settle. But that was something rather more rational and modest than what Mr Wells had settled that it was to settle. To tell a soldier defending his country that it is The War That Will End War is exactly like telling a workman, naturally rather reluctant to do his day's work, that it is The Work That Will End Work. We never promised to put a final end to all war or all work or all worry. We only said that we were bound to endure something very bad because the alternative was something worse. In short, we said what every man on the defensive has to say. Mr Brown is attacked by a burglar and manages to save his life and property. It is absurd to turn round on him and say: "After all, what has come out of the battle in the back-garden? It is the same old Septimus Brown, with the same face, the same trousers, the same temper a little uncertain at breakfast, the same taste for telling the anecdote about the bookmaker at Brighton." It is absurd to complain that Mr Brown has not been turned into a Greek god merely by being bashed on the head by a burglar. He had a right to defend himself; he had a right to save himself; and what he saved was himself, so far no better and no worse. If he had gone out to purify the world by shooting all possible burglars, it would not have been a defensive war. And it would not have been a defensible one.

That is what I mean by saying that for me the War Memorial of Beaconsfield commemorates the rescue of Beaconsfield; not of an ideal Beaconsfield, but of the real Beaconsfield. There are all sorts of things in such an English country town with which I do not agree; there are many which I have tried all my life to alter. I do not like the English landed system, with its absence of peasants and its predominance of squires; I do not like the formless religious compromise of Puritanism turning into Paganism; but I do not want it discredited and flattened out by Prussianism. The defence of its prestige and independence against an inhuman and heathen hegemony was just. But I am far from certain that a War to End War would have been just. I am far from certain that, even if anybody could prevent all protest or defiance under arms, offered by anybody anywhere under any provocation, it would not be an exceedingly wicked thing to do.

This interlude on the intellectual aspects of the War is necessary; because all I say about the passing details of the War period will be unmeaning, if it is assumed that I sympathise with the rather weak-minded reaction that is going on around us. At the first outbreak of the War I attended the conference of all the English men of letters, called together to compose a reply to the manifesto of the German professors. I at least, among all those writers, can say, "What I have written I have written." I wrote several pamphlets against Prussia, which many would consider violent, though in that moment everyone supported their violence. I am still perfectly prepared to support their truth. I hardly know of a word I would alter. I did not take my views from the fever of that fashion; nor with that fever have they passed away.

Immediately after the outbreak of War I was bowled over by a very bad illness, which lasted for many months and at one time came very near to ending so as to cut me off from all newspaper communications and this wicked world. The last thing I did while I was still on my feet, though already very ill, was to go to Oxford and speak to a huge packed mass of undergraduates in defence of the English Declaration of War. That night is a nightmare to me; and I remember nothing except that I spoke on the right side. Then I went home and went to bed, tried to write a reply to Bernard Shaw of which about one paragraph may still exist, and was soon incapable of writing anything. The illness left certain results that prevented me, even when I had recovered, from doing anything more useful than writing. But I set to work to contribute as much as I could both to the general Press and the Government Propaganda; of which there were several departments. And I may remark here that the conduct of the War, whether at home or abroad, was an excellent education for any writer, tending too much to theories, in that complex but concrete matter of the material of mankind; the mystery and inconsistency of man. Man seems to be capable of great virtues but not of small virtues; capable of defying his torturer but not of keeping his temper. And I must admit that I was astounded, when writing propagandist literature at the request of various Government Departments, at the small and spinsterish vanities and jealousies that seemed to divide those Departments; and the way in which they kept up their fussy formalities in the full glare of the Day of Judgment. The facts were really very much as they were so cleverly described by Mr Arnold Bennett in his story of *Lord Raingo*. I could understand a man being a coward and running away from a German; I can understand, and I hope humbly might emulate, a man fighting and standing firm. But that any Englishman should behave as if it were not a fight between an Englishman and a German, but a fight between a Foreign Office clerk and a War Office clerk, is something that altogether escapes my imagination. I daresay every one of those Government officials would have died for England without any fuss at all. But he could not have it suggested that some twopenny leaflet should pass through another little cell in the huge hive of Whitehall, without making a most frightful fuss. I had imagined that I was, for the moment, of one body with Englishmen from whom I differed in the deepest vitals of the soul; one in that hour of death with atheists and pessimists and Manichean Puritans and even with Orangemen from Belfast. But the forms of the Circumlocution Office could still divide men whom neither God nor devil could put asunder. It was a small thing; but it was a part of that realisation of the real riddle of man, which is hidden from boys and comes only to men in their maturity; and which took on more and more the nature of a religious enlightenment; upon the true doctrine of Original Sin and of Human Dignity. It was part of that belated process of growing up, which must unfortunately precede the splendid attainment of second childhood.

When I first recovered full consciousness, in the final turn of my long sickness, I am told that I asked for Land and Water, in which Mr Belloc had already begun his well-known series of war articles, the last of which I had read, or been able to understand, being the news of the new hope from the Marne. When I woke again to real things, the long battles before Ypres were over and the long trench war had begun. The nurse, knowing that I had long been incapable of really reading anything, gave me a copy of the paper at random, as one gives a doll to a sick child. But I suddenly asserted in a loud and clear voice that this was an old number dealing with the first attempt before Nancy; and that I wanted all the numbers of the paper that had appeared since the Battle of the Marne. My mind, such as it is, had suddenly become perfectly clear; as clear as it is now. That also was something of a lesson in the paradox of real things, so different from many modern and merely theatrical things. Since then I have known that everything is not a slow and graduated curve of evolution; but that there is in life and death an element of catastrophe that carries something of the fear of miracle.

At my clear and reiterated request, they brought me the whole huge file of the weekly paper; and I read it steadily through, understanding all the facts and figures and diagrams and calculations, and studying them so closely that I really felt at the end that I had not lost so very much of the general history of the War. I found that the pamphlets I had written were already in circulation, especially abroad; all the more successfully because in a sense secretly. My old friend Masterman, in charge of one Propaganda Department, told me with great pride that his enemies were complaining that no British propaganda was being pushed in Spain or Sweden. At this he crowed aloud with glee; for it meant that propaganda like mine was being absorbed without people even knowing it was propaganda. And I myself saw my very bellicose essay called *The Barbarism of Berlin* appearing as a quiet Spanish philosophical study called "The concept of Barbarism." The fools who baited Masterman would have published it with a Union Jack cover and a picture of the British Lion, so that hardly one Spaniard would read it, and no Spaniard would believe it. It was in matters of that sort that the rather subtle individuality of Masterman was so superior to his political surroundings. In many respects, as I have hinted, he suffered himself to sink too deeply into those surroundings. He allowed himself to be used as a Party hack by Party leaders who were in every way his inferiors. But all that dark humour that was deepest in him came out again, as he grinned over this attack on his success as an intellectual smuggler.

But I am rather proud of the fact that if I wrote a little book called *The Barbarism of Berlin*, I also wrote during the War a rather larger book called *The Crimes of England*. For I was vividly convinced of the folly of England merely playing the Pharisee in this moment of intense moral reality. I therefore wrote a book actually making a list of the real sins of the British Empire in modern history; and then pointing out that in every one of them, not only was the German Empire far worse, but the worst tendencies of Britain had actually been borrowed from Germany. It was a Pro-German policy, the support of the Protestant hero in Prussia or the Protestant princes of Hanover, that had involved us in our mortal quarrel with Ireland and in many worse things. All our recent Imperialism had been praise of Prussia, as an example and an excuse. Nevertheless, to write of the Crimes of England, under that naked title, was at that time liable to misunderstanding; and I believe that in some places the book was banned like a pacifist pamphlet. It was not very pacifist. But all this was to happen later. When I first recovered, I read up, as I have said, the facts of the War. And then, like one resuming the normal routine of his life, I started again to answer Mr Bernard Shaw.

There is some foundation for the anecdote told in Colonel Repington's memoirs; that Mr Belloc and I went on talking through an air-raid and did not know it had begun. I am not sure at what stage we did eventually realise it; but I am quite sure we went on talking. I cannot quite see what else there was to do. But I remember the occasion very well; partly because it was the first air-raid that I had experienced, though I was going to and fro in London all through that period; and secondly because there were other circumstances, which Colonel Repington does not mention, which accentuated the ironic side of the abstractions of conversation and the actuality of bombs. It was at the house of Lady Juliet Duff; and among the guests was Major Maurice

Baring, who had brought with him a Russian in uniform; who talked in such a way as to defy even the interruptions of Belloc, let alone of mere bombs. He talked French in a flowing monologue that suavely swept us all before it; and the things he said had a certain quality characteristic of his nation; a quality which many have tried to define, but which may best be simplified by saying that his nation appears to possess every human talent except common sense. He was an aristocrat, a landed proprietor, an officer in one of the crack regiments of the Czar, a man altogether of the old régime. But there was something about him that is the making of every Bolshevist; something I have felt in every Russian I ever met. I can only say that when he walked out of the door, one felt he might just as well have walked out of the window. He was not a Communist; but he was a Utopian; and his Utopia was far, far madder than any Communism. His practical proposal was that poets alone should be allowed to rule the world. He was himself, as he gravely explained, a poet. But he was so courteous and complimentary as to select me, as being also a poet, to be the absolute and autocratic governor of England. D'Annunzio was similarly enthroned to govern Italy. Anatole France was enthroned to govern France. I pointed out, in such French as could be interposed into such a mild torrent, that government required an *idée generale* and that the ideas of France and D'Annunzio were flatly opposed, rather to the disadvantage of any patriotic Frenchman. But he waved all such doubts away; he was sure that as long as the politicians were poets, or at any rate authors, they could never make any mistakes or fail to understand each other. Kings and magnates and mobs might collide in blind conflict; but literary men could never quarrel. It was somewhere about this stage in the new social structure that I began to be conscious of noises without (as they say in the stage directions) and then of the thrilling reverberations and the thunder of the war in heaven. Prussia, the Prince of the Air, was raining fire on the great city of our fathers; and, whatever may be said against Prussia, she is not governed by poets. We went on talking, of course, with no alteration in the arrangements, except that the lady of the house brought down her baby from an upper floor; and still the great plan unfolded itself for the poetic government of the world. Nobody in such circumstances is entirely without passing thoughts of the possible end; and much has been written about ideal or ironic circumstances in which that end might come. But I could imagine few more singular circumstances, in which to find myself at the point of death, than sitting in a big house in Mayfair and listening to a mad Russian, offering me the Crown of England.

When he had gone, Belloc and I walked across the Park with the last rumblings still echoing in the sky, and heard the All Clear signal as we came out by Buckingham Gate, like the noise of the trumpets of triumph. And we talked a little of the prospects of the War, which were then in the transition stage between the last peril and the last deliverance; and we parted, not without a certain belated emotion of excitement; and I went along Kensington High Road to my mother's home.

Among the legends, not to say the lies, that became current about Belloc among people who knew nothing about him, was the legend that he was what was called an Optimist about the war; or that he exaggerated the German casualties in order to make out a case for mere comfort and reassurance. To anybody who knows Belloc this idea is grotesque in the last degree. To begin with, being an animal endowed with the power of thought, he is quite incapable of supposing it to matter whether you are an Optimist or a Pessimist upon a question of fact; or of recommending anybody to be bright and cheerful so that it will not rain tomorrow. Second, in so far as mood and emotion have their legitimate place in life, his mood and emotion are generally not optimistic enough. And third, those persons who have taken the trouble to go into the actual facts and figures about enemy mortality have agreed that his calculations were substantially correct and those of the other party wildly incorrect. The truth is that, at the very beginning of a novel type of trench warfare, everybody's calculations were for a time incorrect; but his were corrected as early as anybody's and were afterwards continually right while the opposite ones were continually wrong. For the rest, what threw out every scientific estimate of the war was a factor that was moral and not scientific; a standing instance of the change of all material things on the pivot of the human will. It was the revolt in Russia. Nobody worth speaking of predicted it; but Belloc himself said the wisest thing in a general fashion about affairs of the kind. In one of his articles in *Land and Water*, he must have rather puzzled many of his readers, I fear, by an elaborate historical reconstruction of the outlook on the future, in the mind of a Greek official in Byzantium, at the beginning of the sixth century, calculating and combining all the forces of the Roman Empire and the Catholic Church. He noted how such a man might think he had accounted for all the possibilities, the danger of a religious split between East and West, the danger of the barbarian raids on Gaul or Britain, the situation in Africa and Spain, and so on; and then say he had in his hand all the materials of change. "At that moment, far away in a little village of Arabia, Mahomet was eighteen years old."

I need not dwell further on that old and idle quarrel; if the men who ranted about Optimism are remembered at all in serious history, they will be remembered because they quarrelled with Belloc. They were the half-educated proprietors of the Yellow Press of that time, who were annoyed with him for certain relevant remarks he had made about the Sale of Peerages. But it is worth pausing upon for a moment in order to emphasise what was certainly true of all my friends, and I think of all the worthier friends of England; that we never based our convictions on small-minded swagger about Success; that we worked for victory while being entirely ready for defeat; and we never predicted anything about the end of the war, or any other future event; Belloc least of all; as when I heard him say in the first of his London lectures: "It is no part of any speaker or writer to talk about victories being made certain beforehand by this or that. God alone gives victory."

There is another aspect of the way in which the Yellow Press spread panic and political mutiny and called them patriotism and journalistic enterprise. It was apparently supposed that England was in need of being prodded on from behind. My friend Bentley, doing excellent work on the *Daily Telegraph*, described it more truly as England being stabbed in the back. The *Daily Telegraph*, indeed, during those days of fever, did an admirable work of medicinal and moral sanitation. But for me and my little group the quarrel had another effect; that we were, in very varying proportions, fighting upon two fronts; regarding the Hohenzollerns and the Harmsworths as equally successful advertisers and equally unsuccessful statesmen. And it fell to me to give a full expression to this double attitude, for a reason that I could never in common conditions have foreseen.

I became an editor. It would at any time have seemed to me about as probable or promising as that I should become a publisher or a banker or a leader-writer on *The Times*. But the necessity arose out of the continued existence of our little paper, the *New Witness*, which was passionately patriotic and Pro-Ally but as emphatically opposed to the Jingoism of the *Daily Mail*. There were not too many people who could be trusted to maintain these two distinct indignations, without combining them by the disgusting expedient of being moderate. There were not too many of such people; but I was in a manner one of them. And when my brother went to the Front, he left his paper in my hands, requesting me to edit it until he returned. But I went on editing it; because he did not return.

For my brother was destined to prove, in a dark hour of doom, that he alone of all the men of our time possessed the two kinds of courage that have nourished the nation; the courage of the forum and of the field. In the second case he suffered with thousands of men equally brave; in the first he suffered alone. For it is another example of the human irony that it seems easier to die in battle than to tell the truth in politics. Human nature is in any case a strange affair; and, on the news of my brother's death, I as editor of his paper was moved to an odd reaction which I cannot altogether explain, but which I could only express by writing an open letter to Rufus Isaacs, Lord Reading, upon the memories of our great Marconi quarrel. I tried to tell him, with all restraint, that I believed he had really acted against my nation, but in favour of his own blood; and that he who had talked, and doubtless despised even in talking, the tedious Parliamentary foolery about having once met his brother at a family function, had in truth acted throughout from those deep domestic loyalties that were my own tragedy in that hour. But I added, "You are far more unhappy; for your brother is still alive."

It is strange, as I have said, that in a little while his brother was also dead and in the same religious confession as that of my own brother. So ended, symbolically enough, the great Marconi duel; and I continued the editing of my brother's paper, if you can call it editing, and all the other financiers and politicians showed no signs of dying in any faith, or indeed of dying at all. The war worked to its end, in which so many lives were ended; the Germans made their last vast and vain assaults and Foch struck his final blow before Châlons, where Christendom had broken the Huns a thousand years before. But in England the politicians continued to beam benevolently upon us; new noblemen continued to spring into life from somewhat obscure commercial soils; there were any number of flourishing economic ventures, supported by forceful publicity and magnetic personality; and all the powers of the scientific mergers and newspaper combines, that now rule the State, rose slowly into their present power and peace. As the Ancient Mariner remarked, in a moment of melancholy comparison:

> The many men so beautiful
> And they all dead did lie;
> And a thousand thousand slimy things
> Lived on; and so did I.

XII

SOME POLITICAL CELEBRITIES

On almost every occasion when I have met somebody, I have met somebody else. That is, I have met a private man who was oddly different from the public man. Even when the character was not the very contrary of the caricature, as outlined in the newspapers, I might employ a licence of language, by saying that it was even more contrary than a contrary. I mean that the relation was more subtle, and the reality on another plane; that when, after long experience, I discovered with some amazement that a tribute was true, even then the truth was almost the opposite of the tribute. We all rejoiced, for instance, in the chorus of spontaneous tributes to the late King George the Fifth. And yet the very repetition of testimony about the honesty of his public service, gave an indescribable impression of routine which made the impression incomplete. I only met him once myself, at the house of the late Lord Burnham, where he was shooting; and for what my impression is worth, he certainly did strike me as about as genuine a person as I ever met. But he was genuine in a rather unexpected way. He was not only honest but frank, and so free and easy in his likes and dislikes that he might have been called indiscreet. G B S said truly of his public talks that they were indeed the King's English; the private were also decidedly Plain English. He was anything but the supreme Permanent Official many eulogies implied; he was not like some reliable solicitor in whom family secrets are locked up, or some doctor congested with the silence of professional confidences; he was much more like a little sea-captain, who keeps a certain silence and etiquette on his quarter-deck; but plenty of anecdotes, not to say anathemas, in his cabin. But there is no substitute for meeting a man, even meeting him for an hour or two; it will always tell us when a real distortion of history or legend is

171

beginning. And if it should ever happen that I hear before I die, among new generations who never saw George the Fifth, that he is being either praised as a strong silent man, or depreciated as a stupid and empty man, I shall know that history has got the whole portrait wrong.

Sometimes I have had even briefer contacts, with even more curious surprises. I talked to the late Marquess Curzon for only about ten minutes, in an accidental crush, though I had been to his house once or twice; he did not seem to mind the crush; he did not even seem to mind the conversation, or to mind me; he was entirely pleasant and good-tempered. And he said the one thing out of a thousand that hardly anybody, including myself, would have expected Curzon to say. He said how heartily he agreed with me that the cries, catcalls, jokes and jeers of the mob at a public-meeting were very much wittier and more worth hearing than the speeches of statesmen from the platform. I had expressed this view in an *Illustrated London News* article; but he, who was so often the stateliest of statesmen on the most privileged of platforms, would not have occurred to me as the most ardent supporter of the rabble or the buffoon who championed it. Yet it is unquestionably true that he did on many occasions say and do things that provoked and even created the popular legend of his unpopular attitude. He was the one and only example of an English aristocrat who presented himself as a Prussian aristocrat; and this is very odd, because English aristocrats may often be cynics but are not barbarians. In a word, they are mote subtle; but I sometimes fancy that Curzon in some queer way was more subtle than that subtlety. Everyone knows that there was a sort of heroic artificiality about his bodily life; that he sustained his very posture with difficulty; and I suspect that something of that strain turned itself to a sort of stiff and swaggering joke. He came from Oxford when it was the fashion to be a pessimist in philosophy and a reactionary in politics; and rather as the artistic decadents made themselves out worse than they were, he made himself out more undemocratic than he was. It is typical that many of the tales against him are said to have been invented by himself. But in all that I am merely guessing, from a few words said to me by a man who could not have been as stupid as a Prussian; in other cases, in which I had limited but still longer intercourse, I have noticed the same contradiction.

My first illumination, about the contrast between a human being and his political portrait or caricature, came to me with the case of Lord Hugh Cecil. I believe I met him first at the house of Wilfrid Ward, whom I ought to have mentioned long before as an influence enlightening me in many ways; for he had written in the *Dublin Review* a most sympathetic critique of *Orthodoxy*, at a time when many of his world must have thought it a piece of rowdy paradox. He laid down the excellent critical test; that the critics could not understand what he liked, but he could understand what they disliked. "Truth can understand error; but error cannot understand Truth." It was through his kindness that I was, at a later stage, made a member of the Synthetic Society, which was justly proud of its continuity with the Society in which the great Huxley could debate with the equally great Ward (called, God knows why, Ideal Ward), and in which I was privileged to meet several very pivotal persons, such as Baron von Hugel and my old friend Father Waggett of Palestinian days. But if it be asked why I mention it here, the answer is rather curious. For some reason, there were very few literary men in this group devoted to philosophy; except Wilfrid Ward himself, who was an excellent editor and expositor. But there were all the better sort of politicians, or those who might have been statesmen. There I met old Haldane, yawning with all his Hegelian abysses; who appeared to me as I must have appeared to a neighbour in a local debating-club, when he dismissed metaphysical depths and pointed at me, saying, "There is that Leviathan whom Thou hast made to take his sport therein." But I never forgot that England betrayed him in charging him with betraying England, There also I met Balfour, obviously preferring any philosophers with any philosophies to his loyal followers of the Tory Party. Perhaps religion is not the opium of the people, but philosophy is the opium of the politicians. All of which brings me back to Lord Hugh Cecil.

In Liberal caricatures, and in all the letterpress of Liberalism generally, Lord Hugh Cecil was always depicted as a medieval ascetic; it was all very restrained and refined, or he might have been actually denounced as a saint. "F C G" always depicted him in a long cassock and a very Italian-looking biretta; and something like a Gothic stained-glass window was introduced if possible, as the sort of thing he carried about with him. I absorbed all these things in my simplicity; I could not even then feel so much horror of them as did the clientele of the *Daily News*; but that made it all the easier to believe that an obviously intellectual gentleman was really in love with medieval architecture and authority. And then I happened to meet Lord Hugh Cecil at the house of Wilfrid Ward, that great clearing-house of philosophies and theologies; for the vast and valuable work of Wilfrid Ward largely turned upon the very fact that he was more fully in sympathy with the Cecils and the Balfours and the rest than I myself could ever have been. I listened to Lord Hugh's very lucid statements of his position; nobody who loves logic could be unimpressed by so logical a mind; and I formed a number of very definite impressions about him. One was that he had many quite individual ideas of his own; another that he regarded all such ideas, including his own, in what has been called a dry light. But the strongest impression I received, was that he was a Protestant. I was myself still a thousand miles from being a Catholic; but I think it was the perfect and solid Protestantism of Lord Hugh that fully revealed to me that I was no longer a Protestant. He was, and probably still is, the one real Protestant; for his religion is intensely real. From time to time, he startles the world he lives in by a stark and upstanding defence of the common Christian theology and ethics, in which all Protestants once believed. For the Protestant world in England today is a very curious and subtle thing, which it would not become me to criticise; but this may be said of it without offence that, while it is naturally a little disturbed by a Protestant accepting Catholicism, it is far more terribly disturbed by any Protestant who still preserves Protestantism. And then I thought of the dear old Radical caricatures of the medievalist in the cassock; and laughter came as a relief. Old Kensit was a Jesuit compared with Hugh Cecil; for anti-ritualism is only a riotous form of ritualism; and poor old Kensit actually had the simplicity to be photographed with a crucifix in his hand. I once thought it queer that a Cecil should become famous for a revolt against the Reformation. And I have lived to see such men accused by blatant Jingoism of protecting Germany, as once by blatant Radicalism of favouring Rome. But I have lived to realise that Hugh Cecil has been as heroically loyal to his house as to his country. No man has been truer to a tradition than he to the tradition of that great Protestant England, which the genius of the founder of his family established.

It was George Wyndham who once confirmed this notion of mine, by noting what he called the extreme Individualism of Lord Hugh Cecil. The commercial character of that compact and patriotic England of recent centuries had much to do, for instance, with Lord Hugh Cecil being so stubborn a Free-Trader. For he is not only an Old Protestant; this chivalric Tory is also most emphatically an Old Radical. He would have been much more at home in the Manchester School than in the Middle Ages. And I have here dwelt so long on his name, with no other basis than having listened to his luminous conversation, because I do seriously think he stands at the very centre of that recent civilisation today; and might be called the one strong pillar still upholding the England in which I was born. But George Wyndham's ideas were always flowing in a different direction, as were my own; and they were in a sense marked or measured by our common feeling about this other Conservative statesman. For Wyndham was not a Conservative; he was a Tory; that is, he was capable of being a Jacobite, which is something as rebellious as a Jacobin. He did not merely wish to preserve Protestantism or Free Trade, or anything grown native to the nation; he wanted to revive things older and really more international. And my first impressions of the falsity of the Party System came to me, while I was still a Liberal journalist, in the realisation of how much I agreed with Wyndham and how much Wyndham disagreed with Cecil.

I first met George Wyndham at Taplow, at the house of Lord and Lady Desborough, who had long been very good friends to me as to many literary people of all colours and opinions; and I felt almost immediately that Wyndham's opinions were at least of the same general colour as my own. And if ever there was a man of whom the word "colour" in his opinions and everything else, recurs naturally to the mind, it was he. He also suffered, of course, from the silly simplifications of the political comments and cartoons. Because he happened to have been in the Army, he was always depicted as a drawling guardsman; and because he happened to be a handsome man, it was always insinuated that he was merely a ladies' man. In most essential ways it was curiously untrue. Wyndham was very definitely what is called a man's man. He was passionately fond of the particular things that ladies do not generally like; such as sitting up all night to pursue pertinaciously the same interminable argument, upon all sorts of points of detail and pure logic; so that he would not let his guests go till almost daybreak, unless he had settled to his own satisfaction the meaning of "T T" in Shakespeare's Sonnets; or what were the private expectations of Chaucer touching the publication of *Troilus and Cressida*. He was not in any sense a dandy; but in so far as he did dress well, he was totally indifferent to how other men who were his friends might dress, which is another mark of purely masculine companionship. He was a good companion in sporting society as in literary society but in neither was he anything like what is called a society man. He had huge sympathy with gypsies and tramps; and collected many men of letters (including myself) who looked rather like tramps. The inward generosity which gave a gusto or relish to all he did was really at the opposite extreme to all that mere polish, implied by those who slandered him by calling him "charming." He had first written to me some congratulations upon a letter I had sent to the *Westminster Gazette* on Religious Education; in which, even at that early date, I suggested that many Anglicans felt that Christ is not entirely disconnected from His own Mother. Wyndham was supported in this by the deep natural mysticism of his wife; a woman not to be forgotten by anyone who ever knew her, and still less to be merely praised by anyone who adequately appreciated her. She always showed a most moving curiosity about where I picked up this passion for what is called Mariolatry in this Protestant land; and I could assure her with truth, though without any complete explanation, that I had had it in some form from boyhood.

It was at Taplow, at the same time as my first meeting with Wyndham, that I also had my first meeting with the late Earl Balfour; but, though I talked to him fairly often on abstract things, I never came to know him thus personally and certainly never to understand him so well. I do not think he was a very easy person to understand. He was, of course, quite an easy person to misunderstand; having all those external features, whether of elegance or eccentricity, which go to make up a public character; that is, a political cartoon. But in his case the caricatures were even more wildly wide of the mark; and I think that the compliments were worse than the caricatures. His foes in the Press depicted him as Miss Arthur; and his friends in the Press referred to him gracefully as Prince Arthur; and I do not know which of the two was more misleading. There certainly was nothing feminine about him, in the unchivalrous sense in which that word is used for what is silly or weak or wavering; very much the other way. It is typical of these times that he was always criticised as a cloudy and confusing speaker, when he was in fact a remarkably clear speaker; and anybody could follow him who could follow an argument. Only to the Modern Mind it would seem that lucidity is more bewildering than mystification. As for the contemporary pictures of a drooping lily, they might as well have represented his uncle Lord Salisbury as a little broken snowdrop. But there was really something odd about Arthur Balfour. He was always most pleasant and amiable to me; but he had not the general reputation of being pleasant and amiable to everybody. For him alone might have been invented the true definition: "A gentleman is one who is never rude except intentionally." But though he was perhaps an aristocrat to excess, he was not in the least like an ordinary excessive aristocrat. I have met many men of his rank; some arrogant gentlemen; and a few really offensive gentlemen. But they had the simplicity of vanity and ignorance; and the case of Balfour was not simple, as he was not the ordinary bad extreme, nor was he the ordinary good extreme; the good squire or even the good knight. Describing Arthur Balfour as Prince Arthur was far less true than describing George Wyndham as St George. Wyndham really had that romantic or chivalric touch; in Balfour there was something else that I never understood. I have sometimes thought it was national rather than social. Charles II is often quoted as saying that Presbyterianism is no religion for a gentleman; it is less often quoted that he also said Anglicanism was no religion for a Christian. But it is odd that his brief and distorted memory of the Scots made him say that Presbyterianism is no religion for a gentleman, touching the one country where gentlemen were often Presbyterians. Scotland has been much modified by this Puritan creed long ruling among the nobles, like old Argyll of my boyhood's time. And Balfour had something in his blood which I think was the cold ferocity of Calvinism; a bleak streak sometimes felt when the wind changes even in the breezy voyages of Stevenson. The comparison will show that this is without prejudice; for I had from childhood a romantic feeling about Scotland, even that cold, flat, eastern coast. It may not be believed, but I have played golf as a lad on the links a bowshot from Whittinghame, in the days when ordinary English people asked, "What is golf?" It came with a rush over the Border, like the blue bonnets, a year or two later; and grew fashionable largely because Arthur Balfour was the fashion. Whatever else it was, his spell was a Scottish spell; and his pride was a Scottish pride; and there was something hollow-eyed and headachy about his long, fine head, which had nothing in it of the English squires; and suggested to me rather the manse than the castle. Also, as one who went to neither great University, and has many jolly friends from his, very unlike him, I may be allowed to hint that somehow one did *think* of him as a Cambridge man.

I have known practically nothing of politicians after the Age of Asquith and Balfour; but I had some knowledge of one other who is also a Scottish type and another sort of Scottish enigma. To me the mystery about Mr James Ramsay MacDonald was this; that when I knew him slightly in my youth, in the days when we were all Socialists, he had the name of being rather a cold and scientific exponent of Socialism; the more expansive and emotional sort of eloquence seems to have developed late in life; in quite poetical speeches I have heard from him when we have since sat on the same platform, being supposed to do something to restore Rural England. But I remember when I was emotional and expansive, and full of early enthusiasm for Blatchford's *Merrie England*, feeling in MacDonald a more than Fabian frigidity, as he said (neatly enough) that Blatchford's popularisation was like a man fully explaining a motorcar by describing a wheelbarrow. On the later occasion, he was really deploring with me the ravages of the motorcar; though I can hardly picture him carrying rusticity so far as to be wheeled about like Mr Pickwick in a wheelbarrow. But perhaps there was always something about him more suited to tranquil and traditional things. When he was still counted a revolutionary Labour leader with a red tie, I heard Balfour refer to him in Parliament with respectful regret; "confessing myself an admirer of the Parliamentary style of the honourable gentleman," and somehow, when I heard those words, I think I knew that the man with the red tie was destined for a National Ministry. Even then, at least, he looked much more like an aristocrat than most aristocrats do.

But these statesmen were not the kind of men, or even the kind of Scotsmen, with whom I tended to linger. I felt much more kinship with the sort of Scot who, even when he was interested in politics, would never really be allowed in practical politics. A splendid specimen of this type of man was Cunninghame Graham. No Cabinet Minister would ever admire his Parliamentary style; though he had a much better style than any Cabinet Minister. Nothing could prevent Balfour being Prime Minister or MacDonald being Prime Minister; but Cunninghame Graham achieved the adventure of being Cunninghame Graham. As Bernard Shaw remarked, it is an achievement so fantastic that it would never be believed in romance. Nor can it be said in this case, that the Scots are in a conspiracy to praise each other; for I grieve to say that I heard one of these great statesmen deliver a speech full of the noblest ideals with Cunninghame Graham at my elbow, muttering in my ear in a soft but fierce fashion: "I never could stand a Protestant sermon."

There was a small row or scandal, connected with Cunninghame Graham and his candour in politics, which has always stuck in my memory as a symbol. It explains why I, for one, have always got on much better with revolutionists than with reformers; even when I entirely disagreed with the revolutions or entirely agreed with the reforms. In Ireland it would have been different; but in England, during most of my life, the revolutionists were always Socialists; and in theory, almost always State Socialists. And I had early begun to doubt, and later to deny, the Socialist or any other assumption that involved a complete confidence in the State. I think I had begun to doubt it ever since I met the statesmen. On the other hand, I really did agree with the Liberals on many definite points that had become part of the Liberal programme; such as Home Rule for Ireland and a democratic decentralisation many held to be the death of the Empire. But I always felt, and I still feel, more personal sympathy with a Communist like Conrad Noel, than with a Liberal like John Simon; while recognising that both are in their own way sincere. I think the reason is that the revolutionists did, in a sense, judge the world; not justly like the saints; but independently like the saints. Whereas the reformers were so much a part of the world they reformed, that the worst of them tended to be snobs and even the best of them to be specialists. Some of the Liberal specialists, of the more frigid Cambridge type, did faintly irritate me; much more than any mere anarchist or atheist. They seemed so very negative and their criticism was a sort of nagging. One distinguished man, who happened to affect me in this way, was the late J A Hobson, not to be confounded with the S J Hobson whose excellent economic studies still enlighten our debates; but a most high-minded and public-spirited speaker and writer in his own right. I hesitate to name so honest and earnest a man in a critical spirit; but nobody who recalls, with whatever respect, that gaunt figure and keen and bitter countenance, will pretend that his own spirit was not supremely critical. He was one of the most independent and intelligent of the Liberal critics of Imperialism, and on that point I was wholly with the Liberals; I disliked Imperialism; and yet I almost liked it by the time that Hobson had finished speaking against it. I remember one occasion when he took the chair at some meeting of or about Aborigines or the native races of the Empire; and he had Cunninghame Graham on his right, while I had the honour of sitting on the other side. Hobson made a very able political speech, but somehow it seemed to me to be a party speech; concerned more for Liberalism than Liberty. I may be wrong; anyhow, I missed something, as he picked holes in the British Empire until it consisted entirely of holes tied together with red tape. And then Cunninghame Graham began to speak; and I realised what was wanting. He painted a picture, an historical picture like a pageant of Empires; talking of the Spanish Empire and the British Empire as things to be reviewed with an equal eye; as things which brave and brilliant men had often served with double or doubtful effects; he poured scorn on the provincial ignorance which supposes that Spanish Empire-builders or proconsuls had all been vultures of rapine or vampires of superstition; he declared that many of the

Spanish, like many of the English, had been rulers of whom any Empire might be proud. And then he traced such figures against the dark and tragic background of those ancient human populations which they had so often either served or conquered in vain.

Now in the course of this speech Cunninghame Graham had occasion to say in passing, touching some local riot and crime; "I have never been able to feel myself that tyrannicide, in certain circumstances, is intrinsically and inevitably indefensible." Will it be believed that there was immediately a horrible howling fuss about these words; that they were the only words of the speech that anybody bothered to remember; that these were only remembered as an execrable example of the frenzy of the foes of Empire; and that all the funny people on that platform were lumped together as gory regicides who went about drinking the blood of kings? And all the time, I had been saying to myself that Cunninghame Graham at least had been fair to Empires as Empires, whereas J A Hobson had not been fair to the British Empire at all. There was nothing particularly unprecedented or preposterous in what the Scottish Socialist had said about tyrannicide, though we may disagree with it for particular moral or religious reasons. He only said what practically all the great Pagans would have said; what all the admirers of Hermodius and Aristogiton would have said; what many Renaissance theorists, Catholic and non-Catholic, would have said; what all the great French Revolutionists would have said; what practically all the classic poets and tragedians down to modern times would have said. It was no more than was implied in a hundred sacred pictures of Judith or a hundred secular praises of Brutus. But Mr Hobson would have been shocked, I fear, at the faintest suggestion of the killing of an evil king; but he was not in the least shocked at the implied impossibility of the power of a good king, or the modern ignorance of all that men have meant by kingship.

It was the irritant of this irritation, which seemed to me a little local irritation, against any large views either of loyalty or liberty, that slowly estranged me from political liberalism. But it would not be fair to say so, without adding that I did know men capable of working with the party, who were really full of something that was not liberalism but liberality. Two men of that type remain in my memory; and it is for their sake and in their sense that I say I am a Liberal. One was Augustine Birrell, who enlivened his politics through literature; and the other was the last Gladstonian, G W E Russell, who did it by inheriting the very real religion of Gladstone. They were both very Victorian, as became their generation; but they inherited an appreciation of all the great Victorians, which covered a great variety. Birrell was a Nonconformist with a very rich comprehension of Newman. Russell was a High Churchman with a quite detached admiration for Matthew Arnold. And they both drew out of these deeper and wider things a certain rich repose in humour denied to the mere men of the Party System. I shall never forget the occasion when old Birrell, roused by the rather vulgar refinement of the popular Puritan press, as expressed by a suave editor who patronised the polysyllabic style of Dr Johnson, rose like a white-maned lion at the dinner-table where the editor had spoken, and told him that if he wanted to understand the style of Dr Johnson, he should consult the passage in which Dr Johnson called somebody the son of a bitch. It was spat out with such virile anger that it sounded alarmingly like a personal remark. And I shall never forget the other occasion, in which Russell figured in what might seem the opposite fashion; for Russell was a sleek, slow-moving, heavy man and had the name of a sybarite; but he was never afraid of being in a minority; and he took the chair at a Pro-Boer dinner when Pro-Boers were most unpopular. At the end his health was proposed by Sir Wilfrid Lawson, the celebrated teetotal fanatic, or shall we say enthusiast, who was also a brave man, and could fight for the few. He was by this time an old man; and anyhow, by some accident, he confused the terms of the toast; calling it a vote of thanks; or what not. I only know that, for some reason, the last scene of this dinner is also astonishingly vivid in my memory. For Russell rose like some vast fish, gazing upwards insolently at the ceiling as he always did, and began: "This toast, which Sir Wilfrid Lawson seems to have a post-prandial difficulty in enunciating..."

There were many others, of course, who were complete exceptions to anything I have said here about the atmosphere of political Liberalism. One to whom I owe more than to many other people was Philip Wicksteed, the Dante lecturer; but there again, the modern mind had been broadened by a study of narrow medieval dogmas. But on the whole, I must confess that I reached a point of practical separation; I did not in the least desire to come any nearer to the imperialism of Curzon, or the cynical patriotism of Balfour, or the patriotic pacifism of Cecil; I am not a Conservative, whatever I am; but the general atmosphere of liberality was too illiberal to be endured.

Mr Lloyd George's Insurance Act roughly marks the moment of my disappearance; for I thought it a step to the Servile State; as legally recognising two classes of citizens; fixed as masters and servants. But a comic coincidence helped it; for I had just written *The Flying Inn*; containing a verse of violent abuse of Cocoa. After all these years, it can do no harm to mention that a Liberal editor wrote me a very sympathetic but rather sad letter, hoping that no personal attack was meant on some of the pillars of the Party. I assured him that my unaffected physical recoil from cocoa was not an attack on Mr Cadbury; also that the Praise of Wine was a traditional thing not intended as an advertisement for Mr Gilbey. So I left the Liberal paper and wrote for a Labour paper, which turned ferociously Pacifist when the War came; and since then I have been the gloomy and hated outcast you behold, cut off from the joys of all the political parties.

XIII

SOME LITERARY CELEBRITIES

I am just old enough to remember what were called Penny Readings; at which the working-classes were supposed to have good literature read to them, because they were not then sufficiently educated to read bad journalism for themselves. As a boy, or even a child, I passed one evening in something curiously called the Progressive Hall; as if the very building could not stand still, but must move onward like an omnibus along the path of progress. There was a little chairman with eyeglasses, who was nervous; and a big stout staring schoolmaster called Ash, who was not at all nervous; and a programme of performers if not eminent no doubt excellent. Mr Ash read "The Charge of the Light Brigade" in resounding tones; and the audience awaited eagerly the change to a violin solo. The chairman explained hastily that Signor Robinsoni was unfortunately unable to perform that evening, but Mr Ash had kindly consented to read "The May Queen." The next item on the programme was a song, probably called "Sea Whispers," to be sung by Miss Smith accompanied by Miss Brown. But it was not sung by Miss Smith or accompanied by Miss Brown; because, as the chairman somewhat feverishly explained, they were unable to attend; but we were solaced by the announcement that Mr Ash had kindly consented to read "The Lord of Burleigh." At about this point a truly extraordinary thing occurred; extra-ordinary at any time, to any one who knows the patience and politeness of the English poor; still more astonishing in the less sophisticated poor of those distant days. There arose slowly in the middle of the room, like some vast leviathan arising from the ocean, a huge healthy simple-faced man, of the plastering profession, who said in tones as resounding as Mr Ash's, and far more hearty and human, "Well, I've just 'ad about enough of this. Good evening, Mr Ash; good evening, ladies and gentlemen." And with a wave of universal benediction, he shouldered his way out of the Progressive Hall with an unaffected air of complete amiability and profound relief.

I hardly know why, but that giant has remained in my memory as the one original titan who first rebelled against the Victorians. And I still vastly prefer his colossal common sense and complete good humour to the often petty and sometimes spiteful sneers or sniggers of more recent and cultured critics against the Victorian conventions. But it has warned me that, both for good reasons and bad, there is now a tendency to regard some Victorians as bores, or at least the subject as a bore; and my own memory of men older than myself, in the world of letters, is necessarily a memory of the Victorians, if only of the late Victorians. Even in this respect, of course, the present fashion is very patchy and paradoxical. For instance, there seems to be a much more vivid interest in the lives of such literary men than in their literary works. Any amount is written and rewritten about the romance of Mr and Mrs Browning, in plays and pages of biography and gossip. But though their story is rewritten, I rather doubt whether Browning is reread, or whether Mrs Browning is read at all. There seem to be more details remembered out of the story of the Brontes than there are details remembered out of the Bronte stories. It is a queer ending for all the aesthetic talk about an artist being only important in his art. Queerest of all, there is more popularity for a book about a man like Palmerston, whose politics are quite dead, than for a book by a man like Carlyle, whose politics would seem partly applicable in these days of reaction and dictatorship. On the whole, despite the giant shadow of the plasterer, I can advance shamelessly as a late Victorian from under the very shadow of Queen Victoria; whose shadow never grows less.

The first great Victorian I ever met, I met very early, though only for a brief interview: Thomas Hardy. I was then a quite obscure and shabby young writer awaiting an interview with a publisher. And the really remarkable thing about Hardy was this; that he might have been himself an obscure and shabby young writer awaiting a publisher; even a new writer awaiting his first publisher. Yet he was already famous everywhere; he had written his first and finest novels culminating in *Tess*; he had expressed his queer personal pessimism in the famous passage about the President of the Immortals. He had already the wrinkle of worry on his elvish face that might have made a man look old; and yet, in some strange way, he seemed to me very young. If I say as young as I was, I mean as simply pragmatical and even priggish as I was. He did not even avoid the topic of his alleged pessimism; he defended it, but somehow with the innocence of a boys' debating-club. In short, he was in a sort of gentle fuss about his pessimism, just as I was about my optimism. He said something like this: "I know people say I'm a pessimist; but I don't believe I am naturally; I like a lot of things so much; but I could never get over the idea that it would be better for us to be without both the pleasures and the pains; and that the best experience would be some sort of sleep." I have always had a weakness for arguing with anybody; and this involved all that contemporary nihilism against which I was then in revolt; and for about five minutes, in a publisher's office, I actually argued with Thomas Hardy. I argued that non-existence is not an experience; and there can be no question of preferring it or being satisfied with it. Honestly, if I had been quite simply a crude young man, and nothing else, I should have thought his whole argument very superficial and even silly. But I did not think him either superficial or silly.

For this was the rather tremendous truth about Hardy; that he had humility. My friends who knew him better have confirmed my early impression; Jack Squire told me that Hardy in his last days of glory as a Grand Old Man would send poems to the Mercury and offer to alter or withdraw them if they were not suitable. He defied the gods and dared the lightning and all the rest of it; but the great Greeks would have seen that there was no thunderbolt for him, because he had not ὕβρις or insolence. For what heaven hates is not impiety but the pride of impiety. Hardy was blasphemous but he was not proud; and it is pride that is a sin and not blasphemy. I have been blamed for an alleged attack on Hardy, in a sketch of Victorian literature; it was apparently supposed that talking about the village atheist brooding on the village idiot was some sort of attack. But this is not an attack on Hardy; this is the defence of Hardy. The whole case for him is that he had the sincerity and simplicity of the village atheist; that is, that he valued atheism as a truth and not a triumph. He was the victim of that decay of our agricultural culture, which gave men bad religion and no philosophy. But he was right in saying, as he said essentially to me all those. years ago, that he could enjoy things, including better philosophy or religion. There come back to me four lines, written by an Irish lady in my own little paper:

> Who can picture the scene at the starry portals,
> Truly, imagination fails,
> When the pitiless President of the Immortals
> Shows unto Thomas the print of the nails?

I hope it is not profane to say that this hits the right nail on the head. In such a case, the second Thomas would do exactly what Prometheus and Satan never thought of doing; he would pity God.

I must leap a long stretch of years before I come to my meeting with the other great Victorian novelist so often bracketed with Hardy; for by that time I had made some sort of journalistic name, which was responsible for my wife and myself being invited to visit George Meredith. But even across the years, I felt the curious contrast. Hardy was a well, covered with the weeds of a stagnant period of scepticism, to my view; but with truth at the bottom of it; or anyhow with truthfulness at the bottom of it. But Meredith was a fountain. He had exactly the shock and shining radiation of a fountain in his own garden where he entertained us. He was already an old man, with the white pointed beard and the puff of white hair like thistle-down; but that also seemed to radiate. He was deaf; but the reverse of dumb. He was not humble; but I should never call him proud. He still managed to be a third thing, which is almost as much the opposite of being proud; he was vain. He was a very old man; and he was still magnificently vain. He had all those indescribable touches of a quite youthful vanity; even, for instance, to the point of preferring to dazzle women rather than men; for he talked the whole time to my wife rather than to me. We did not talk to him very much; partly because he was deaf but much more because he was not dumb. On an honest review, I doubt whether we could either of us have got in a word or two edgeways. He talked and talked, and drank ginger-beer, which he assured us with glorious gaiety he had learned to like quite as much as champagne.

Meredith was not only full of life, but he was full of lives. His vitality had that branching and begetting genius of the novelist, which is always inventing new stories about strange people. He was not like most old novelists; he was interested in what was novel. He did not live in the books he had written; he lived in the books he had not written. He described a number of novels that were really novel; especially one about the tragedy of Parnell. I do not think I agreed very much with his interpretation; for he held that Parnell might easily have recovered popularity, if he had been capable of wanting it; but that he was naturally secretive and solitary. But I doubt whether that Irish squire was really any more secretive than any number of speechless English squires, who were at the same moment conducting exactly the same sort of sex intrigue, and would have been equally angry and equally inarticulate if they had been discovered. Only they never were discovered. For there was no hope that the discovery might delay the deliverance of a Christian nation. But that was the quality that struck me personally about Meredith. Ever on the jump, he could jump to conclusions; so great a man could never be called superficial; but, in a sense, being so swift means being superficial. Many cheap parodies of Sherlock Holmes have made him a blunderer; we have yet to read a real comedy of a Sherlock Holmes who was really clever with insufficient data. We talk of a devouring thirst for information; but real thirst does not devour but swallow. So Meredith, for instance, swallowed the current racial theory of dividing the nations by the Teuton and the Celt.

The name of James Barrie dates also from my youth, though of course he was younger than Meredith or Hardy; he has lived to be my very good friend; but he is of all friends the least egotistical; and I connect him largely with intensely interesting memories of these other men and their contemporaries.

He remains especially as a witness to the greatness of Meredith; in a world which has rather strangely forgotten him; but he also told me many tales of the men I never met; such as Stevenson and Henley and Wilde; with Wells and Shaw I have dealt in another place in another connection. But there is one impression that has been left on my mind by such memories of such men; and that is the strangely fugitive character of the controversies even about the greatest literary men. Like anybody writing any memoirs, I find that my first difficulty is to convey how immensely important certain individuals appeared at certain epochs. For those men are no longer topics, even when they are still classics. I remember Barrie giving me a most amusing account of a violent scene of literary controversy, in which Henley hurled his crutch across the room and hit some other eminent literary critic in the stomach. That will illustrate a certain importance that seemed to attach itself to certain intellectual tastes and preferences. For this piece of creative critical self-expression was apparently provoked by the statement, during a discussion about Ibsen and Tolstoy, that one of these great men was great enough to hang the other on his watch-chain. But what strikes me as the grand and grim joke of the whole business, is that the narrator had apparently entirely forgotten whether Ibsen was to hang Tolstoy on his watch-chain or Tolstoy to hang Ibsen on his watch-chain. From which I venture to infer that neither of those giants now seems quite so gigantic to anybody as they then seemed to somebody.

But I have seen Sir James Barrie many times since, and could say many other things about him; only there is something in his own humorous self-effacement that seems to create round him a silence like his own. In the case of the elder Victorians, it was generally true that I met the man only once, upon a sort of privileged embassy; and such impressions may easily be illusions. If it was so in the case of Meredith, it was much mote so in the case of Swinburne. For by the time I saw him, he was a sort of god in a temple, who could only be approached through a high-priest. I had a long conversation with Watts-Dunton and then a short conversation with Swinburne. Swinburne was quite gay and skittish, though in a manner that affected me strangely as spinsterish; but he had charming manners and especially the courtesy of a consistent cheerfulness. But Watts-Dunton, it must be admitted, was very serious indeed. It is said that he made the poet a religion; but what struck me as odd, even at the time, was that his religion seemed to consist largely of preserving and protecting the poet's irreligion. He thought it essential that no great man should be contaminated with Christianity. He shook his head over Browning's temptations to that creed… "Anybody so *borne* as poor Browning was." He then referred me to his friend's "Hertha" as the crest of his creation; "Then he was quite on top of the wave." And I, who knew my Swinburne backwards, delighting in the poetry and already rather despising the philosophy, thought it was a queer metaphor to use about the real and sincere Swinburne:

> It is not much that a man can save
> On the sands of life, in the straits of time,
> Who swims in sight of the great third wave
> That never a swimmer shall cross or climb.

I did not think it had been crossed or climbed in the monstrously muddled pantheism of "Hertha;" in which a later Swinburne absurdly attempted to deduce a revolutionary ethic, of the right to resist wrongs, from a cosmic monism which could only mean that all things are equally wrong or right.

Of course, I have only noted here a name or two, because they are the most famous; I do not even say that they ate the most worthy of fame. For instance, supposing that we each keep a private collection of our pet pessimists, I have always been more intellectually impressed by A E Housman than by Thomas Hardy. I do not mean that I have been impressed by anybody with the intellectual claims of pessimism, which I always thought was piffle as well as poison; but it seems to me that Housman has, more than Hardy, a certain authority of great English literature; which is all the more classic because its English is such very plain English. I could never quite digest Hardy as a poet, much as I admire him as a novelist; whereas Housman seems to me one of the one or two great classic poets of our time. I have had both friends and fellowship in discontent with the Socialists; indeed, I was not discontented with them about conditions with which they were discontented; but rather about the prospects with which they were contented. And there was a sort of official optimism, when the collectivist ticket-collector of the Fabian tram called out, "Next stop, Utopia," at which something in me not merely heathen, was always stirred to a sympathy with the words of that high heathen genius:

> The troubles of our proud and angry dust
> Are from eternity and shall not fail.

As everyone knows, the poet was also a professor, and one of the first authorities on the old Pagan literature. I cherish a story about him which happens to concern this double character of the classical and the poetical. It may be a familiar story; it may be a false story. It describes the start of an after-dinner speech he made at Trinity, Cambridge; and whoever made it or invented it had a superb sense of style. "This great College, of this ancient University, has seen some strange sights. It has seen Wordsworth drunk and

Porson sober. And here am I, a better poet than Porson, and a better scholar than Wordsworth, betwixt and between."

But Hardy and Housman, like Henley and Swinburne, and most of the other great men among my elders for that matter, produced on my mind a curious cloudy impression of being all one background of Pagan pessimism; though what it was in the foreground, to which they were a background, I did not really know; or at least I was very vague. But some sense of sameness in these very varied persons and positions took the form, in my case, of making me wonder why they were so much divided into literary groups; and what the groups were *for*. I was puzzled by culture being cut up into sections that were not even sects. Colvin kept one court, which was very courtly; Henley kept another, which was not exactly courtly, or was full of rather rowdy courtiers; in the suburbs Swinburne was established as Sultan and Prophet of Putney, with Watts-Dunton as a Grand Vizier. And I could not make out what it was all about; the prophet was not really a commander of the faithful because there was no faith; and as for the doubt, it was equally common to all the rival groups of the age. I could not understand why it should matter so very much to Mr Watts-Dunton, if Colvin chose to like one particular new poet or Henley chose to dislike another.

I have known one or two isolated cases also of the mere man of imagination. It is always difficult to give even an outline of men of this kind; precisely because an outline is always the line at which a thing touches other things outside itself. I have already suggested very vaguely, for instance, something of the position of W B Yeats; but that is precisely because Yeats does touch some things outside his own thoughts; and suggests controversies about Theosophy or Mythology or Irish politics. But he who is simply the imaginative man can only be found in the images he makes and not in the portraits of him that other people make. Thus I could mention a number of detached and definite things about Mr Walter de la Mare; only that they would not, strictly speaking, be about him. I could say that he has a dark Roman profile rather like a bronze eagle, or that he lives in Taplow not far from Taplow Court, where I have met him and many other figures in the landscape of this story; or that he has a hobby of collecting minute objects, of the nature of ornaments, but hardly to be seen with the naked eye. My wife happens to have the same hobby of collecting tiny things as toys; though some have charged her with inconsistency on the occasion when she collected a husband. But she and de la Mare used to do a trade, worthy of Goblin Market, in these pigmy possessions. I could mention the fact that I once found a school, somewhere in the wilds of the Old Kent Road, if I remember right, where all the little girls preserved a sort of legend of Mr de la Mare, as of a fairy uncle, because he had once lectured there ever so long ago. I've no idea what spells he may have worked on that remote occasion; but he had certainly in the words of an elder English poet, knocked 'em in the Old Kent Road. But even a thing like this has not, strictly speaking, anything to do with the subject; the centre and fullness of the subject. And I have never been able to say anything that is, in that sense, about the subject. The nearest I could ever come to judging imaginative work would be simply to say this; that if I were a child, and somebody said to me no more than the two words Peacock Pie, I should pass through a certain transforming experience. I should not think of it especially as being a book. I should not even think of it as being a man; certainly not as something now so sadly familiar as a literary man. A sacramental instinct within me would give me the sense that there was somewhere and somehow a substance, gorgeously coloured and good to eat. Which is indeed the case. Nor would any doubts and differences about the theoretical or ethical edges of Mr Yeats' personality affect my appetite, even now that I am no longer a child, for the silver apples of the moon and the golden apples of the sun.

The images of imaginative men are indisputable; and I never wanted to dispute about them. The ideas of logical and dogmatic men (especially the sceptics, those very dogmatic men) are disputable; and I always wanted to dispute about them. But I never wanted to dispute about tastes where there are no tests. I have never taken sides where there are neither tastes held in common nor theses held in controversy; and this has kept me out of many movements. But then I am conscious of a gap or defect in my mind about such matters. I always feel it yawning in me like an abyss (yawning is the correct description so far as I am concerned), when people tell me that something ought to be done for the sake of "the Drama." I think Shaw's *Caesar and Cleopatra* is a good drama; though to my ethical tastes it is both too Pacifist and too Imperialist. I think *Are You a Mason?* is a good drama; and my appreciation has nothing to do with a Popish suspicion about Masonry. But to talk about helping "the drama," sounds to me like helping the typewriter or the printing-press. It seems, to my simple mind, to depend a good deal on what comes out of it.

But among these literary figures, there was one figure whom I shall put last because I ought to put first. It was the figure of a contemporary and companion of all that world of culture; a close friend of Meredith; an artist admired as artistic by the aesthetes and even by the decadents. But Alice Meynell, though she preferred to be aesthetic rather than an aesthetic, was no aesthete; and there was nothing about her that can decay. The thrust of life in her was like that of a slender tree with flowers and fruit for all seasons; and there was no drying up of the sap of her spirit, which was in ideas. She could always find things to think about; even on a sick bed in a darkened room, where the shadow of a bird on the blind was more than the bird itself, she said, because it was a message from the sun. Since she was so emphatically a craftsman, she was emphatically an artist and not an aesthete; above all, she was like that famous artist who said that he always mixed his paints with brains. But there was something else about her which I did not understand at the time, which set her apart as something separate from the time. She was strong with deep roots where all the Stoics were only stiff with despair; she was alive to an immortal beauty where all the Pagans could only mix beauty with mortality. And though she passed through my own life fitfully, and far more rarely than I could wish, and though her presence had indeed something of the ghostly gravity of a shadow and her passing something of the fugitive accident of a bird, I know now that she was not fugitive and she was not shadowy. She was a message from the Sun.

XIV

PORTRAIT OF A FRIEND

Apart from vanity or mock modesty (which healthy people always use as jokes) my real judgment of my own work is that I have spoilt a number of jolly good ideas in my time. There is a reason for this; and it is really rather a piece of autobiography than of literary criticism. I think *The Napoleon of Notting Hill* was a book very well worth writing; but I am not sure that it was ever written. I think that a harlequinade like *The Flying Inn* was an extremely promising subject, but I very strongly doubt whether I kept the promise. I am almost tempted to say that it is still a very promising subject – for somebody else. I think the story called *The Ball and the Cross* had quite a good plot, about two men perpetually prevented by the police from fighting a duel about the collision of blasphemy and worship, or what all respectable people would call, "a mere difference about religion." I believe that the suggestion that the modern world is organised in relation to the most obvious and urgent of all questions, not so much to answer it wrongly, as to prevent it being answered at all, is a social suggestion that really has a great deal in it; but I am more doubtful about whether I got a great deal out of it, even in comparison with what could be got out of it. Considered as stories, in the sense of anecdotes, these things seem to me to have been more or less fresh and personal, but considered as novels, they were not only not as good as a real novelist would have made them, but they were not as good as I might have made them myself, if I had really even been trying to be a real novelist. And among many more abject reasons for not being able to be a novelist, is the fact that I always have been and presumably always shall be a journalist.

But it was not the superficial or silly or jolly part of me that made me a journalist. On the contrary, it is such part as I have in what is serious or even solemn. A taste for mere fun might have led me to a public-house, but hardly to a publishing-house. And if it led me to a publishing-house, for the publishing of mere nonsense rhymes or fairy-tales, it could never thus have led me to my deplorable course of endless articles and letters in the newspapers. In short, I could not be a novelist; because I really like to see ideas or notions wrestling naked, as it were, and not dressed up in a masquerade as men and women. But I could be a journalist because I could not help being a controversialist. I do not even know if this would be called mock modesty or vanity, in the modern scale of values; but I do know that it is neither. It occurs to me that the best and most wholesome test, for judging how far mere incompetence or laziness, and how far a legitimate liking for direct democratic appeal, has prevented me from being a real literary man, might be found in a study of the man of letters I happen to know best; who had the same motives for producing journalism, and yet has produced nothing but literature.

In the days when Belloc was known to Bentley and Oldershaw, but not to me, when they were all together in the Radical group at Oxford, Belloc himself chiefly frequented a much smaller group which called itself the Republican Club. So far as I can make out, the Republican Club never consisted of more than four members, and generally less; one or more of them having been solemnly expelled either for Toryism or for Socialism. This was the club which Belloc celebrated in the fine dedication of his first book; of which two lines have passed into popularity. "There's nothing worth the wear of winning but laughter and the love of friends;" but in the course of which he also described in more detail the ideals of this fastidious fellowship.

> We kept the Rabelaisian plan
> We dignified the dainty cloisters
> With Natural Law, the Rights of Man,
> Song, Stoicism, Wine and Oysters.
>
> We taught the art of writing things
> On men we still would like to throttle,
> And where to get the blood of kings
> At only half-a-crown a bottle.

Of the other three corners of this very Four-Square Gospel of Citizenship, that is of Belloc's three constant colleagues in the old Republican Club, one is still, I believe a distinguished exile and official in Burma; or as his old friends loved to say with sour smiles of affectionate resignation, "a Satrap;" as if he had somehow medised or condescended to the oriental barbarism which we call Imperialism. I have no doubt that as a fact he was a happy and highly satisfactory Satrap; but he was the one member of the group whom I never met. The other two Republicans, who were Belloc's most intimate friends at Oxford, have both in different ways played a considerable part in my own life. One was John Swinnerton Phillimore, son of the old Admiral whose name made a sort of background for the Kensington of my boyhood, afterwards Latin Professor at Glasgow University and one of the first classical authorities of his time; now alas, only an ever-deepening memory. The other was Francis Yvon Eccles, the distinguished French scholar, whom I now meet all too seldom through his gravitation towards a home in France.

Eccles, like Belloc, was the child of one French and one English parent; but there was a certain misleading comedy about the names, as if they had been interchanged like labels. For Eccles, who happened to have the English surname, looked much more like a Frenchman, and Belloc, with the French surname, looked much more like an Englishman; indeed he ended by being the one solitary but symbolic Englishman really looking like the traditional John Bull. It is true that he reached this traditional type through the possession of a square chin like that of the great Emperor of the French, and the subsequent assumption of side-whiskers to satisfy the conventions of the Spaniards. But the combined effect of these foreign influences was that he looked exactly like what all English farmers ought to look like; and was, as it were, a better portrait of Cobbett than Cobbett was. Moreover, the symbol was true; for the roots that hold him to the Downs and the deep ploughlands of South England were even deeper, so far as instinct is concerned, than the marble foundations of the abstract Republic of the Republican Club. I remember drinking a pot of beer with a publican not far from Horsham and mentioning my friend's name; and the publican, who obviously had never heard of books or such bosh, merely said, "Farms a bit, doesn't he?" and I thought how hugely flattered Belloc would be.

I knew Eccles in Fleet Street, from the first days of the old Pro-Boer *Speaker*, of which he was largely the literary adviser; yet it was always inevitable to think of him as sitting outside a café in Paris rather than in London. His head, his hat, his arched eyebrows and wrinkled forehead of quite disinterested curiosity, his Mephistophelean tuft, his type of patient lucidity, were far more French than his friend with the French name. Whether or no these externals commonly correspond to characters, they certainly do not always correspond to careers. Thus, John Phillimore, the son of a sailor and coming largely of a family of sailors, himself looked very much more like a sailor than like a don. His dark compact figure and bright brown face might have been on any quarter-deck. On the other hand, by another such carnival comedy of exchange, I always thought that his cousin, who is, I believe, a distinguished Admiral, looked much more like a don or a professor. But John Phillimore, as things fell out, had to be a rather unique sort of don; and at once a popular and a pugnacious professor. You could not conduct classes amid the racial and religious chaos of Glasgow, full of wild Highlanders and wild Irish, and young fanatical Communists and old fanatical Calvinists, without possessing some of the qualities of the quarter-deck. Most of the stories about Phillimore read like tales of mutiny on the high seas. It was shrewdly said of him that the effect of the word, "gentlemen," as said by him, was like the famous effect of the word, "Quirites," as said by Caesar. On a similar occasion an insubordinate but intelligent Glasgow crowd seems to have instantly grasped the gratifying irony of his appeal, "Gentlemen, gentlemen! I have not yet ceased casting my pearls."

The chief fact relevant to this chapter, however, is that Belloc's career began with the ideals of the Republican Club. To those who talk about ideals, but do not think about ideas, it may seem odd that both he and Eccles have ended as strong Monarchists. But there is a thin difference between good despotism and good democracy; both imply equality with authority, whether the authority be impersonal or personal. What both detest is oligarchy; even in its more human form of aristocracy, let alone its present repulsive form of plutocracy. Belloc's first faith was in the impersonal authority of the Republic, and he concentrated on its return in the eighteenth century, but rather specially touching its military aspect. His first two books were the very fine monographs on the two most famous of the French Revolutionists; and he was, in that sense, very heartily revolutionary. But I mention the matter here for a special reason, in connection with something in which he was and is rather unique in this country; native and rooted as is his real relation to this country. I have already remarked that to know him well is to know that, as a man, he is English and not French. But there is another aspect in his curious case. In so far as he is a traditionalist, he is an English traditionalist. But when he was specially a revolutionist, he was in the very exact sense a French Revolutionist. And it might be roughly symbolised by saying that he was an English poet but a French soldier. Now I thought I knew all about Revolutionists long before I met the representative of the Republican Club. I had talked to them in dirty taverns or untidy studios, or more depressing vegetarian hostels. I knew there were differences in cut and colour; and that some were more really revolutionary than others. I knew that some wore pale green neckties and gave lectures on decorative art; while some wore red neckties and made speeches on Trade Union platforms. I have sung "The Red Flag" in hearty chorus with the latter, and Edward Carpenter's "England, arise" in more refined accents with the former. And though I knew nothing of the comparison with another method, I did more and more realise, with an ever sinking heart, that for some reason we had not got a decent revolutionary song to our name; and that in the matter of producing any respectable sort of Hymn of Hate, my countrymen were a washout.

One weakness of these popular war-songs was that they were not war-songs. They never gave the faintest hint of how anybody could ever make war on anything. They were always waiting for the Dawn; without the least anticipation that they might be shot at dawn, or the least intelligent preparation for shooting anybody else at dawn. "England arise; the long long night is over; faint in the east behold the dawn appear." They were all like that; they were all Songs Before Sunrise; as if the sun that rose on the just and the unjust did not also rise on the conquered and the conqueror. But the English revolutionary poet wrote as if he owned the sun and was certain to be the conqueror. In other words, I found that the Socialist idea of war was exactly like the Imperialist idea of war; and I was strengthened and deepened in my detestation of both of them. I heard many arguments against the idea of a Class War; but the argument which discredits it for me is the fact that the Socialists, like the Imperialists, always assumed that they would win the war. I am no Fascist; but the March on Rome gave them the surprise they needed. To say the least, it considerably halted the inevitable proletarian triumph; just as the Boers had halted the inevitable British triumph. And I do not like inevitable triumphs. Also I do not believe in them. I do not think that any social solution, even a more manly one like that of Morris, should be called "as sure as that tomorrow's sun will rise."

And then Belloc wrote a poem called "The Rebel," and nobody noticed the interesting point about it. It is a very violent and bitter poem; it would be much too revolutionary for most of the revolutionists; even those with red ties would blush, and those with pale green ties would turn pale with sickness, at such threats against the rich as break out here… "and slash their pictures in their frames" … "and hack their horses at the knees and hew to death their timber trees;" and the very fine ending, "and all these things I mean to do; for fear perhaps my little son should break his hands as I have done."

That is not a Song Before Sunrise. That is an attack before sunrise. But the peculiar point I wish to note here, appears in the previous verse about the actual nature of the attack. It is the only revolutionary poem I ever read that suggested that there was any plan for making any attack. The first two lines of the verse run: "When we shall find them where they stand, a mile of men on either hand." The Comrades of the Dawn always seemed to be marching in column, and singing. They never seemed to have heard of deploying; into the long line that faces the foe for battle. The next two lines are: "I mean to charge them right away, and force the flanks of their array." Whoever heard of the Comrades of the Dawn having so complicated an idea as that of turning the enemy's flank? Then comes the encirclement:

> And press them inward from the plains
> And drive them clamouring down the lanes,

> And gallop and harry and have them down,
> And carry the gates and hold the town.

The Pursuit; and then the Holding of the Bridgehead. Now that is the only Song of the Class War I ever read that has the haziest notion of what a war would be like. In this wild lyric, full of vindictive violence and destruction, there is also in quite swift lyrical form a perfectly clear tactical plan and military map; a definite description of how men may storm a fortress, if it has to be stormed. The violence of this democratic, though doubtless dramatic, utterance goes far beyond anything that any Communist will reach in a hundred years. But it involves also the real character of battle; and a battle, like every human work, is at once designed in its beginning and doubtful in its end. Now the Comrades of the Dawn already annoyed me; because their revolution was wildly undesigned in its beginning, but had no doubt about its end. Just like Imperialism; and the South African War.

That is what I mean by saying that Belloc is an English poet but a French soldier. The man at rest, and therefore the man in reality, is the man of Sussex; but he has been enlarged, or some would say infected, by the foreign influence of those who have known real revolutions and invasions; and if he were called upon to conduct a revolution, he would conduct it as logically as a Parisian mob still conducts a riot. As he once remarked, such a democratic mob can deploy. But I have only taken this chance example to illustrate a general truth about a very remarkable man. I have taken the fact that the ordinary song of revolt is only militant, but his is also military. I mean that it is full of the notion, not only of fighting for the faith, but of getting to grips with the fact. If we are going to fight the rich, or fight the revolt against the rich, or fight resistance to a reasonable redistribution of riches, or fight anything else, this is how it is done. And when I remember all the other romantic revolutionary songs it does not at all surprise me, at least in this country, to realise that no fighting has been done.

Now that is exactly how his contemporaries have missed the whole point about Belloc at every point of his action; for instance, in his historic study of The Servile State. Because the English, of whom I am one, are romantic, and because they delight in the romance that the French are romantic, and delight in the more delirious romance that Belloc is French, they have simply been stone-blind to him when he is entirely scientific. His study of the Servile State is as strictly scientific as a military map is military. There is nothing romantic about it; nothing rollicking about it; nothing even particularly amusing about it, except the two admirable words, "this fool," which occur in the calm procession of a thousand impartial words, in the chapter on The Practical Man. And even excepting that is like accusing Euclid of making a joke, when he proves a proposition with a *reductio ad absurdum*. Anyone who knows the place of reason in the modern scheme, can imagine what happened. First, before reading what Belloc wrote, the critics started to criticise what Belloc would probably write. They said he threatened us with a horrible nightmare called the Servile State. As a fact, it was his whole point that it was not a nightmare, but something that we were already almost as habituated to accepting as to accepting the daylight. All the time, a thesis as pivotal as that of Adam Smith or Darwin is hardly realised, or even criticised, by anybody as what it is, though it has been criticised quite wildly, conjecturally and at random, as everything that it is not. Bernard Shaw roundly asserted that it was a mere revival of Herbert Spencer's description of all dependence on the State as slavery. And when we pointed out that he could not have read a page of Belloc's book if he really thought it was like Herbert Spencer's book, he replied with characteristic gaiety that it was Herbert Spencer's that he had not read. Many supposed that it was a sort of satiric description of a Socialist State; something between Laputa and Brave New World. Others seem still to suppose that the Servile State is a general term for any tyranny or oppressive official State; and even use the term currently in that sense. For it is typical of our time and country that, while no one could say the book was popular, the title of the book was immediately and vastly popular. There was a time when errand-boys and railway-porters said "Servile State;" they did not know what it meant; but they knew about as much as the book-reviewers and even the dons.

The thesis of the book is that the Socialist movement does not lead to Socialism. This is partly because of compromise and cowardice; but partly also because men have a dim indestructible respect for property, even in its disgusting disguise of modern monopoly. Therefore, instead of the intentional result, Socialism, we shall have the unintentional resultant: Slavery. The compromise will take the form of saying, "We must feed the poor; we won't rob the rich; so we will tell the rich to feed the poor, handing them over to be the permanent servants of a master-class, to be maintained whether they are working or no, and in return for that complete maintenance giving a complete obedience." All this, or the beginnings of it, can be seen in a hundred modern changes, from such things as Insurance Acts, which divide citizens by law into two classes of masters and servants, to all sorts of proposals for preventing strikes and lock-outs by compulsory arbitration. Any law that sends a man back to his work, when he wants to leave it, is in plain fact a Fugitive Slave Law.

Now I take that one example of a scientific thesis maintained in a purely scientific way, to show how very little the intellectual importance of Belloc's work has been understood. The reason of that misunderstanding lies in the other fact about him, which is really foreign and relatively French; the habit of separating in his own mind the scientific from the artistic; the ornamental from the useful. It is true that when a Frenchman designs a park as an ornamental park the paths are very curly indeed because they are only ornamental. When he designs a road, he makes it as straight as a ramrod, like the roads down which French soldiers used to march with all their ramrods; because a toad is meant to be useful and is most short when it is straight. Belloc's little Arcadian lyric, "When I was not much older than Cupid and bolder," is very like an ornamental French garden; and his book on the Servile State is very like a French military road. No man is more instinctively witty; and no man can be more intentionally dull.

These two voices of Belloc, so to speak, were so distinct that he could sometimes pass from one to the other and make it seem like two persons speaking; effecting a transition on a platform almost as dramatic as the dialogue of a ventriloquist with his doll. When he stood as a Liberal member for Salford, he often managed to bewilder his hecklers by spraying them with these sharply alternated showers of cold and hot water. Salford was a poor and popular constituency, in which there were many strata of simple and provincial people, retaining the prejudices of our great-grandfathers; one of them being the touching belief that anybody with a French name could be made to cower and grovel by any allusion to the Battle of Waterloo. This was probably the only battle of which the heckler himself had ever heard; and his information about it was limited to the partly inaccurate statement that it was won by the English. He therefore used to call out at intervals, "Who won Waterloo?" And Belloc would affect to take this with grave exactitude, as a technical question put to him upon a tactical problem, and would reply with the laborious lucidity of a lecturer, "The issue of Waterloo was ultimately determined, chiefly by Colborne's manoeuvre in the centre, supported by the effects of Van der Smitzen's battery earlier in the engagement. The Prussian failure in synchrony was not sufficiently extensive, etc." And then, while the unfortunate patriot in the audience was still endeavouring to grapple with this unexpected growth of complexity in the problem he had propounded, Belloc would suddenly change his own note to the ringing directness of the demagogue, would openly boast of the blood of that Pyrenean soldier who had followed the revolutionary army of Napoleon, and risen in its ranks, through all the victories that established a code of justice all over a continent and restored citizenship to civilisation. "It is good democratic blood; and I am not ashamed of it."

This transition of tone had a tremendous effect, the whole hail rose at him roaring with applause and the investigator of the Belgian campaign was left isolated. But that is exactly the point; that he really was isolated. It is a point, not only in the subtlety of that blend of French and English blood; but also of the rather special subtlety of the English. The English are insular, not so much in the sense of being insolent but simply of being ignorant; but they are not spiteful. Other things being equal, they would rather cheer a Frenchman who was proud of being a Frenchman, as they cheered Napoleon's Marshal at the Coronation of Queen Victoria, than remind him of Napoleon's misfortune at Waterloo. And the same interesting distinction cuts the other way also. We have been told in a tiresome way from childhood about something that was called French rhetoric. To our shame, we have forgotten that there was until very lately a noble thing called English rhetoric. And as distinct from his irony or his objective scientific militarism, the rhetoric of Belloc was thoroughly English rhetoric. There was nothing in it that could not have been said by Cobbett or even by Fox, in the days when the genuine English Radical could address the genuine English crowd. What has weakened that direct popular appeal has been the change that turned nearly all Englishmen into a sort of imitation Londoners; and the rhetoric of Westminster grew more and more pompous and hypocritical while the wit of Whitechapel grew more and more acrid and flippant. But it has been possible, even in my own time, to hear occasionally the voice historic and a virile English demagogue; talking in plain English about primary emotions. Nobody ever did it better, when he chose, than old John Burns, for whom I have spoken and voted so often in the days when I lived in Battersea. To mention one case, as a sort of model; it was natural enough that the old Dock-Strike agitator, having become a Cabinet Minister and in many ways a rather Conservative force, should be assailed by more revolutionary groups as an extinct volcano if not a surrendered fortress. But Burns knew how to deal with that sort of thing when speaking to democrats; by cutting deeper into human facts instead of sliding away upon legal fictions. He was taunted by some Socialists at a Battersea meeting with not having opposed the Royal Grant to Queen Mary or some princess at the celebrations on the appearance of an heir. I can imagine how the smoother sort of Lib-Lab. social climber, passing through Parliament into the governing class, would explain away his position in terms of the etiquette of the House. John Burns said, "I am the son of my mother and the husband of my wife. And if you ask me to put a public insult upon a woman who has just borne a child, I will not do it." That is English rhetoric; and it is as good as any in the world.

But while it is quite a mistake to suppose that there was anything particularly French about the direct democratic oratory that Belloc used in those days, there was another quality which he also used, which I think may really be called a rather French speciality. We generally have some very silly and inadequate notion in our minds when we talk about French wit; and the full richness of that fruit of culture is seldom covered even when we talk of French irony. For the best French irony is nothing so simple as merely saying one thing and meaning the opposite. It is at once exhibiting and withdrawing, in one flash, a series of aspects of a thing; like a man twirling a jewel with twenty facets. And the more brief it is, the more flippant it is, the more seemingly superficial it is, the more there is in that irony an element of mystery. There is always a touch of bewilderment, for the simple, in the tale of such tags as that of Voltaire; "To succeed in the world it is not sufficient to be stupid, you must also be well-mannered." Curiously enough, there is exactly that quality in an ordinary military dispatch, sent out by a very silent and practical soldier; by Foch at the supreme crisis of the Marne. "My right is hard pressed; my left is retreating; situation excellent; I attack." For it might be all sorts of things besides the quite prosaic and practical thing that it is; it might be a paradox; or a boast; or a bitter jest of despair; and all the time it is in fact a quite correct description of the advantages of his own immediate tactical situation, as exact as a military map. I have never so vividly felt that there was really something French about Belloc, as when he would from time to time suddenly say things like that on a public platform before an entirely puzzled audience. I remember once when he was lecturing on the same campaign in the Great War; a purely technical lecture full of plans and figures. And he paused to say parenthetically that perhaps nobody would ever understand why Von Kluck made his one big blunder before Paris. "Perhaps," said Belloc, like a man for a moment bemused; "perhaps he was inspired."

Now you can make all sorts of things out of that; in all sorts of opposite directions. You could make it a Voltairean sneer at divine inspiration, and the disasters it brings; or a dark mysterious judgment like that suggested when "the Lord hardened Pharaoh's heart," or all kinds of other fine shades between the two. But you could never be quite certain that you had got to the bottom of it. So that shining ornamental pond which looks so shallow, and is called French wit, is indeed the deepest of all wells and truth lies at the bottom of it. Finally, it may be remarked, that this very diversity in one man's methods, and his own habit of keeping these diverse things distinct, is the explanation of the accident by which many people have been disappointed or bewildered or even bored by Belloc in different aspects; because they were looking for the revelation of one of the legends about him, when he happened to be concentrating with cold ferocity on something much more prosaic or precise. In debating with Bernard Shaw about the Law of Rent, he observed austerely that if they were discussing economics, he would discuss economics, but if Mr Shaw was making jokes he would be happy to reply in comic verse. To which Mr Shaw, ever ready to rise to a sporting event, pursued the subject in some delightful doggerel; which Belloc acknowledged with the song about "the strip to the south of the Strand;" then including the Adelphi. But it is typical that his song simply was a song, and could have been sung in any pub as a drinking-song.

One of the most amusing events of my life occurred when I took the chair for a private celebration of Belloc's sixtieth birthday. There were about forty people assembled, nearly all of them were what is called important in the public sense, and the rest were even more important in the private sense; as being his nearest intimates and connections. To me it was that curious experience, something between the Day of Judgment and a dream, in which men of many groups known to me at many times, all appeared together as a sort of resurrection. Anybody will understand that feeling who has had, as most people have had, the experience of some total stranger stopping him in the street and saying, "And how are the old set?" On such occasions I become acutely conscious of having belonged to a large number of old sets. Most of the people I knew well enough; but some of the younger I had known quite lately and others long ago; and they included, as do all such gatherings, those whom I had intended to enquire about, and never carried out my intention. Anyhow, they were of all sorts except the stupid sort; and the renewed comradeship stirred in me the memory of a hundred controversies. There was my old friend Bentley, who dated from my first days at school; and Eccles, who reminded me of the earliest political rows of the Pro-Boers; and Jack Squire (now Sir John) who first floated into my circle in the days of the *Eye-Witness* and my brother's campaign against corruption; and Duff Cooper, a rising young politician I had met but a month or so before, and A P Herbert of somewhat similar age; and the brilliant journalist I had long known as Beachcomber, and only recently known as Morton. It was to be, and was, a very jolly evening; there were to be no speeches. It was specially impressed upon me that there were to be no speeches. Only I, as presiding, was to be permitted to say a few words in presenting Belloc with a golden goblet modelled on certain phrases in his heroic poem in praise of wine, which ends by asking that such a golden cup should be the stirrup-cup of his farewell to friends:

> And sacramental raise me the divine
> Strong brother in God and last companion, wine.

I merely said a few words to the effect that such a ceremony might have been as fitting thousands of years ago, at the festival of a great Greek poet; and that I was confident that Belloc's sonnets and strong verse would remain like the cups and the carved epics of the Greeks. He acknowledged it briefly, with a sad good humour, saying he found that, by the age of sixty, he did not care very much whether his verse remained or not. "But I am told," he added with suddenly reviving emphasis, "I am told that you begin to care again frightfully when you are seventy. In which case, I hope I shall die at sixty-nine." And then we settled down to the feast of old friends, which was to be so happy because there were no speeches.

201

Towards the end of the dinner somebody whispered to me that it would perhaps be better if a word were said in acknowledgment of the efforts of somebody whose name I forget, who was supposed to have arranged the affair. I therefore briefly thanked him; and he still more briefly thanked me, but added that it was quite a mistake, because the real author of the scheme was Johnnie Morton, otherwise *Beachcomber*, who sat immediately on his right. Morton rose solemnly to acknowledge the abruptly transferred applause; glanced to his own right, and warmly thanked whoever happened to be sitting there (I think it was Squire) for having inspired him with this grand conception of a banquet for Belloc. Squire arose, and with many courteous gestures, explained that the gentleman on his own right, Mr A P Herbert, had been the true and deep and ultimate inspiration of this great idea; and that it was only fitting that the secret of his initiative should be now revealed. By this time, the logic of the jest was in full gallop and could not be restrained; even if I had wished to restrain it. A P Herbert rose to the occasion with superb presence of mind, and gave the series quite a new and original turn. He is an excellent speaker; and, as we all know, an admirable author; but I never knew before that he is an admirable actor. For some reason best known to himself, he chose to pretend to be the oratorical official of some sort of Workmen's Benevolent Society, like the Oddfellows or the Foresters. He did not need to tell us that he was taking this part; in the tone of his voice, he told it in the first few words. I shall never forget the exactitude of the accent with which he said, "I'm sure, friends, we're all very pleased to see ex-Druid Chesterton among us this evening." But he also gave his speech a definite logical direction. He said it was not to 'im, but to our old and faithful friend Duff Cooper that this pleasant evening was really due. Duff Cooper, sitting next to him, then rose and in resolute and ringing tones delivered an imitation of a Liberal platform speech, full of invocations of his great leader Lloyd George. He explained, however, that Mr E C Bentley on his right, and not himself, had arranged this tribute to that pillar of political Liberalism, Mr Belloc. Bentley gave one glance to his own right, and rose with exactly that supercilious gravity that I had seen forty years ago in the debating-clubs of our boyhood; the memory of his balanced eye-glasses and bland solemnity came back to me across my life with such intensity as stirs the tears that are born of time. He said, with his precise enunciation, that he had himself followed through life one simple and sufficient rule. In all problems that arose, he had been content to consult exclusively the opinion of Professor Eccles. In every detail of daily life, in his choice of a wife, of a profession, of a house, of a dinner, he had done no more than carry out whatever Professor Eccles might direct. On the present occasion, any appearance he might have had of arranging the Belloc banquet was in fact a mask for Professor Eccles' influence, Professor Eccles responded in a similar but even more restrained fashion, merely saying that he had been mistaken for the man next to him, the real founder of the feast; and so by fatal and unfaltering steps, the whole process went round the whole table; till every single human being there had made a speech. It is the only dinner I have ever attended, at which it was literally true that every diner made an after-dinner speech. And that was the very happy ending of that very happy dinner, at which there were to be no speeches.

I did not myself make another speech; though I was far from thinking that there had been too much speechifying. Only certain fragmentary words, a memory of a late Victorian poet whom I knew, Sir William Watson, floated on the surface of my mind; and it was those words that I should have said, if I had said anything. For what the poet said to his friend is all that I could have added, in a merely personal spirit, to the many things that were said that night about Hilaire Belloc; and I should not have been ashamed if the words had sounded like a vaunt:

> Nor without honour my days ran,
> Nor yet without a boast shall end;
> For I was Shakespeare's countryman,
> And were not you my friend.

XV

THE INCOMPLETE TRAVELLER

If these my memoirs are not exactly lavishly dated, as indeed my letters are never dated at all, I hope no one will suspect me of any lack of reverence for that great academic school of history now generally known as 1066 and All That. I have some rudiments of knowledge about what may be called 1066; for instance, I know that the Conquest did not really happen till 1067. But I think the point somewhat unimportant, as compared, let us say, with the current view that the Normans reared towers over Galilee and reigned in Sicily, and helped to give birth to St Thomas Aquinas, solely that they might make Anglo-Saxons yet more Anglo-Saxon, in the far-off hope of their becoming Anglo-American. In short, I have the deepest respect for 1066; but I shall continue in a humble way to wage a relentless war with All That.

But for me, in any case, compromise and amendment would come too late. I have written several books that were supposed to be biographies; and lives of really great and remarkable men, meanly refusing them the most elementary details of chronology; and it would be a more than mortal meanness that I should now have the arrogance to be accurate about my own life, when I have failed to be thus accurate about theirs. Who am I that I should be dated more carefully than Dickens or Chaucer? What blasphemy if I reserved for myself what I had failed to render to St Thomas and St Francis of Assisi. It seems to be a clear case, in which common Christian humility commands me to continue in a course of crime.

But if I do not date my letters, or my literary sketches, when I am at home, and am to some extent regulated by the clock and the calendar, still less do I feel capable of such punctuality when the timeless spirit of holiday travel has not only hurled me through space, but knocked me out of time. I shall give only this short chapter to a few notes of travel; because most of the note-books have already been turned into some other sort of books; on Ireland and America, on Palestine and Rome. I will only touch here on a few things that I happen not to have recorded elsewhere; a visit to Spain; my second visit to America; and my first, but I hope not my last, visit to Poland.

Let me first feed the hunger for dates upon the date-palm of Palestine, if the flippancy be forgiven; and so at least get the first few journeys in their right order; even if I consider some of the subsequent cases in more general style. I can proudly claim that I do know the date of my pilgrimage to Jerusalem; partly because it was a year after the close of the Great War, and partly because when my publishers suggested my going to the Holy Land, it sounded to me like going to the moon. It was the first of my long journeys, through a country still imperilled and under arms; it involved crossing the desert at night in something like a cattle-truck; and parts even of the Promised Land had some of the qualities of a lunar landscape. One incident in that wilderness still stands out in my memory for some strange reason; there is no need to recur here to Palestinian politics; but I was wandering about in the wilderness in a car with a zealous little Zionist; he seemed at first almost monomaniac, of the sort who answers the statement, "It's a fine day," with the eager reply, "Oh, yes, the climate is perfect for our project." But I came to sympathise with his romance; and when he said, "It's a lovely land; I should like to put the Song of Solomon in my pocket and wander about," I knew that, Jew or Gentile, mad or sane, we two were of the same sort. The lovely land was a wilderness of terraced rock to the horizon, and really impressive; there was not a human thing in sight but ourselves and the chauffeur, who was a black-browed giant, the rare but real Jewish type that turns prize-fighter. He was an excellent driver; and the rule in those parts is that a Ford can go anywhere if it keeps off the road. He had gone ahead to clear some fallen stones and I remarked on this efficiency. The swarthy little professor beside me had taken a book from his pocket, but replied dispassionately, "Yes; I only know him slightly; between ourselves, I believe he is a murderer; but I made no indelicate enquiries." He then continued to read the Song of Solomon, and savoured those spices that rise when the south wind blows upon the garden. The hour was full of poetry; and not without irony.

The dates of my first and second visits to America have some true significance; for one was about a year after the Palestinian visit, and the other was comparatively recently; in 1930. This is not only because the first was very near the beginning and the second very near the end of the prolonged freak of Prohibition. I will not stop here to argue with any fool who thinks there is something funny about objecting to Prohibition. What is part of the same process is this; that one began with the Boom and the other saw the start of the Slump and, what is more important, a profound revolution in the highly intelligent American people. It is not trivial that, touching Prohibition, they had wholly changed; at the beginning even those who disliked it believed in it; at the end even those who liked it disbelieved in it. But it is much more important that, by the end, lifelong Republicans told me of their intention to vote for Franklin Roosevelt; even those who had cursed the demagogy of Theodore Roosevelt. The Americans have seen more plutocracy than anybody; but I am not sure they may not see through it sooner than anybody else.

For the rest, my last American tour consisted of inflicting no less than ninety lectures on people who never did me any harm; and the remainder of the adventure, which was very enjoyable, breaks up like a dream into isolated incidents. An aged negro porter, with a face like a walnut, whom I discouraged from brushing my hat, and who rebuked me saying, "Ho, young man. Yo's losing yo dignity before yo times. Yo's got to look nice for de girls." A grave messenger who came to me in a Los Angeles hotel, from a leading film magnate, wishing to arrange for my being photographed with the Twenty-four Bathing-Beauties; Leviathan among the Nereids; an offer which was declined amid general surprise. An agonising effort to be fair to the subtleties of the evolutionary controversy, in addressing the students of Notre Dame, Indiana, in a series on "Victorian Literature," of which no record remained except that one student wrote in the middle of his blank note-book, "Darwin did a lot of harm." I am not at all certain that he was wrong; but it was something of a simplification of my reasons for being agnostic about the agnostic deductions, in the debates about Lamarck and Mendel. A debate about the history of religion with a very famous sceptic; who, when I tried to talk about Greek cults or Asiatic asceticism, appeared to be unable to think of anything except Jonah and the Whale. But it is the curse of this comic career of lecturing that it seems to bring on the lighter stage nothing except comedies; and I have already said that I do not think America takes them any more seriously than I do. The real American commentary was serious and sound; and none more so than that of an industrial master of machinery, who said to me, "People must go back to the farm."

I had pottered about in France ever since my father took me there as a boy; and Paris was the only foreign capital I knew. I owe it to him that I was at least a traveller and not a tripper. The distinction is not snobbish; indeed it is one rather of epoch than education; half the trouble about the modern man is that he is educated to understand foreign languages and misunderstand foreigners. The traveller sees what he sees; the tripper sees what he has come to see. A true traveller in a primitive epic or folk-tale did not pretend to like a beautiful princess because she was beautiful. It is still true of a poor sailor; of a tramp; in short, of a traveller. Thus he need form no opinion of Paris newspapers; but if he wanted to, he would probably read them. The tripper never reads them, calls them rags, and knows as much about the rags as the *chiffonnier* who picks them up with a spike. I will give only one case, since it recalls my connection with a very early controversy. All England came to two great moral conclusions about a man called Zola; or rather about two men both called Zola. The first was merely a filthy Frenchman; a pornographer we jailed by proxy even in his publisher. The second was a hero and a martyr for the truth, presumably tortured by the Inquisition – just like Galileo. The truth concerned the Dreyfus case; and as a journalist behind the scenes I soon found out the truth was not so simple. Déroulède said, "Dreyfus may or may not be guilty; but France is not guilty." I say Dreyfus may have been innocent, but Dreyfusards were not always innocent; even when they were English editors. It was my first awful eye-opener about our Press propaganda. I am not talking of the conclusion but of the methods of the Dreyfusards. A quite independent, intelligent Scot, an Oxford friend of Oldershaw, told me they had practically proposed forgery, by falsifying the size of handwriting. But the only point here is Zola, who was first nasty and then noble; even in his very pictures, his brow grew loftier and his neck less thick. Now I would not go to either extreme about poor Zola; but I happened to be in Paris on the day of his funeral at the Pantheon. Paris was fiercely divided; and I bought one of the fanatical rags in a café, in which Maurice Barrès, a pretty detached *littérateur*, gave his reasons for having voted against the apotheosis; and wrote in one sentence all that I have tried to say here about the pessimists and the atheists and the realists and the rest. He said he did not object to obscenity; "I do not care how far down you force the mind of man; so long as you do not break the spring."

Most of us would not look at such rags as that, of course; but they are full of remarks of that sort, for anyone who, not content even with condescending to look at them, has the morbid curiosity to read them. And the remark seems to me a more important comment on what Zola stood for than the mere fact that he stood for the Dreyfusard Party, even if he was as trustworthy about Dreyfus as he was certainly untrustworthy about Lourdes. Now we have not that sort of comment in England; for bulk and business methods and good printing do not provide it. But we have good things of our own to balance its absence; and the best of them are things we hardly ever hear anything about.

After all, the strangest country I ever visited was England; but I visited it at a very early age, and so became a little queer myself. England is extremely subtle; and about the best of it there is something almost secretive; it is amateur even more than aristocratic in tradition; it is never official. Among its very valuable and hardly visible oddities is this. There is one type of Englishman I have very frequently met in travel and never met in books of travel. He is the expiation for the English tripper; he may be called the

English exile. He is a man of good English culture quite warmly and unaffectedly devoted to some particular foreign culture. In some sense, he has already figured in this story; for Maurice Baring had exactly that attitude towards Russia and Professor Eccles towards France. But I have met a particularly charming Anglo-Irish academic gentleman doing exactly the same work of penetrating with sympathy the soul of Poland; I have met another searching out the secrets of Spanish music in Madrid; and everywhere they are dotted about on the map, doing not only something for Europe but very decidedly something for England; proving to Lithuanian antiquaries or Portuguese geographers that we are not all bounders and boosters, but come of the people that could interpret Plutarch and translate Rabelais. They are a microscopically small minority; like nearly every English group that really knows what is going on; but they are a seed and therefore a secret. It can only be a comic coincidence, but it is a curious fact, that they are mostly of a certain personal type; tending to slight baldness and agreeable smiles under old-fashioned moustaches. If sociology were a science, which is absurd, I would set up a claim like a Darwinian scientist to have discovered a species. It is in remembering these men that I find it easiest to range rapidly, for the purpose of this short chapter, over the different countries in which they are our very unofficial diplomatists.

I love France; and I am glad I saw it first, when I was young. For if an Englishman has understood a Frenchman, he has understood the most foreign of foreigners. The nation that is nearest is now the furthest away. Italy and Spain, and rather especially Poland, are much more like England than that square fortress of equal citizens and Roman soldiers; full of family councils and *patria potestas* and private property under the Roman Law; the keep and citadel of Christendom. This is evident, for a first example, in the case of Italy. When I first went to Florence, I had only a confused impression that this Italian city was full of English ladies; and that they were all Theosophists. But when I first went to Assisi after I had been to Rome (in more senses than one), I saw that this is not quite fair. There really is a sympathy between English and Italian culture, which there is not as yet between English and French culture. There is really something warm-hearted and romantic gilding those stark cliffs that look across the plain to Perugia; and it is in touch with two nations. The English do appreciate St Francis as they do not appreciate Pascal or the Cur d'Ars. The English can read Dante in a translation, even when they cannot read Italian. They cannot read Racine, even when they can read French. In short, they have some comprehension of medievalism in Italy; when they have not a glimmer of the granite grandeur of classicism in France. The surname of Rossetti was not altogether an accident. The devotion of my old friend Philip Wicksteed to

Dante was an excellent example of what I mean by the typical Englishman with a foreign hobby.

I felt the same when I went to lecture in Madrid; and met that shy and polite Englishman who could have lectured to the Spaniards on their own Spanish tunes and songs. I did not feel that Spanish people were in a difficult sense different from English people, but only that a stupid Puritanism had forbidden the English to show the hearty and healthy emotions the Spanish are allowed to show. The most manifest emotion, as it struck me, was the pride of fathers in their little boys. I have seen a little boy run the whole length of one of the tree-lined avenues in the great streets, in order to leap into the arms of a ragged workman, who hugged him with more than maternal ecstacy. It may, of course, be said that this is un-English; which seems an ungenerous reflection on the English. I prefer to say that the Spanish workman, only too probably, had not been to an English public school. But really there are very few English people who would not *like* it to happen. Puritanism is only a paralysis; which stiffens into Stoicism when it loses religion. That sort of warmth and casualness was my impression of Spain. Oh, yes, I saw the Escorial. Yes, thank you, I visited Toledo; it is glorious, but I remember it best by a more glorious peasant woman who poured out wine by the gallon and talked all the time.

I recently revisited Spain, if the Catalans will allow me to call it Spain (opinions apart, I am sincerely sympathetic with such sensitive points), for I revisited it with a rush in a car that could only charge down the eastern coast to Tarragona. If I say that I charged, the motion is metaphorical; the motive power was a motor driven by Miss Dorothy Collins who acted as secretary, courier, chauffeuse, guide, philosopher and above all, friend, without whom my wife and I would have often been without friends and in need of philosophy. For after crossing France and cresting the Pyrenees like Charlemagne and the Alps like Napoleon (or like Hannibal accompanied by an elephant) she brought me again to Florence, to deliver some lecture, and then returned through Switzerland to Calais, where the great campaign began.

In the course of it, I had two curious experiences in two foreign cafés. One was outside Barcelona, where the proprietor was an authentic American gangster who had actually written a book of confessions about his own organised robbing and racketeering. Modest, like all great men, about the ability he had shown in making big business out of burglary and highway robbery, he was very proud of his literary experiment, and especially of his book; but, like some other literary men, he was dissatisfied with his publishers. He said he had rushed across just in time to find that they had stolen nearly all his royalties. "It was a shame," I said sympathetically, "why it was simply robbery." "I'll say it was," he said with an indignant blow on the table. "It was just plain robbery."

The other day was dateless, even for my dateless life; for I had forgotten time and had no notion of anything anywhere, when in a small French town I strolled into a café noisy with French talk. Wireless songs wailed unnoted; which is not surprising, for French talk is much better than wireless. And then, unaccountably, I heard a voice speaking in English; and a voice I had heard before. For I heard the words, "...wherever you are, my dear people, whether in this country or beyond the sea," and I remembered Monarchy and an ancient cry; for it was the King; and that is how I kept the Jubilee.

Returning through France, I remembered again the riddle, that I had found those far countries so near; but that the two nations that are nearest are those we never understand; Ireland and France. About Ireland, I have already written much; and I have nothing to say because I have nothing to unsay. I have written about Ireland in the hour of her tragedy, after the red dawn of the Easter Rising and the nightmare threat of conscription; and again in the hour of her triumph, when the Eucharistic Congress blazed before millions in the Phoenix Park; and all the swords and the trumpets saluted what was a Phoenix indeed. But there is one more nation, not unlike her in that tragedy and triumph, with a note on which I will end. Some day perhaps I may attempt a fuller study. Here in this chapter I only recall one or two things; not those I could remember, but those I cannot forget.

When I visited Poland I was honoured by an invitation from the Government; but all the hospitality I received was far too much alive to remind me of anything official. There is a sort of underground tavern in Warsaw, where men drink Tokay, which would cure any official of officialism; and there they sang the marching songs of the Poles. Cracow is now even more the national city because it is not the capital; and its secrets are better explored by men like Professor Roman Dyboski than by anybody entangled in statecraft. But I saw something of that difficult statesmanship, enough to know that nothing but nonsense is talked about it in the newspapers which discuss what they call the Polish Corridor. The fairest generalisation is this: recent events would be better understood if everybody saw the self-evident fact that the Poles always have a choice of evils. I met the great Pilsudski; and that grand and rather grim old soldier of fortune practically told me that, *of the two*, he preferred Germany to Russia. It is equally clear that his rival Dmowski, who also entertained us delightfully in his rural retreat, had decided that, *of the two*, he preferred Russia to Germany. I had met this interesting man before; for Dr Sarolea brought him to my house; where the Belgian, in his impish way, had taunted the Pole with his Anti-Semitism, saying persuasively: "After all, your religion came from the Jews." To which the Pole answered: "My religion came from Jesus Christ, who was murdered by the

Jews." Pilsudski was also very sympathetic with Lithuania; though Lithuanians and Poles were quarrelling at the time. He was enthusiastic for Wilno; and I afterwards found on the frontier a historic site where Poles and Lithuanians are at peace – even when they are at war.

I was driving with a Polish lady, who was very witty and well-acquainted with the whole character of Europe, and also of England (as is the barbarous habit of Slavs); and I only noticed that her tone changed, if anything to a sort of coolness, as we stopped outside an archway leading to a side-street, and she said: "We can't drive in here." I wondered; for the gateway was wide and the street apparently open. As we walked under the arch, she said in the same colourless tone: "You take off your hat here." And then I saw the open street. It was filled with a vast crowd, all facing me; and all on their knees on the ground. It was as if someone were walking behind me; or some strange bird were hovering over my head. I faced round, and saw in the centre of the arch great windows standing open, unsealing a chamber full of gold and colours; there was a picture behind; but parts of the whole picture were moving like a puppet-show, stirring strange double memories like a dream of the bridge in the puppet-show of my childhood; and then I realised that from those shifting groups there shone and sounded the ancient magnificence of the Mass.

One other memory I will add here. I made the acquaintance of a young Count whose huge and costly palace of a country house, upon the old model (for he had quite different notions himself), had been burned and wrecked and left in ruins by the retreat of the Red Army after the Battle of Warsaw. Looking at such a mountain of shattered marbles and black and blasted tapestries one of our party said: "It must be a terrible thing for you to see your old family home destroyed like this." But the young man, who was very young in all his gestures, shrugged his shoulders and laughed, at the same time looking a little sad. "Oh, I do not blame them for that," he said. "I have been a soldier myself, and in the same campaign; and I know the temptations. I know what a fellow feels, dropping with fatigue and freezing with cold, when he asks himself what some other fellow's armchairs and curtains can matter, if he can only have fuel for the night. On the one side or the other, we were all soldiers; and it is a hard and horrible life. I don't resent at all what they did here. There is only one thing that I really resent. I will show it to you."

And he led us out into a long avenue lined with poplars; and at the end of it was a statue of the Blessed Virgin, with the head and the hands shot off. But the hands had been lifted; and it is a strange thing that the very mutilation seemed to give more meaning to the attitude of intercession; asking mercy for the merciless race of men.

XVI

THE GOD WITH THE GOLDEN KEY

Some time ago, seated at ease upon a summer evening and taking a serene review of an indefensibly fortunate and happy life, I calculated that I must have committed at least fifty-three murders, and been concerned with hiding about half a hundred corpses for the purpose of the concealment of crimes; hanging one corpse on a hat-peg, bundling another into a postman's bag, decapitating a third and providing it with somebody else's head, and so on through quite a large number of innocent artifices of the kind. It is true that I have enacted most of these atrocities on paper; and I strongly recommend the young student, except in extreme cases, to give expression to his criminal impulses in this form; and not run the risk of spoiling a beautiful and well-proportioned idea by bringing it down to the plane of brute material experiment, where it too often suffers the unforeseen imperfections and disappointments of this fallen world, and brings with it various unwelcome and unworthy social and legal consequences. I have explained elsewhere that I once drew up a scientific table of Twenty Ways of Killing a Wife and have managed to preserve them all in their undisturbed artistic completeness, so that it is possible for the artist, after a fashion, to have successfully murdered twenty wives and yet keep the original wife after all; an additional point which is in many cases, and especially my own, not without its advantages. Whereas, for the artist to sacrifice his wife and possibly his neck, for the mere vulgar and theatrical practical presentation of one of these ideal dramas, is to lose, not only this, but all the ideal enjoyment of the other nineteen. This being my strict principle, from which I have never wavered, there has been nothing to cut short the rich accumulation of imaginative corpses; and, as I say, I have already accumulated a good many. My name achieved a certain notoriety as that of a writer of these murderous short stories, commonly called detective stories; certain publishers and magazines have come to count on me for such trifles; and are still kind enough, from time to time, to write to me ordering a new batch of corpses; generally in consignments of eight at a time.

Any who have come upon traces of this industry may possibly know that a large number of my little crime stories were concerned with a person called Father Brown; a Catholic priest whose external simplicity and internal subtlety formed something near enough to a character for the purposes of this sketchy sort of storytelling. And certain questions have arisen, especially questions about the identity or accuracy of the type, which have not been without an effect on more important things.

As I have said, I have never taken my novels or short stories very seriously, or imagined that I had any particular status in anything so serious as a novel. But I can claim at the same time that it was novel enough to be novel, in the sense of not being historical or biographical; and that even one of my short stories was original enough to do without originals. The notion that a character in a novel must be "meant" for somebody or "taken from" somebody is founded on a misunderstanding of the nature of narrative fancy, and especially of such slight fancies as mine. Nevertheless, it has been generally said that Father Brown had an original in real life; and in one particular and rather personal sense, it is true.

The notion that a novelist takes a character bodily and in all its details from a friend or an enemy is a blunder that has done a great deal of harm. Even the characters of Dickens, at once so plainly creations and so plainly caricatures, were measured against mere mortals, as if there were any mortals who could fit exactly the magnificent mock-heroic statute of Weller or Micawber. I remember my father telling me how some of his contemporaries indignantly purged themselves of the charge of being the model of Mr Pecksniff; and especially of how the well-known S C Hall, the Spiritualist, cleared himself with an eloquence which some found too sublime to be convincing. "How can I be said to resemble Pecksniff?" said this worthy man to my father. "You know me. The world knows me. The world knows that I have devoted my life to the good of others, that I have lived a pure and exalted life devoted to the highest duties and ideals, that I have sought always to set an example of truth, of justice, of probity, of purity, and of public virtue. What resemblance can there be between me and Pecksniff?"

When a writer invents a character for the purposes of fiction, especially of light or fanciful fiction, he fits him out with all sorts of features meant to be effective in that setting and against that background. He may have taken, and probably has taken, a hint from a human being. But he will not hesitate to alter the human being, especially in externals, because he is not thinking of a portrait but of a picture. In Father Brown, it was the chief feature to be featureless. The point of him was to appear pointless; and one might say that his conspicuous quality was not being conspicuous. His commonplace exterior was meant to contrast with his unsuspected vigilance and intelligence; and that being so, of course, I made his appearance shabby and shapeless, his face round and expressionless, his manners clumsy, and so on. At the same time I did take some of his inner intellectual qualities from my friend, Father John O'Connor of Bradford, who has not, as a matter of fact, any of these external qualities. He is not shabby, but rather neat; he is not clumsy, but very delicate and dexterous; he not only is but looks amusing and amused. He is a sensitive and quick-witted Irishman, with the profound irony and some of the potential irritability of his race. My Father Brown was deliberately described as a Suffolk dumpling from East Anglia. That, and the rest of his description, was a deliberate disguise for the purpose of detective fiction. But for all that, there is a very real sense in which Father O'Connor was the intellectual inspiration of these stories; and of much more important things as well. And in order to explain these things, especially the important things, I cannot do better than tell the story of how the first notion of this detective comedy came into my mind.

In those early days, especially just before and just after I was married, it was my fate to wander over many parts of England, delivering what were politely called lectures. There is a considerable appetite for such bleak entertainments, especially in the North of England, the South of Scotland, and among certain active Nonconformist centres even in the suburbs of London. With the mention of bleakness there comes back to me the memory of one particular chapel, lying in the last featureless wastes to the north of London, to which I actually had to make my way through a blinding snowstorm, which I enjoyed very much; because I like snowstorms. In fact, I like practically all kinds of English weather except that particular sort of weather that is called "a glorious day." So none need weep prematurely over my experience, or imagine that I am pitying myself or asking for pity. Still, it is the fact that I was exposed to the elements for nearly two hours either on foot or on top of a forlorn omnibus wandering in a wilderness; and by the time I arrived at the chapel I must have roughly resembled the Snow Man that children make in the garden. I proceeded to lecture, God knows on what, and was about to resume my wintry journey, when the worthy minister of the chapel, robustly rubbing his hands and slapping his chest and beaming at me with the rich hospitality of Father Christmas, said in a deep, hearty, fruity voice: "Come, Mr Chesterton; it's a bitter cold night! Do let me offer you an oswego biscuit." I assured him gratefully that I felt no such craving; it was very kind of him, for there was no possible reason, in the circumstances, for his offering me any refreshment at all. But I confess that the thought of returning through the snow and the freezing blast, for two more hours, with the glow of that one biscuit within me and the oswego fire running through all my veins, struck me as a little out of proportion. I fear it was with considerable pleasure that I crossed the road and entered a public-house immediately opposite the chapel, under the very eyes of the Nonconformist Conscience.

This is a parenthesis; and I could add a good many parentheses about distant days of vagabond lecturing. Of those days the tale is told that I once sent a telegram to my wife in London, which ran: "Am in Market Harborough. Where ought I to be?" I cannot remember whether this story is true; but it is not unlikely or, I think, unreasonable. It was in the course of such wanderings that I made many friends whose friendship I value; such as Mr Lloyd Thomas, then in Nottingham, and Mr McClelland of Glasgow. But I mention these here only as leading up to that very accidental meeting in Yorkshire, which was to have consequences for me rather beyond the appearance of accident. I had gone to give a lecture at Keighley on the high moors of the West Riding, and stayed the night with a leading citizen of that little industrial town; who had assembled a group of local friends such as could be conceived, I suppose, as likely to be patient with lecturers; including the curate of the Roman Catholic Church; a small man with a smooth face and a demure but elvish expression. I was struck by the tact and humour with which he mingled with his very Yorkshire and very Protestant company; and I soon found out that they had, in their bluff way, already learned to appreciate him as something of a character. Somebody gave me a very amusing account of how two gigantic Yorkshire farmers, of that district, had been deputed to go the rounds of various religious centres, and how they wavered, with nameless terrors, before entering the little presbytery of the little priest. With many sinkings of heart, they seem to have come finally to the conclusion that he would hardly do them any serious harm; and that if he did, they could send for the police. They really thought, I suppose, that he had his house fitted up with all the torture engines of the Spanish Inquisition. But even these farmers, I was told, had since accepted him as a neighbour, and as the evening wore on his neighbours decidedly encouraged his considerable powers of entertainment. He expanded, and was soon in the middle of reciting that great and heartsearching dramatic lyric which is entitled, "My Boots are Tight." I liked him very much; but if you had told me that ten years afterwards I should be a Mormon Missionary in the Cannibal Islands, I should not have been more surprised than at the suggestion that, fully fifteen years afterwards, I should be making to him my General Confession and being received into the Church that he served.

Next morning he and I walked over Keighley Gate, the great wall of the moors that separates Keighley from Wharfedale, for I was visiting friends in Ilkley; and after a few hours' talk on the moors, it was a new friend whom I introduced to my old friends at my journey's end. He stayed to lunch, he stayed to tea; he stayed to dinner; I am not sure that, under their pressing hospitality, he did not stay the night; and he stayed there many nights and days on later occasions; and it was there that we most often met. It was in one of these visits that the incident occurred, which led me to take the liberty of putting him, or rather part of him, into a string of sensational stories. But I mention it, not because I attach any importance to those stories, but because it has a more vital connection with the other story; the story that I am telling here.

I mentioned to the priest in conversation that I proposed to support in print a certain proposal, it matters not what, in connection with some rather sordid social questions of vice and crime. On this particular point he thought I was in error, or rather in ignorance; as indeed I was. And, merely as a necessary duty and to prevent me from falling into a mare's nest, he told me certain facts he knew about perverted practices which I certainly shall not set down or discuss here. I have confessed on an earlier page that in my own youth I had imagined for myself any amount of iniquity; and it was a curious experience to find that this quiet and pleasant celibate had plumbed those abysses far deeper than I. I had not imagined that the world could hold such horrors. If he had been a professional novelist throwing such filth broadcast on all the bookstalls for boys and babies to pick up, of course he would have been a great creative artist and a herald of the Dawn. As he was only stating them reluctantly, in strict privacy, as a practical necessity, he was, of course, a typical Jesuit whispering poisonous secrets in my ear. When we returned to the house we found it full of visitors, and fell into special conversation with two hearty and healthy young Cambridge undergraduates, who had been walking or cycling across the moors in the spirit of the stern and vigorous English holiday. They were no narrow athletes, however, but interested in various sports and in a breezy way in various arts; and they began to discuss music and landscape with my friend Father O'Connor. I never knew a man who could turn with more ease than he from one topic to another, or who had more unexpected stores of information, often purely technical information, upon all. The talk soon deepened into a discussion on matters more philosophical and moral; and when the priest had left the room, the two young men broke out into generous expressions of admiration, saying truly that he was a remarkable man, and seemed to know a great deal about Palestrina or Baroque architecture, or whatever was the point at the moment. Then there fell a curious reflective silence, at the end of which one of the undergraduates suddenly burst out: "All the same, I don't believe his sort of life is the right one. It's all very well to like religious music and so on, when you're all shut up in a sort of cloister and don't know anything about the real evil in the world. But I don't believe that's the right ideal. I believe in a fellow coming out into the world, and facing the evil that's in it, and knowing

217

something about the dangers and all that. It's a very beautiful thing to be innocent and ignorant; but I think it's a much finer thing not to be afraid of knowledge."

To me, still almost shivering with the appallingly practical facts of which the priest had warned me, this comment came with such a colossal and crushing irony, that I nearly burst into a loud harsh laugh in the drawing-room. For I knew perfectly well that, as regards all the solid Satanism which the priest knew and warred with all his life, these two Cambridge gentlemen (luckily for them) knew about as much of real evil as two babies in the same perambulator.

And there sprang up in my mind the vague idea of making some artistic use of this comic yet tragic cross-purposes; and constructing a comedy in which a priest should appear to know nothing and in fact know more about crime than the criminals. I afterwards summed up the special idea in the story called "The Blue Cross," otherwise very slight and improbable, and continued it through the interminable series of tales with which I have afflicted the world. In short, I permitted myself the grave liberty of taking my friend and knocking him about; beating his hat and umbrella shapeless, untidying his clothes, punching his intelligent countenance into a condition of pudding-faced fatuity, and generally disguising Father O'Connor as Father Brown. The disguise, as I have said, was a deliberate piece of fiction, meant to bring out or accentuate the contrast that was the point of the comedy. There is also in the conception, as in nearly everything I have ever written, a good deal of inconsistency and inaccuracy on minor points; not the least of such flaws being the general suggestion that Father Brown had nothing in particular to do, except to hang about in any household where there was likely to be a murder. A very charming Catholic lady I know once paid my detective priest the appropriate compliment of saying: "I am very fond of that officious little loafer."

Nevertheless, the incident of the Cambridge undergraduates, and their breezy contempt for the fugitive and cloistered virtue of a parish priest, stood for much more serious things in my life than my unfortunate, but merely professional, heap of corpses or massacre of characters. It brought me in a manner face to face once more with those morbid but vivid problems of the soul, to which I have earlier alluded and gave me a great and growing sense that I had not found any real spiritual solution of them; though in certain external ways of proportion and practice, they trouble a man less in manhood than they do in youth. They still troubled me a good deal; but I might have sunk more and more into some sort of compromise or surrender of mere weariness, but for this sudden glimpse of the pit that is at all our feet. I was surprised at my own surprise. That the Catholic Church knew more about good than I did was easy to believe. That she knew more about evil than I did seemed incredible.

When people ask me, or indeed anybody else, "Why did you join the Church of Rome?" the first essential answer, if it is partly an elliptical answer, is, "To get rid of my sins." For there is no other religious system that does *really* profess to get rid of people's sins. It is confirmed by the logic, which to many seems startling, by which the Church deduces that sin confessed and adequately repented is actually abolished; and that the sinner does really begin again as if he had never sinned. And this brought me sharply back to those visions or fancies with which I have dealt in the chapter about childhood. I spoke there of the indescribable and indestructible certitude in the soul, that those first years of innocence were the beginning of something worthy, perhaps more worthy than any of the things that actually followed them. I spoke of the strange daylight, which was something more than the light of common day, that still seems in my memory to shine on those steep roads down from Campden Hill, from which one could see the Crystal Palace from afar. Well, when a Catholic comes from Confession, he does truly, by definition, step out again into that dawn of his own beginning and look with new eyes across the world to a Crystal Palace that is really of crystal. He believes that in that dim corner, and in that brief ritual, God has really re-made him in His own image. He is now a new experiment of the Creator. He is as much a new experiment as he was when he was really only five years old. He stands, as I said, in the white light at the worthy beginning of the life of a man. The accumulations of time can no longer terrify. He may be grey and gouty; but he is only five minutes old.

I am not here defending such doctrines as that of the Sacrament of Penance; any more than the equally staggering doctrine of the Divine love for man. I am not writing a book of religious controversy; of which I have written several and shall probably, unless violently restrained by my friends and relatives, write several more. I am here engaged in the morbid and degrading task of telling the story of my life; and have only to state what actually were the effects of such doctrines on my own feelings and actions. And I am, by the nature of the task, especially concerned with the fact that these doctrines seem to me to link up my whole life from the beginning, as no other doctrines could do; and especially to settle simultaneously the two problems of my childish happiness and my boyish brooding. And they specially affected one idea; which I hope it is not pompous to call the chief idea of my life; I will not say the doctrine I have always taught, but the doctrine I should always have liked to teach. That is the idea of taking things with gratitude, and not taking things for granted. Thus the Sacrament of Penance gives a new life, and reconciles a man to all living, but it does not do it as the optimists and the hedonists and the heathen preachers of happiness do it. The gift is given at a price, and is conditioned by a confession. In other words, the name of the price is Truth, which may also be called Reality; but it is facing the reality about oneself. When the process is only applied to other people, it is called Realism.

I began by being what the pessimists called an optimist; I have ended by being what the optimists would very probably call a pessimist. And I have never in fact been either, and I have never really changed at all. I began by defending vermilion pillar-boxes and Victorian omnibuses although they were ugly. I have ended by denouncing modern advertisements or American films even when they are beautiful. The thing that I was trying to say then is the same thing that I am trying to say now; and even the deepest revolution of religion has only confirmed me in the desire to say it. For indeed, I never saw the two sides of this single truth stated together anywhere, until I happened to open the Penny Catechism and read the words, "The two sins against Hope are presumption and despair."

I began in my boyhood to grope for it from quite the other end; the end of the earth most remote from purely supernatural hopes. But even about the dimmest earthly hope, or the smallest earthly happiness, I had from the first an almost violently vivid sense of those two dangers; the sense that the experience must not be spoilt by presumption or despair. To take a convenient tag out of my first juvenile book of rhymes, I asked through what incarnations or pre-natal purgatories I must have passed, to earn the reward of looking at a dandelion. Now it would be easy enough, if the thing were worth while even for a commentator, to date that phrase by certain details, or guess that it might have been worded otherwise at a later time. I do not believe in Reincarnation, if indeed I ever did; and since I have owned a garden (for I cannot say since I have been a gardener) I have realised better than I did that there really is a case against weeds. But in substance what I said about the dandelion is exactly what I should say about the sunflower or the sun, or the glory which (as the poet said) is brighter than the sun. The only way to enjoy even a weed is to feel unworthy even of a weed. Now there are two ways of complaining of the weed or the flower; and one was the fashion in my youth and another is the fashion in my later days; but they are not only both wrong, but both wrong because the same thing is right. The pessimists of my boyhood, when confronted with the dandelion, said with Swinburne:

> I am weary of days and hours,
> Blown buds of barren flowers,
> Desires and dreams and powers
> And everything but sleep.

And at this I cursed them and kicked at them and made an exhibition of myself; having made myself the champion of the Lion's Tooth, with a dandelion rampant on my crest. But there is a way of despising the dandelion which is not that of the dreary pessimist, but of the more offensive optimist. It can be done in various ways; one of which is saying, "You can get much better dandelions at Selfridge's," or "You can get much cheaper dandelions at Woolworth's." Another way is to observe with a casual drawl, "Of course nobody but Gamboli in Vienna really understands dandelions," or saying that nobody would put up with the old-fashioned dandelion since the super-dandelion has been grown in the Frankfurt Palm Garden; or merely sneering at the stinginess of providing dandelions, when all the best hostesses give you an orchid for your buttonhole and a bouquet of rare exotics to take away with you. These are all methods of undervaluing the thing by comparisons; for it is not familiarity but comparison that breeds contempt. And all such captious comparisons are ultimately based on the strange and staggering heresy that a human being has a right to dandelions; that in some extraordinary fashion we can demand the very pick of all the dandelions in the garden of Paradise; that we owe no thanks for them at all and need feel no wonder at them at all; and above all no wonder at being thought worthy to receive them. Instead of saying, like the old religious poet, "What is man that Thou carest for him, or the son of man that Thou regardest him?" we are to say like the discontented cabman, "What's this?" or like the bad-tempered Major in the club, "Is this a chop fit for a gentleman?" Now I not only dislike this attitude quite as much as the Swinburnian pessimistic attitude, but I think it comes to very much the same thing; to the actual loss of appetite for the chop or the dish of dandelion tea. And the name of it is Presumption and the name of its twin brother is Despair.

This is the principle I was maintaining when I seemed an optimist to Mr Max Beerbohm; and this is the principle I am still maintaining when I should undoubtedly seem a pessimist to Mr Gordon Selfridge. The aim of life is appreciation; there is no sense in not appreciating things; and there is no sense in having more of them if you have less appreciation of them. I originally said that a cockney lamp-post painted pea-green was better than no light or no life; and that if it was a lonely lamp-post, we might really see its light better against the background of the dark. The Decadent of my early days, however, was so distressed by it that he wanted to hang himself on the lamp-post, to extinguish the lamp, and to let everything relapse into aboriginal darkness. The modern millionaire comes bustling along the street to tell me he is an Optimist and has two million five thousand new lamp-posts, all ready painted not a Victorian pea-green, but a Futuristic chrome yellow and electric blue, and that he will plant them over the whole world in such numbers that nobody will notice them, especially as they will all look exactly the same. And I cannot quite see what the Optimist has got to be Optimistic about. A lamp-post can be significant although it is ugly. But he is not making lamp-posts significant; he is making them insignificant.

In short, as it seems to me, it matters very little whether a man is discontented in the name of pessimism or progress, if his discontent does in fact paralyse his power of appreciating what he has got. The real difficulty of man is not to enjoy lamp-posts or landscapes, not to enjoy dandelions or chops; but to enjoy enjoyment. To keep the capacity of really liking what he likes; that is the practical problem which the philosopher has to solve. And it seemed to me at the beginning, as it seems to me now in the end, that the pessimists and optimists of the modern world have alike missed and muddled this matter; through leaving out the ancient conception of humility and the thanks of the unworthy. This is a matter much more important and interesting than my opinions; but, in point of fact, it was by following this thin thread of a fancy about thankfulness, as slight as any of those dandelion-clocks that are blown upon the breeze like thistledown, that I did arrive eventually at an opinion which is more than an opinion. Perhaps the one and only opinion that is really more than an opinion.

For this secret of antiseptic simplicity was really a secret; it was not obvious, and certainly not obvious at that time. It was a secret that had already been almost entirely left to, and locked up with, certain neglected and unpopular things. It was almost as if the dandelion-tea really were a medicine, and the only recipe or prescription belonged to one old woman, a ragged and nondescript old woman, rather reputed in our village to be a witch. Anyhow, it is true that both the happy hedonists and the unhappy pessimists were stiffened by the opposite principle of pride. The pessimist was proud of pessimism, because he thought nothing good enough for him; the optimist was proud of optimism, because he thought nothing was bad enough to prevent him from getting good out of it. There were valuable men of both these types; there were men with many virtues; but they not only did not possess the virtue I was thinking of, but they never thought of it. They would decide that life was no good, or that it had a great deal of good; but they were not in touch with this particular notion, of having a great deal, of gratitude even for a very little good. And as I began to believe mote and more that the clue was to be found in such a principle, even if it was a paradox, I was more and more disposed to seek out those who specialised in humility, though for them it was the door of heaven and for me the door of earth.

For nobody else *specialises* in that mystical mood in which the yellow stat of the dandelion is startling, being something unexpected and undeserved. There are philosophies as varied as the flowers of the field, and some of them weeds and a few of them poisonous weeds. But they none of them create the psychological conditions in which I first saw, or desired to see, the flower. Men will crown themselves with flowers and brag of them, or sleep on flowers and forget them, or number and name all the flowers for a parade of learning and pedantry, or cultivate the flowers only in order to grow a super-flower for the Imperial International Flower Show; or, on the other hand, trample the flowers like a stampede of buffaloes, or root up the flowers as a childish camouflage of the cruelty of nature, or tear the flowers with their teeth to show that they are enlightened philosophical pessimists. But this original problem with which I myself started, the utmost possible imaginative appreciation of the flower – about that they can make nothing but blunders, in that they are ignorant of the elementary facts of human nature; in that, working wildly in all directions, they are all without exception going the wrong way to work. Since the time of which I speak, the world has in this respect grown even worse. A whole generation has been taught to talk nonsense at the top of its voice about having "a right to life" and "a right to experience" and " a right to happiness." The lucid thinkers who talk like this generally wind up their assertion of all these extraordinary rights by saying that there is no such thing as tight and wrong. It is a little difficult, in that case, to speculate on where their rights came from; but I, at least, leaned more and more to the old philosophy which said that their real rights came from where the dandelion came from; and that they will never value either without recognising its source. And in that ultimate sense uncreated man, merely in the position of the babe unborn, has no right even to see a dandelion; for he could not himself have invented either the dandelion or the eyesight.

I have here fallen back on one idle figure of speech from a fortunately forgotten book of verses; merely because such a thing is light and trivial, and the children puff it away like thistledown; and this will be most fitting to a place in which formal argument would be quite a misfit. But lest anyone should suppose that the notion has no relation to the argument, but is only a sentimental fancy about weeds or wild flowers, I will lightly and briefly suggest how even the figure fits in with all the aspects of the argument. For the first thing the casual critic will say is "What nonsense all this is; do you mean that a poet cannot be thankful for grass and wild flowers without connecting it with theology; let alone your theology?" To which I answer: "Yes; I mean he cannot do it without connecting it with theology, unless he can do it without connecting it with thought. If he can manage to be thankful when there is nobody to be thankful to, and no good intentions to be thankful for, then he is simply taking refuge in being thoughtless in order to avoid being thankless." But indeed the argument goes beyond conscious gratitude, and applies to any sort of peace or confidence or repose, even unconscious confidence or repose. Even the nature-worship which Pagans have felt, even the nature-love which Pantheists have felt, ultimately depends as much on some implied purpose and positive good in things, as does the direct thanksgiving which Christians have felt. Indeed, Nature is at best merely a female name we give to Providence when we are not treating it very seriously; a piece of feminist mythology. There is a sort of fireside fairytale, more fitted for the hearth than for the altar; and in that what is called Nature can be a sort of fairy godmother. But there can only be fairy godmothers because there are godmothers; and there can only be godmothers because there is God.

What has troubled me about sceptics all my life has been their extraordinary slowness in coming to the point; even to the point of their own position. I have heard them denounced, as well as admired, for their headlong haste and reckless rush of innovation; but my difficulty has always been to get them to move a few inches and finish their own argument. When first it was even hinted that the universe may not be a great design, but only a blind and indifferent growth, it ought to have been perceived instantly that this must for ever forbid any poet to retire to the green fields as to his home, or to look at the blue sky for his inspiration. There would be no more of any such traditional truth associated with green grass than with green rot or green rust; no more to be recalled by blue skies than by blue noses amputated in a freezing world of death. Poets, even Pagans, can only directly believe in Nature if they indirectly believe in God; if the second idea should really fade, the first is bound to follow sooner or later; and, merely out of a sad respect for human logic, I wish it had been sooner. Of course a man might have an almost animal appreciation of certain accidents of form or colour in a rock or a pool, as in a rag-bag or a dustbin; but that is not what the great poets or the great Pagans meant by the mysteries of Nature or the inspiration of the elemental powers. When there is no longer even a vague idea of purposes or presences, then the many-coloured forests really is a rag-bag and all the pageant of the dust only a dustbin. We can see this realisation creeping like a slow paralysis over all those of the newest poets who have not reacted towards religion. Their philosophy of the dandelion is not that all weeds are flowers; but rather that all flowers are weeds. Indeed it reaches to something like nightmare; as if Nature itself were unnatural. Perhaps that is why so many of them try desperately to write about machinery; touching which nobody has yet disputed the Argument from Design. No Darwin has yet maintained that motors began as scraps of metal, of which most happened to be scrapped; or that only those cars, which had grown a carburettor by accident, survived the struggle for life in Piccadilly. But whatever the reason, I have read modern poems obviously meant to make grass seem something merely scrubby and prickly and repugnant, like an unshaven chin.

That is the first note; that this common human mysticism about the dust or the dandelion or the daylight or the daily life of man does depend, and always did depend on theology, if it dealt at all in thought. And if it be next asked why this theology, I answer here – because it is the only theology that has not only thought, but thought of everything. That almost any other theology or philosophy contains a truth, I do not at all deny; on the contrary, that is what I assert; and that is what I complain of. Of all the other systems or sects I know, every single one is content to follow a truth, theological or theosophical or ethical or metaphysical; and the more they claim to be universal, the more it means that they merely take something and apply it to everything. A very brilliant Hindu scholar and man of science said to me, "There is but one thing, which is unity and universality. The points in which things differ do not matter; it is only their agreement that matters." And I answered, "The agreement we really want is the agreement between agreement and disagreement. It is the sense that things do really differ, although they are at one." Long afterwards I found what I meant stated much better by a Catholic writer, Coventry Patmore: "God is not infinite; He is the synthesis of infinity and boundary." In short, the other teachers were always men of one idea, even when their one idea was universality. They were always especially narrow when their one idea was breadth. I have only found one creed that could not be satisfied with a truth, but only with the Truth, which is made of a million such truths and yet is one. And even in this passing illustration about my own private fancy, this was doubly demonstrated. If I had wandered away like Bergson or Bernard Shaw, and made up my own philosophy out of my own precious fragment of truth, merely because I had found it for myself. I should soon have found that truth distorting itself into a falsehood. Even in this one case, there are two ways in which it might have turned on me and rent me. One would have been by encouraging the delusion to which I was most prone; and the other by excusing the falsehood which I thought most inexcusable. First, the very exaggeration of the sense that daylight and dandelions and all earthly experience are a sort of incredible vision would, if unbalanced by other truths, have become in my case very unbalanced indeed. For that notion of seeing a vision was dangerously near to my old original natural nightmare, which had led me to move about as if I were in a dream; and at one time to lose the sense of reality and with it much of the sense of responsibility. And again, on the side of responsibility, in the more practical and ethical sphere, it might have forced on me a sort of political Quietism, to which I was really as much of a conscientious objector as to Quakerism. For what could I have said, if some tyrant had twisted this idea of transcendental contentment into an excuse for tyranny? Suppose he had quoted at me my verses about the all-sufficiency of elementary existence, and the green vision of life, had used them to prove that the poor should be content with anything, and had said, like the old oppressor, "Let them eat grass."

In a word, I had the humble purpose of not being a maniac, but especially of not being a monomaniac; and above all, of not being a monomaniac about a notion merely because it was my own. The notion was normal enough, and quite consistent with the Faith; indeed it was already a part of it. But only as a part of it could it have remained normal. And I believe this to be true of practically all the notions of which my ablest contemporaries have made new philosophies; many of them normal enough at the start. I have therefore come to the conclusion that there is a complete contemporary fallacy about the liberty of individual ideas; that such flowers grow best in a garden, and even grow biggest in a garden; and that in the wilderness they wither and die.

Here again, I am well aware that somebody will ask the natural and normally reasonable question: "Do you really mean that a man cannot object to people being asked to eat grass, unless he accepts your particular creed?" To which I will only answer for the moment, "Yes; I do mean that; but not exactly as you mean it." I will only add here, in passing, that what really revolts me and everybody else about that famous taunt of the tyrant is that it conveys some suggestion of treating men like beasts. I will also add that it would not remove my objection, even if the beasts had enough grass, or if the botanists had proved that grass is the most nutritious diet.

Now why do I offer here this handful of scrappy topics, types, metaphors all totally disconnected? Because I am not now expounding a religious system. I am finishing a story; rounding off what has been to me at least a romance, and very much of a mystery story. It is a purely personal narrative that began in the first pages of this book; and I am answering at the end only the questions I asked at the beginning. I have said that I had in childhood, and have partly preserved out of childhood, a certain romance of receptiveness, which has not been killed by sin or even by sorrow; for though I have not had great troubles, I have had many. A man does not grow old without being bothered; but I have grown old without being bored. Existence is still a strange thing to me; and as a stranger I give it welcome. Well, to begin with, I put that beginning of all my intellectual impulses before the authority to which I have come at the end; and I find it was there before I put it there. I find myself ratified in my realisation of the miracle of being alive; *not* in some hazy literary sense such as the sceptics use, but in a definite dogmatic sense; of being made alive by that which can alone work miracles.

I have said that this rude and primitive religion of gratitude did not save me from ingratitude; from sin which is perhaps most horrible to me because it is ingratitude. But here again I have found that the answer awaited me. Precisely because the evil was mainly of the imagination, it could only be pierced by that conception of confession which is the end of mere solitude and secrecy. I had found only one religion which dared to go down with me into the depths of myself. I know, of course, that the practice of Confession, having been reviled through three or four centuries and through the greater part of my own life, has now been revived in a belated fashion. The scientific materialists, permanently behind the times, have revived all that was reviled in it, as indecent and introspective. I have heard that a new sect has started once more the practice of the most primitive monasteries, and treated the confessional as communal. Unlike the primitive monks of the desert, it seems to find a satisfaction in performing the ritual in evening-dress. In short, I would not be supposed to be ignorant of the fact that the modern world, in various groups, is now prepared to provide us with the advantages of Confession. None of the groups, so far as I know, professes to provide the minor advantage of Absolution.

I have said that my morbidities were mental as well as moral; and sounded the most appalling depths of fundamental scepticism and solipsism. And there again I found that the Church had gone before me and established her adamantine foundations; that she had affirmed the actuality of external things; so that even madmen might hear her voice; and by a revelation in their very brain begin to believe their eyes.

Finally, I said that I had tried, however imperfectly, to serve justice; and that I saw our industrial civilisation as rooted in injustice, long before it became so common a comment as it is today. Anybody who cares to turn up the files of the great newspapers, even those supposed to be Radical newspapers, and see what they said about the Great Strikes, and compare it with what my friends and I said at the same date, can easily test whether this is a boast or a brute fact. But anybody reading this book (if anybody does) will see that from the very beginning my instinct about justice, about liberty and equality, was somewhat different from that current in our age; and from all the tendencies towards concentration and generalisation. It was my instinct to defend liberty in small nations and poor families; that is, to defend the rights of man as including the rights of property; especially the property of the poor. I did not really understand what I meant by Liberty, until I heard it called by the new name of Human Dignity. It was a new name to me; though it was part of a creed nearly two thousand years old. In short, I had blindly desired that a man should be in possession of something, if it were only his own body. In so far as materialistic concentration proceeds, a man will be in possession of nothing; not even his own body. Already there hover on the horizon sweeping scourges of sterilisation or social hygiene, applied to everybody and imposed by nobody. At least I will not argue here with what are quaintly called the scientific authorities on the other side. I have found one authority on my side.

This story, therefore, can only end as any detective story should end, with its own particular questions answered and its own primary problem solved. Thousands of totally different stories, with totally different problems, have ended in the same place with their problems solved. But for me my end is my beginning, as Maurice Baring quoted of Mary Stuart, and this overwhelming conviction that there is one key which can unlock all doors brings back to me my first glimpse of the glorious gift of the senses; and the sensational experience of sensation. And there starts up again before me, standing sharp and clear in shape as of old, the figure of a man who crosses a bridge and who carries a key; as I saw him when I first looked into fairyland through the window of my father's peepshow. But I know that he who is called Pontifex, the Builder of the Bridge, is called also Claviger, the Bearer of the Key; and that such keys were given him to bind and loose when he was a poor fisher in a far province, beside a small and almost secret sea.

G K Chesterton

St Francis of Assisi

Chesterton examines the life of St Francis, 'a very real historical human being', from the standpoint of the 'ordinary modern thinker and enquirer'. With his characteristic discernment he tells how St Francis turned his back on his home and family and explains why, for the 'sake of his vision, he denied himself all sense of place and possession'.

Chaucer

Chesterton expounds the 'genius of Geoffrey Chaucer' in this literary biography that explores both the writer and his time. He claims that Chaucer and his Age were 'more sane, more normal and more cheerful than writers that came after him' and the characters he portrayed have an immediate contemporary relevance.

Beautifully and sensitively written, this biography about the 'Father of English Poetry' will inform and inspire.

G K Chesterton

Criticisms and Appreciations of the Works of Charles Dickens

Written with intelligence and authority, these twenty-three essays provide an insight into the works of the literary genius of Charles Dickens.

Chesterton greatly admired Dickens as a social prophet and defender of the common man. Here, he focuses both on the style and the ideology of Dickens and provides the critical insight into his work with his characteristic perceptive generosity. Chesterton is still regarded by many as one of the most accomplished and perceptive critics of Dickens.

As much about Chesterton's strongly held beliefs as about Dickens, this volume is sure to inform and give pleasure to advocates of both writers.

George Bernard Shaw

The book traces in some detail Shaw's work as a critic (puritanical opposition to Shakespeare) and as a dramatist.

Chesterton was ideally placed to write this critical biography of the literary works and political views of George Bernard Shaw. He was a personal friend and yet an ardent opponent of Shaw's progressive socialism. The lightness of tone and the humour of his other works are equally present in his examination of Shaw. The book presents a perceptive and far from dated critique of Shaw's philosophy and politics and, through them, the emerging progressive orthodoxy of the 20th century.

The book represents an excellent introduction to Shaw's work and the spirit of the age in which it was created.

OTHER TITLES BY G K CHESTERTON AVAILABLE DIRECT
FROM HOUSE OF STRATUS

Quantity		£	$(US)	$(CAN)	€
GENERAL FICTION:					
	THE BALL AND THE CROSS	6.99	12.95	19.95	13.50
	THE MAN WHO KNEW TOO MUCH	6.99	12.95	19.95	13.50
	THE MAN WHO WAS THURSDAY	6.99	12.95	19.95	13.50
	MANALIVE	6.99	12.95	19.95	13.50
	THE NAPOLEON OF NOTTING HILL	6.99	12.95	19.95	13.50
	THE PARADOXES OF MR POND	6.99	12.95	19.95	13.50
	THE POET AND THE LUNATICS	6.99	12.95	19.95	13.50
	THE RETURN OF DON QUIXOTE	6.99	12.95	19.95	13.50
	TALES OF THE LONG BOW	6.99	12.95	19.95	13.50
FATHER BROWN SERIES:					
	THE INNOCENCE OF FATHER BROWN	6.99	12.95	19.95	13.50
	THE WISDOM OF FATHER BROWN	6.99	12.95	19.95	13.50
	THE INCREDULITY OF FATHER BROWN	6.99	12.95	19.95	13.50
	THE SECRET OF FATHER BROWN	6.99	12.95	19.95	13.50
	THE SCANDAL OF FATHER BROWN	6.99	12.95	19.95	13.50

ALL HOUSE OF STRATUS BOOKS ARE AVAILABLE FROM GOOD BOOKSHOPS
OR DIRECT FROM THE PUBLISHER:

Internet: www.houseofstratus.com including synopses and features.

Email: sales@houseofstratus.com
              info@houseofstratus.com
              (please quote author, title and credit card details.)

OTHER TITLES BY G K CHESTERTON AVAILABLE DIRECT
FROM HOUSE OF STRATUS

Quantity	£	$(US)	$(CAN)	€
BIOGRAPHY:				
ST THOMAS AQUINAS	8.99	13.95	20.95	15.00
ST FRANCIS OF ASSISI	8.99	13.95	20.95	15.00
WILLIAM BLAKE	8.99	13.95	20.95	15.00
ROBERT BROWNING	8.99	13.95	20.95	15.00
CHAUCER	8.99	13.95	20.95	15.00
WILLIAM COBBETT	8.99	13.95	20.95	15.00
CHARLES DICKENS	8.99	13.95	20.95	15.00
GEORGE BERNARD SHAW	8.99	13.95	20.95	15.00
ROBERT LOUIS STEVENSON	8.99	13.95	20.95	15.00
OTHER WORKS:				
THE BALLAD OF THE WHITE HORSE	6.99	12.95	19.95	13.50
CRITICISMS AND APPRECIATIONS OF THE WORKS OF CHARLES DICKENS	8.99	13.95	20.95	15.00
HERETICS	8.99	13.95	20.95	15.00
ORTHODOXY	8.99	13.95	20.95	15.00
THE VICTORIAN AGE IN LITERATURE	8.99	13.95	20.95	15.00

ALL HOUSE OF STRATUS BOOKS ARE AVAILABLE FROM GOOD BOOKSHOPS
OR DIRECT FROM THE PUBLISHER:

Tel: **Order Line**
            0800 169 1780 (UK)
            International
            +44 (0) 1845 527700 (UK)

Fax: **+44 (0) 1845 527711 (UK)**
            (please quote author, title and credit card details.)

Send to: **House of Stratus Sales Department**
            Thirsk Industrial Park
            York Road, Thirsk
            North Yorkshire, YO7 3BX
            UK

PAYMENT

Please tick currency you wish to use:

☐ £ (Sterling)   ☐ $ (US)   ☐ $ (CAN)   ☐ € (Euros)

Allow for shipping costs charged per order plus an amount per book as set out in the tables below:

CURRENCY/DESTINATION

	£(Sterling)	$(US)	$(CAN)	€ (Euros)
Cost per order				
UK	1.50	2.25	3.50	2.50
Europe	3.00	4.50	6.75	5.00
North America	3.00	3.50	5.25	5.00
Rest of World	3.00	4.50	6.75	5.00
Additional cost per book				
UK	0.50	0.75	1.15	0.85
Europe	1.00	1.50	2.25	1.70
North America	1.00	1.00	1.50	1.70
Rest of World	1.50	2.25	3.50	3.00

PLEASE SEND CHEQUE OR INTERNATIONAL MONEY ORDER
payable to: HOUSE OF STRATUS LTD or card payment as indicated

STERLING EXAMPLE

Cost of book(s):. . . . . Example: 3 x books at £6.99 each: £20.97

Cost of order:. . . . . Example: £1.50 (Delivery to UK address)

Additional cost per book: . . . . Example: 3 x £0.50: £1.50

Order total including shipping: . . . . Example: £23.97

VISA, MASTERCARD, SWITCH, AMEX:

☐☐☐☐☐☐☐☐☐☐☐☐☐☐☐☐☐☐☐

Issue number (Switch only):

☐☐☐

Start Date: **Expiry Date:**

☐☐/☐☐   ☐☐/☐☐

Signature: _____

NAME: _____

ADDRESS: _____

COUNTRY: _____

ZIP/POSTCODE: _____

Please allow 28 days for delivery. Despatch normally within 48 hours.

Prices subject to change without notice.
Please tick box if you do not wish to receive any additional information. ☐

House of Stratus publishes many other titles in this genre; please check our website
(**www.houseofstratus.com**) for more details.